About the Author

Pierre Berton, well-known and well-loved Canadian author,
journalist, and media personality, hailed from Whitehorse, Yukon.
During his career, he wrote fifty books for adults and twenty-two
for children, popularizing Canadian history and culture and
reflecting on his life and times. With more than thirty literary
awards and a dozen honorary degrees to his credit, Berton
was also a Companion of the Order of Canada.

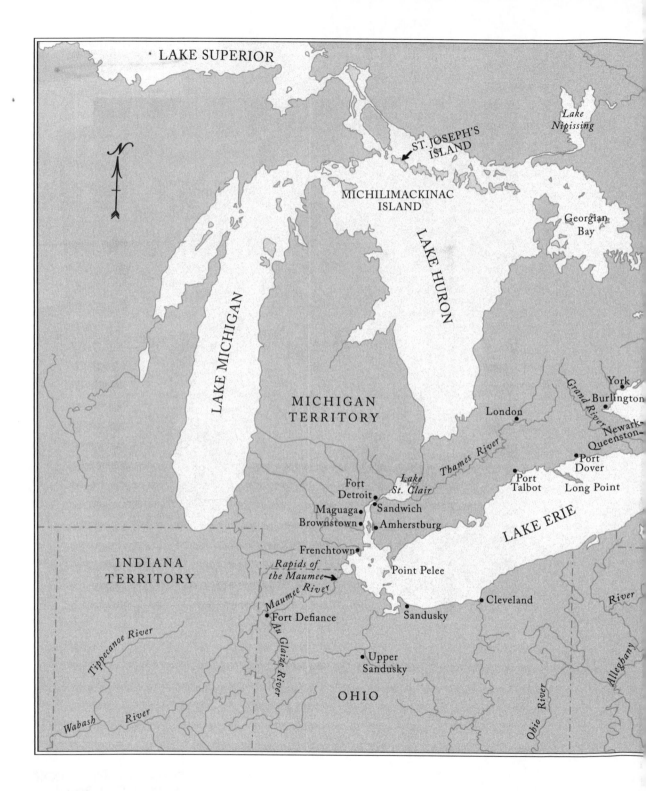

LAKE SUPERIOR

Lake Nipissing

ST. JOSEPH'S ISLAND

MICHILIMACKINAC ISLAND

Georgian Bay

LAKE HURON

LAKE MICHIGAN

MICHIGAN TERRITORY

York
Burlington

Grand River

London

Newark-
Queenston-

Thames River

Port Dover

Port Talbot

Long Point

Fort Detroit

Lake St. Clair

Maguaga

Sandwich

Brownstown

Amherstburg

LAKE ERIE

Frenchtown

INDIANA TERRITORY

Rapids of the Maumee River

Point Pelee

Tippecanoe River

Maumee River

Fort Defiance

Au Glaize River

Sandusky

Cleveland

River

Upper Sandusky

Wabash River

OHIO

Ohio River

Alleghany

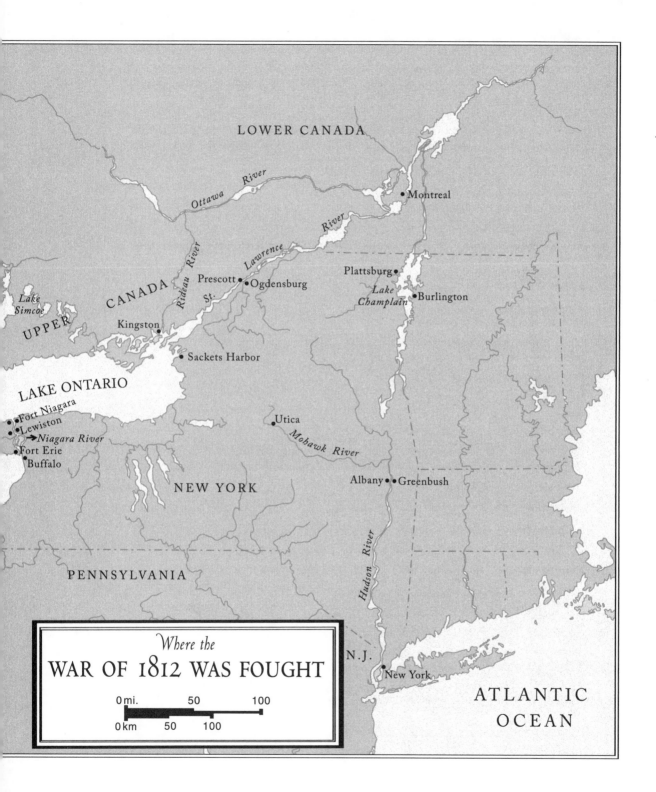

LOWER CANADA

Ottawa River

Montreal

Rideau River

St. *Lawrence River*

UPPER CANADA

Lake Simcoe

Prescott • •Ogdensburg

Plattsburg•

Lake Champlain •Burlington

Kingston

• Sackets Harbor

LAKE ONTARIO

•Fort Niagara
•Lewiston
→*Niagara River*
•Fort Erie
•Buffalo

•Utica

Mohawk River

NEW YORK

Albany• •Greenbush

PENNSYLVANIA

Hudson River

N.J.

New York

ATLANTIC OCEAN

Where the
WAR OF 1812 WAS FOUGHT

0 mi.   50   100

0 km   50   100

Cover and interior design by John Luckhurst
Maps by Brian Smith / Articulate Eye
Front cover image *The Battle of Queenston Heights*, Major James B. Dennis (The Weir Foundation, Queenston, Ontario, 982.2)
Back cover image *The Meeting of Brock and Tecumseh*, C. W. Jefferys (Archives of Ontario, AC621231)
Copyedited by Joan Tetrault
Proofread by Ann Sullivan
Scans by ABL Imaging

A Note on the Type:
The type in this book is set in Minion, Cloister Open Face, and Delphin IIA.

The publisher gratefully acknowledges the support of The Canada Council for the Arts and the Department of Canadian Heritage.

THE CANADA COUNCIL | LE CONSEIL DES ARTS
FOR THE ARTS | DU CANADA
SINCE 1957 | DEPUIS 1957

We acknowledge the financial support of the Government of Canada through the Book Publishing Industry Development Program (BPIDP) for our publishing activities.

Printed in Canada by Transcontinental

10 09 08 07 06 / 5 4 3 2 1

First published in the United States in 2006 by
Fitzhenry & Whiteside
121 Harvard Avenue, Suite 2
Allston, MA 02134

Library and Archives Canada Cataloguing in Publication

Berton, Pierre, 1920-
The battles of the War of 1918 / Pierre Berton.

Includes index.
ISBN-13: 978-1-897252-01-7
ISBN-10: 1-897252-01-3

1. Canada--History--War of 1812--Campaigns--Juvenile literature.
I. Title.

FC442.B462 2006   j971.03'4   C2006-902916-4

FIFTH HOUSE LTD.
A Fitzhenry & Whiteside Company
1511, 1800-4 St. SW
Calgary, Alberta T2S 2S5

1-800-387-9776
www.fitzhenry.ca

The Battles of the War of 1812
An Omnibus

Pierre Berton

FIFTH
HOUSE

CONTENTS

Foreword *by Charlotte Gray*

You can almost smell the battle—the stink of sour sweat and fear, the bitter reek of cordite, the acrid stench of flames licking at tar-covered ropes. And you can hear the rumbles of gun carriages, the thud of cannonballs, the whistle of grapeshot, and the piercing, relentless howls of agony as bullets find their mark.

When Pierre Berton describes a battle, you are right *there*. You get to know the commanders; you meet some of the eager young soldiers; you *care* about what happens to them. Once the guns start firing, you are both exhilarated and fearful. Will General Isaac Brock beat the Yankees back across the Niagara River? Will the great Shawnee warrior Tecumseh achieve his dream of uniting different Indian peoples and creating an independent Native state? Will Commodore Oliver Perry, in charge of the American fleet on Fort Erie, get his big new ships across the sand bar at Presqu'Isle in time to do battle? Will twelve-year old George Jarvis live to tell the tale of the day he followed General Brock up Queenston Heights?

I met Pierre Berton only a couple of times, but in each case I was instantly aware that he was someone who gave himself heart and soul to whatever project he was engaged in. Brown eyes twinkling, he radiated energy. On one occasion, we were both being interviewed on CBC Radio about how to get Canadians, and particularly young adults, fired up about our history. I remember him leaning towards the microphone, clenching his fists as though ready for a brawl, and insisting, "Forget dates. You don't need a string of dates. You need to tell 'em what happened—who won, who lost, and why it mattered!"

Now, reading Berton's dramatic descriptions of the battles of the War of

1812, I realize that is exactly what he did. Berton's thrilling blow-by-blow descriptions of these battles are grounded in his sheer enthusiasm for getting in the middle of the fight. When I peer into the smoke above the battlegrounds, I can almost see Berton's tall, lean, white-haired figure, waving his musket in the air and shouting, "C'mon, boys, follow me!"

Like any good military leader, he was well prepared. He immersed himself in the details of each side's strengths and weaknesses, each commander's strategies, and the unpredictable factors that make the difference between victory and defeat. Berton was *really* good at research. One piece of advice he gave any rookie writer was, "Always check the weather records for the period you are describing."

All the true stuff Berton dug up meant he could recreate a scene so vividly that reading it is like watching a movie of the battle. Imagine, for example, being a young sailor on the American flagship *Lawrence*, during the Battle of Lake Erie, and seeing first a red-hot canon-ball crashing into a pan of boiling peas, and then a runaway pig guzzling up the spilt peas as buckshot hailed down from the skies. Or imagine catching a bunch of Kentucky soldiers, after the battle on the Thames River, skinning the body of an Indian to make souvenir razor strops.

Berton also tells us why these battles mattered.

The War of 1812 barely rates a mention in many of the weighty tomes covering the history of North America. A minor conflict in which the United States attempted to invade Canada, it was overshadowed by major clashes on the other side of the Atlantic Ocean. For almost a decade, Napoleon Bonaparte's France had been pitted against the rest of Europe. The number of casualties sustained in a single Napoleonic battle surpassed the entire population of Upper Canada. The leaders of the great European powers paid scant attention to a few messy skirmishes between tiny, ill-equipped armies in remote and distant American territories. They certainly weren't particularly concerned when, in 1812, U.S. President Madison declared that he was going to invade British North America to punish Britain for arrogantly capturing American ships in the Atlantic. A whiff of "Who cares?" drifted towards Britain's beleaguered colonists.

But along the disputed border, these hostilities completely disrupted the rhythms of the pioneer farms and tiny market towns. Until 1812, the men and women who lived along the border had all but ignored it. Residents each side of the border were linked by trade, language, family ties, and the common struggle to wrest a living from the wilderness. Once war broke out, settlers also had to cope with hungry soldiers breaking down fences, stealing supplies, and burning barns. At harvest time, army commanders quickly discovered that half their soldiers deserted to bring in the crops. When winter set in, it was too cold to fight, so the conflict was put on hold until icicles melted in the spring. And in the end, after bloody skirmishes had spluttered along for thirty months, none of the participants—the Canadian settlers, the Americans, or the Indians—made significant gains in land, power, or prestige. The Indians were betrayed by both sides. At one level, it was, as Berton says, "a very silly war," which ended in a stalemate.

At a deeper level, however, the war mattered big-time. The Canadians had neither expected nor wanted the war. Yet despite their distaste for the fight, they had managed to repel five separate American attacks. They had watched Americans burn their parliament buildings in York (which would soon be renamed Toronto), but they and their fledgling colony had survived. As Berton himself put it so well, "The plain people ... developed a sense of pride and a sense of community."

It was a pride in Canada that Berton himself relished as he plunged into the battles of 1812. Pierre Berton never underestimated the sheer horrors of war: the agonies of the wounded as they watched the amputation of their shattered limbs; the aching hunger of ill-equipped soldiers under canvas during a winter so cold it made their teeth rattle. But Berton understood how individual tragedy and heroism shape a larger story. And throughout his own career, as a public personality and writer, he was a passionate Canadian nationalist. As he leads us all into an exploration of the last war fought on Canadian soil, I can still hear his voice ("C'mon, readers, follow me!"). It was a war that helped create the Canada we see today—a Canada that the late, great Pierre Berton loved.

Charlotte Gray
June 2006

"William Hull" (1753–1825),
by James Sharples Sr. Hull was an American general who
surrendered Fort Detroit to Canada's General Isaac Brock
at the beginning of the War of 1812.

THE CAPTURE OF DETROIT

CONTENTS

The Peculiar War

WHEN WAR BROKE OUT BETWEEN THE UNITED STATES AND CANADA IN JUNE OF 1812, JOHN RICHARDSON RUSHED TO JOIN THE COLOURS. HE WAS ONLY 15 — A SLIGHT, CURLY-HEADED, CLEAN-SHAVEN YOUTH — BUT, UNLIKE SO MANY OF HIS NEIGHBOURS, HE WAS EAGER TO SERVE HIS COUNTRY.

Many of his neighbours on the Detroit River were recent arrivals from the United States, reluctant to fight their former compatriots. But Richardson came of solid Canadian stock. His mother's father, John Askin, was a famous fur trader. His grandmother was an Ottawa Indian of the Algonquin nation. And so young John, to his considerable delight, found himself accepted as a "gentleman volunteer" in a regular regiment—the British 41st—stationed in Fort Amherstburg not far from the present site of Windsor. In the next thirty months, he probably saw more of the War of 1812 than any other teenager in Upper Canada.

After fifteen months of fighting, Richardson was captured by the Americans—a capture that tells us a good deal about that most peculiar of wars. Unlike so many prisoners in so many jail cells around the world, he could be fairly sure of decent treatment by his enemies, because he knew so many of them. His grandfather, John Askin, had only to write a note to the American colonel at Fort Detroit asking him to look after the boy. After all, that colonel was Askin's son-in-law. The man in charge of his prison was another relative.

The War of 1812, then, must be seen as a civil war fought by men and women on both sides of a border that all had ignored until hostilities broke out. Many were former neighbours who spoke the same language and were often related to one another. Unlike the Richardsons, three out of every five were former Americans.

Some had come up from the United States after the American Revolution. These "Tories," as their compatriots called them, were fiercely loyal to the British Crown. Canadians know them as "United Empire Loyalists." They formed the backbone of the volunteer civilian army, known as the militia.

The others were more recent arrivals. They came to Canada because the land was cheap and taxes almost non-existent. They wanted to be left alone to clear the land of stumps, to drain the marshes, till the soil, and harvest their crops of wheat, barley, and corn, or tend the apple, pear, and cherry trees that grew so abundantly along the border.

For them, life was hard enough without war. They built their own cabins and barns with the help of their neighbours and, since there was scarcely anything resembling a shop or a store, they made everything themselves, from farm implements to the homespun clothing that was the universal dress. Those villages that existed at all were mere huddles of shacks. Communication was difficult and sometimes impossible. Newspapers were virtually unknown. In the single room schoolhouses, children learned to read, write, and figure—not much more.

It was, like so many conflicts, a very silly war. Communication was so bad that hundreds of soldiers, not to mention generals, had no idea it had begun.

These people didn't want to fight any more than their counterparts, the civilian soldiers south of the border. It was indeed a peculiar war that moved along in fits and starts, like a springless buggy bumping over a dirt track. At harvest time and seeding, farmers on both sides deserted or were sent off to tend to their crops. In winter, nothing moved; it was too cold to fight, and so each autumn all activity was postponed until spring.

It was, like so many conflicts, a very silly war. Communication was so bad that hundreds of soldiers, not to mention generals, had no idea it had begun. The last bloody battle was fought long after peace had been declared. The problems that had caused the war in the first place—Great Britain's attacks on American shipping—were solved well before the war ended. But the war went on—men were maimed and killed, farms were vandalized, barns were burned, whole communities were put to the torch, and "traitors" were hanged for no purpose.

Why were young Canadians like John Richardson fighting young Americans along the international border? The Canadians who fought did so to protect their country from attack. The Americans were fighting for something less tangible—their honour. Once again, they felt, the British were pushing them around. The War of 1812 was in many ways a continuation of the War of Independence fought forty years before.

It started with Napoleon Bonaparte, the dictator of France. Bonaparte wanted to conquer all of Europe, and so the British found themselves locked in a long and bloody struggle with him—a struggle that began with the great British naval victory at Trafalgar and ended a decade later with the famous battle of Waterloo.

But in their zeal to conquer Napoleon, the British pushed the Americans too far. By boarding American ships on the high seas and kidnapping American sailors for service in the Royal Navy—on the grounds that these seamen were actually British deserters—they got the Americans' backs up. Then, in order to strangle the French by a sea blockade, the British announced they would seize any ship that dared sail directly for a French port. By 1812, they had captured four hundred American vessels, some within sight of the U.S. coast.

That was too much. The United States at last declared war on Great Britain. Since it couldn't attack England directly, it determined to give the British a bloody nose by invading its colony, Canada.

To President Thomas Jefferson, that seemed "a mere matter of marching." Surely the United States, with a population of eight million, could easily defeat a mere three hundred thousand Canadians!

The odds, however, weren't quite as unequal as Jefferson supposed. Great Britain had 17,000 regular troops stationed in Upper and Lower Canada. The entire U.S. regular army numbered only 7,000, many of them badly trained.

Moreover, the British controlled the water routes—Lakes Huron, Erie, and Ontario, and also the St. Lawrence River. For that was the key to both mobility and communication. The roads were almost worthless when they existed at all—not much more than rutted cart tracks. Everything—supplies, troops, and weapons—moved by water.

When the war broke out, the Americans were prevented from using this water highway by the presence of the Royal Navy on the lakes. A British express canoe could move swiftly and fearlessly all the way to Lake Superior, carrying dispatches. But the American high command had difficulty communicating at all, which explains why its outposts didn't know for a month that the war was on. The Americans had to use express riders—bold men on horseback, plunging through a jungle of forest and swamp and exposed at every turn to an Indian ambush.

No wonder, then, that almost from the outset the War of 1812 developed into a shipbuilding contest, with both sides feverishly hammering men-of-war to completion in a race to control the lakes.

The Indians were another asset for the British. The Americans had turned them into enemies, burning their crops and villages and hunting them down like wild animals. In American eyes, the Indians were an obstruction to be pushed aside or eliminated as the pioneers and settlers moved resolutely westward. But the Canadians hadn't fought the Indians since the days of the French-English wars fifty years before. They saw them as harvesters of furs, or, as in the case of the Mohawks of the Grand Valley, loyal subjects of the King.

The American attitude caused John Richardson's boyhood friend, Tecumseh, to move into Upper Canada from the U.S. with his followers to fight on the British side. The Native allies numbered no more than two thousand in all, but with their woodcraft they made a formidable enemy. The Americans were terrified of the Indians. The mere hint that a force of Natives was advancing could send a chill through the blood of the citizen soldiers of Ohio or Kentucky.

As a member of the regular army, John Richardson wore a scarlet uniform and carried a musket almost as tall as himself. This awkward, muzzle-loading "Brown Bess" was the basic infantry weapon—and a notoriously inaccurate one. The little one-ounce (30-g) ball, wobbling down the smooth barrel, could fly off in any direction. Richardson and his fellow soldiers didn't bother to aim their weapons; they pointed them in the direction of the enemy, waited for the command, and then fired in unison.

The effect of several hundred men, marching in line and in step, shoulders touching, and advancing behind a spray of lead, could be devastating. The noise alone was terrifying. The musket's roar makes the crack of a modern rifle sound like a popgun. Smokeless powder was unknown; after the first volley the battlefield was shrouded in a thick fog of grey.

It required twelve separate movements to load and fire a musket. A well-drilled soldier could get off two or three shots a minute. By that time he was usually close enough to the enemy to rely on his bayonet.

Young Richardson learned to remove a paper cartridge from his pouch, tear off the top with his teeth, and pour a little powder in the firing pan and the rest down the barrel. Then he stuffed it with wadding, tapped it tight with his ramrod, and dropped in the ball. When he pulled the trigger it engaged the flintlock whose spark (he hoped) would ignite the powder in the pan and send a flash through a pinhole, exploding the charge in the barrel. As Richardson himself discovered at the Battle of Frenchtown later that year, it didn't always work. The phrase "a flash in the pan" comes down to us from those days.

> *It required twelve separate movements to load and fire a musket. A well-drilled soldier could get off two or three shots a minute. By that time he was usually close enough to the enemy to rely on his bayonet.*

Some of the American woodsmen used the famous Tennessee rifle, a far more accurate weapon because of the spiral groove inside the barrel. That put a spin on the ball—in the same way a pitcher does in baseball—making it far easier to hit the target. However, it was slower to load and was used mainly by snipers or individual soldiers.

A more terrible weapon was the cannon, which operated on the same flintlock principle as the musket. From the tiny three-pounders (1.4-kg) to the big twenty-four-pounders (11-kg), these weapons were identified by the weight of shot they hurled at the ramparts of the defenders. A sixteen-pound (7-kg) ball of solid pig iron (known as "roundshot") could knock down a file of two dozen men. Bombs—hollowed out shot, crammed with powder and bric-a-brac, and fused to explode in mid-air—were even more devastating. Every soldier feared the canister and grape shot—sacks or metal canisters filled with musket balls that broke apart in the air, sending scores of projectiles whirling above the enemy.

Crude as they seem to us now, these weapons caused a dreadful havoc for the soldiers who fought in the war. Men with mangled limbs and jagged wounds faced searing pain because anaesthetics had not been invented. Yet, grievously wounded men pleaded with army surgeons to amputate a wounded limb as quickly as possible for fear of gangrene. They swallowed a tot of rum or whisky, held a bullet ("biting the bullet") between their gritted teeth, and endured fearful agony as the knives and saws did their work.

Sanitation in the field was primitive, for science had not yet discovered that diseases were caused by germs. Measles, typhus, typhoid, influenza, and dysentery probably put more men out of action than the enemy. The universal remedy was liquor—a daily glass of strong Jamaica rum for the British, a quarter pint (200 mL) of raw whisky for the Americans. In battle after battle, the combatants on both sides were at least half drunk. Hundreds of youths who had never touched hard liquor in their lives learned to stiffen their resolve through alcohol in the War of 1812.

These were civilian soldiers, members of the militia. In Canada, the Sedentary Militia, largely untrained, was available in times of crisis. Every fit male between eighteen and sixty was required to serve in it when needed. Few had uniforms, and those who did were as tattered as beggars. Often they were sent home to their farms after a battle, to be called up later.

Some signed up in the Incorporated Militia of Upper Canada for the duration of the war. These were young men inspired by patriotism, a sense of adventure, or the bounty of eighty dollars paid to every volunteer upon enlistment. In Lower Canada, a similar body of the Select Embodied Militia, composed of men between eighteen and twenty-five, was drawn by lot to serve for a minimum of two years. They were paid and trained as regular soldiers. In addition, some regular units were also recruited in Canada, bearing such names as the Glengarry Fencibles or the Canadian Voltigeurs.

The American draftees and volunteers were engaged by the various states for shorter periods—as little as a month, as much as a year. Most refused to serve beyond that period; few were properly trained. Born of revolution and dedicated to absolute democracy, the United States had decided against a large standing army. The citizen soldiers even elected their own officers—an awkward and not very efficient process, sneered at by the regulars. And they were recruited to fight *only* in defence of their country.

That caused a major problem for the United States. Legally, the state militia didn't have to cross the border. Hundreds who had been drafted reluctantly used that excuse when their superiors tried to goad them into attacking Canada. Jefferson had said it was "a mere matter of marching," but when the armies reached the border, the marching stopped.

They didn't want to fight any more than their former compatriots, now tilling the fields and tending the orchards on the other side. That was one of the reasons why this peculiar war ended in stalemate. The Americans derived very little benefit from it; nor did the Indians, who were eventually betrayed by both sides when the peace talks were held. The only real victors were the Canadians, who got no territory but gained something less tangible, yet in the end more precious. Having helped to hurl back five American armies, the plain people who had once been so indifferent to the war developed both a sense of pride and a sense of community. They had come through the fire and they had survived. In a very real sense the War of 1812 marked the first faint stirrings of a united Canadian nation.

CHAPTER ONE

Isaac Brock's Secret Message

THERE WAS A TIME, AT THE TURN OF THE NINETEENTH CENTURY, WHEN THE CITY OF DETROIT WAS NOTHING MORE THAN A PALISADED FORT IN THE WILDERNESS. WINDSOR DID NOT YET EXIST, EXCEPT IN THE VILLAGE OF SANDWICH, NOW A WINDSOR SUBURB. A FEW KILOMETRES DOWN THE DETROIT RIVER, AS IT ENTERS LAKE ERIE, WAS THE BRITISH FORT AMHERSTBURG, WHICH THE AMERICANS CALLED FORT MALDEN. AND IT WAS HERE THAT THE WAR OF 1812 BEGAN.

It was from Fort Detroit that the Americans hoped to invade Canada in the summer of 1812. It seemed simple enough. The British fort was lightly held and a large American force of 2,200 men was advancing toward the border. But, as it turned out, it wasn't simple at all. Instead of surrendering to superior numbers, the Canadians, British, and Indians turned the tables on the invaders and seized not only Fort Detroit but most of Michigan Territory with scarcely a drop of blood spilled.

How did they do it? How did they capture an entire American army? The answer has less to do with soldiers and guns than with the personalities of the two opposing commanders: the British general, Isaac Brock, who hated and despised his job, and his American opposite number, William Hull, an old soldier who didn't really want to fight.

Both had a long experience of war, but Hull at fifty-eight was in decline while Brock, a vibrant forty-two, was fairly itching for battle.

It tells you something about Hull that his men thought him closer to seventy. As governor of Michigan Territory, he saw himself as a father figure, protecting his people from the ravages of the Indians who had been driven to the British side by American policies. Certainly, he looked like a grandfather with his distinguished features gone to flesh and his shock of

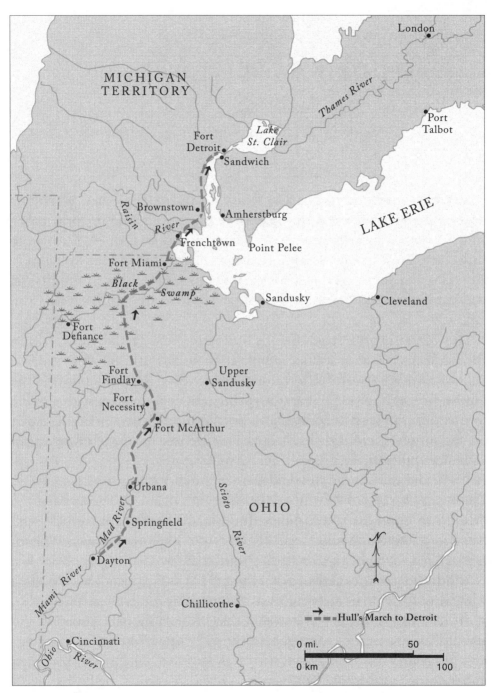

London

MICHIGAN
TERRITORY

Thames River

Port
Talbot

Fort
Detroit

*Lake
St. Clair*

Sandwich

Brownstown

Raisin

River

Amherstburg

LAKE ERIE

Frenchtown

Point Pelee

Fort Miami

Black   *Swamp*

Sandusky

Cleveland

Fort
Defiance

Fort
Findlay

Upper
Sandusky

Fort
Necessity

Fort McArthur

Urbana

Scioto

OHIO

Mad River

Springfield

River

Dayton

N

Chillicothe

→ Hull's March to Detroit

Miami River

0 mi.   50

0 km   100

Cincinnati

Ohio   *River*

Detroit *and vicinity*

dead-white hair. He chewed tobacco unceasingly, especially when he was nervous; then his jaws worked overtime.

During the American Revolution, Hull had been a bold and gallant officer who fought with distinction, survived nine battles, and received the official thanks of Congress. But now he was fading away.

Brock, on the other hand, breathed hell fire. Let us look at him a few months before the war—the date is February 27—seated in his study in Little York, the future site of Toronto, composing a secret letter that will affect the future of his country. We see a remarkably handsome soldier with a fair complexion, a broad forehead, clear eyes of grey blue, and sparkling white teeth. Isaac Brock fitted the kind of role that Hollywood casting directors have in mind when they need an actor to play a British officer.

He was a massive figure, was Brock, big-boned and powerful, almost six foot, three inches (2 m) in height, with a slight tendency to portliness and the flush of middle age on his cheeks. But in his own words—and his own words survive in his letters and documents—he was "hard as nails." He was popular, too—especially with his soldiers—but he was also aloof. He took few into his confidence.

Behind that formidable exterior there was concealed a frustrated soul. Brock was the most powerful man in Upper Canada; president and chief administrator of the province and head of the army—a virtual dictator, in short, who took his orders from the Governor General in Montreal. But he was not happy. He wanted desperately to be in on the *real* fighting in Europe, where the Duke of Wellington was locked in a life-and-death struggle with Napoleon's armies.

Brock didn't care for Canada. To him it was a frontier backwater, especially York, which he found as unsophisticated as it was muddy. A gourmet, a lover of fine wines, an omnivorous reader, and a spirited dancer at society balls, he longed for a larger community. He despised the local legislature and was quite prepared to ride over it roughshod if necessary. General Brock was no democrat. Democracy to him was an American concept—and a poisonous one.

Now, in this very month of February, he had been handed exactly what he desired—permission from the Governor General to escape from his colonial prison and join Wellington in Europe. Bitterly, he realized he could not go. Canada was on the verge of war; the general must stay; duty would have to take precedence over personal whim. Or was that strictly true? Perhaps, expecting war, Brock welcomed it. He was, after all, a warrior. Glory, honour, adventure all beckoned; all these—and even death.

Like a good commander, Brock put himself in the shoes of his antagonists. For five years, ever since the British had begun to harry the Americans on the high seas, he had been certain that war would come. For five years he had been preparing for it. Already he was planning to reinforce Fort Amherstburg. Meanwhile, the secret letter he was scribbling in his study that February afternoon was to form part of his plan for the defence of Canada.

The letter was addressed to a strange frontier figure far out on the western plains. His real name was Robert Dickson, but the Sioux knew him as Mascotopah—the Red-Haired Man. Brock desperately needed him to arouse the various western tribes—Menomenee, Winnebago, Ottawa, Chippewa, as well as the Sioux—to fight the Americans. Many were old enemies; Brock would need the respected Mascotopah to weld them into a fighting force.

Through their hunger for land, the Americans had made enemies of the Indians on the northwestern frontier. In Brock's view, the Indians were the key to victory; the security of Canada depended upon them. For it he could rouse the tribes with Dickson's help. The United States would have to waste much of its limited military strength trying to subdue them. That would weaken the invading army.

This was the substance of his secret communication. Dickson was born a Scot but he was as close to being an Indian as any white could be. His wife was the sister of a Sioux chief. His domain covered the present-day states of Iowa, Wisconsin, and Minnesota.

Dickson was out there somewhere in that empty wilderness—nobody knew quite where—a white man living like an Indian and exercising all the powers of a Sioux chief. Brock had to find him before the war began and that would not be easy.

He knew that the Indians would fight the Americans only if they were convinced the British were winning. If he could seize the American island of Michilimackinac (known simply as Mackinac and pronounced "Mackinaw"), he knew the tribes would take heart.

This little rock was immensely significant and, if you look at the map, you will see why. It sits in the channel that joins three of the Great Lakes—Michigan, Superior, and Huron. Any force entering any of these lakes would have to come under its guns. If Dickson and his followers could seize it, they would control the water highway of the Northwest.

Isaac Brock believed that offence is the best defence. If Michilimackinac fell, then Dickson's Indians would help him attack Detroit. There, they would be joined by another Native force—those disenchanted members of several American tribes who had come together under the great Shawnee war chief, Tecumseh, to do battle on the British side. And if Detroit fell, more Indians would join—even, he hoped, the Mohawks who, to this time, had been distressingly neutral.

And so he sent off his secret missive addressed only "To Mr. Robert Dickson residing with the Indians near Missouri." Almost five months went by before he received his answer, an answer that was already outdated by events. Long before that, the Red-Haired Man and his friends, anticipating Brock, had departed for Canada to prepare for the invasion of the unsuspecting island.

CHAPTER TWO

The Americans March North

BROCK WAS DEAD RIGHT. IT WAS THE INDIANS WHO DICTATED WASHINGTON'S
PLANS IN A WAR THAT WAS NOT YET DECLARED. TECUMSEH AND HIS FOLLOWERS
WERE CREATING CHAOS IN THE INDIANA AND MICHIGAN TERRITORIES. THE
UNITED STATES WOULD HAVE TO DEAL WITH THEM BEFORE ATTACKING
MONTREAL.

To advance the American war plans, the administration invited William
Hull, the governor of Michigan Territory, to come to Washington to discuss
the defence of the northwestern frontier. Washington believed in Hull.
Because he had a reputation for sound judgment, personal courage, and
decisive command, President Madison listened carefully to his advice.

Hull pointed out that the United States must secure Lake Erie by reinforcing the tiny fort at Detroit and by building warships to command the
water routes. Only in that way could they be sure of the swift movement of
men and supplies.

Hull realized, as Brock did, that the Indians held the key to defeat or victory. A formidable army at Detroit, denying the lake to British ships, could
cut the Indians off from the British and perhaps prevent a general uprising
of the tribes. Hull was convinced that without the Indians "the British cannot hold Upper Canada."

The government agreed, and Hull was told to raise an army of twelve
hundred volunteers from the Ohio Militia. With that force he would have
to cut a road through forest and swamp for two hundred miles (320 km)
from Urbana, Ohio, to Detroit, and thus secure the frontier.

It all made sense on paper. But it depended on inspired leadership, swift
communications, careful timing, well-trained troops, an efficient war
department, and a united, enthusiastic nation. Unfortunately for the
Americans, none of these conditions existed.

The men seemed anxious enough to fight. By May, Ohio's quota of twelve hundred volunteers was oversubscribed. Sixteen hundred answered the call. The new general joined his troops at Dayton, Ohio, after a journey that left him weak from cold and fever. In spite of his reputation, he was a flabby old soldier, tired of war, hesitant of command, and suspicious of the militia, who he knew were untrained and suspected were untrustworthy.

He paraded his troops on May 25—an unruly lot: noisy, disobedient, untrained. He was appalled. Their arms were unfit for use, the leather covering the cartridge boxes was rotten, many had no blankets or clothing. No armourers had been provided to repair the weapons, no means adopted to furnish the missing clothing, no stores of arms or supplies existed. The powder in the magazines was useless. America wasn't ready for battle. It hadn't contemplated an offensive war—or even a defensive one—at any time since the Revolution.

When Hull and his staff set off to view the troops with a fife and drum corps leading the way, there was a note of farce. The sound of the drums frightened the ponies. The general's horse shied. Hull's feet slipped out of the stirrups, he lost his balance, his hat flew off, and he was forced to cling to the animal's mane in a most unsoldierly fashion until it slowed to a walk. It was not a happy beginning for the invasion of Canada.

The volunteers were formed into three regiments. Because they elected their own leaders, their officers had to act as politicians. In fact the three regimental commanders had been politicians in civilian life. Hull had his trouble with these three, one of whom called him "a weak old man." Hull was just as contemptuous of the volunteers as they were of him.

The army started to march north on June 1. A few days later at the frontier community of Urbana, the last outpost of civilization, Hull's suspicions were reinforced. From that point to Detroit the troops faced two hundred miles (320 km) of wilderness with no pathway, not even an Indian trail to follow. The volunteers turned ugly. They had been promised an advance of fifty dollars each for a year's clothing; they got only sixteen. They rode one unpopular officer out of camp on a rail and, when the orders came to march, scores refused to move. Only the regular infantry was able to prod the wavering volunteers into action.

Off they went, hacking away through jungle and forest, as much a mob as an army. The rain fell all the time. The newly built road became a swamp. Wagons were mired and had to be hoisted by brute strength. The troops kept their spirits up on corn liquor supplied by friendly settlers.

They plunged through the pelting rain into the no man's land of the Black Swamp, a labyrinth of deadfalls and ghostly trees behind whose trunks Tecumseh's unseen Indian spies kept watch. A fog of insects clogged the soldiers' nostrils and bloated their faces; a gruel of mud and water rotted their boots and swelled their ankles. They could not rest at day's end until they hacked out a barricade against Indian attack.

Strung out for two miles (3.2 km), day after day, the human serpent finally wriggled to a halt, blocked by rising water and unbridgeable streams. Hull camped his men in ankle-deep mud and built a blockhouse, which he named Fort Necessity. There, the sodden army waited until the floods ebbed. Yet Hull himself was not cast down. He had more than two thousand rank and file under his command and still believed his force superior to any that might oppose it.

The troops finally moved out and reached a branch of the Maumee River. And there a letter caught up with Hull from the secretary of war urging him to advance with all possible haste to Fort Detroit, to await further orders. That letter was dated June 18. It must have been written on the morning of that day, because it failed to include the one piece of information essential to prevent a major blunder.

On the afternoon of June 18, the United States officially declared war on Great Britain.

CHAPTER THREE

The Red-Haired Man

ON THE VERY DAY THAT WAR WAS DECLARED, BROCK'S COURIER CAUGHT UP AT LAST WITH THE RED-HAIRED MAN. HE FOUND HIM AT THE WISCONSIN-FOX PORTAGE IN ILLINOIS TERRITORY. ROBERT DICKSON WAS A MAN OF COMMANDING PRESENCE, A MASSIVE AND CHEERFUL SIX-FOOTER (2 M), WITH A FLAMING SHOCK OF RED HAIR AND A RUDDY FACE TO MATCH. EVERYBODY LIKED HIM. THERE WAS AN EASY SOCIABILITY ABOUT DICKSON — A DIGNITY, A SENSE OF HONOUR AND PRINCIPLE. MEN OF EVERY COLOUR TRUSTED HIM. HE WAS ALSO HUMANE. HE HAD TRIED TO TEACH THE INDIANS NOT TO KILL AND SCALP WHEN THEY TOOK PRISONERS. THE GREATEST WARRIORS, HE TOLD HIS PEOPLE, WERE THOSE WHO SAVED THEIR CAPTIVES RATHER THAN DESTROYED THEM.

What was he doing out here in this lonely land? He lived often in great squalor, existing for weeks on wild rice, corn, and pemmican or sometimes on nothing but melted snow, going for months without hearing his native tongue, trudging for kilometres on snowshoes or struggling over long portages with back-breaking loads; he was never at rest. He knew no real home but moved ceaselessly along his string of trading posts like a trapper tending a trapline.

His two brothers, who also emigrated from Scotland, preferred the civilized life. But Robert Dickson had spent twenty years in Indian country. Why? Certainly not for profit. He had little money; the fur trade was a risky business. Not for glory, for there was no glory. For power? He could have had more in the white man's world. The answer seems to be that he was here, like so many of his countrymen, for the adventure of the frontier—the risks, the dangers, the excitement, and now, perhaps, because after two decades these were his people, and this wild, untravelled land was his home.

Beyond the Great Lakes there were others like him, living among the Indians, exploring the land. Most were Scotsmen.

Dickson liked the Indians for themselves. He was faithful to his Indian wife, prided himself that he was educating his half-Indian children, and was angered by the treatment his people received from American frontiersmen who saw the Indian as a dangerous animal to be exterminated. His patriotism needed no fuelling. He was more than delighted to aid his countrymen.

He lost no time. That very day he sent a reply to Brock and dispatched it to Fort Amherstburg with thirty Menomenee warriors. Then with 130 Sioux, Winnebago, and Menomenee, he set off for St. Joseph's Island, the British outpost at the western entrance to Lake Huron. There he waited for orders.

They came by express canoe on July 15. The British commander at St. Joseph's Island, Captain Charles Roberts, was told to "adopt the most prudent measure either of offence or defence which circumstances might point out." Roberts resolved to make the most of these ambiguous instructions. The following morning to the skirl of fife and the roll of drum—banners waving, Indians whooping—his polyglot army embarked upon the glassy waters of the lake.

Off sailed the gunboat *Caledonia* (seized from the Montreal-based North West Company, or Nor'Westers), loaded with two brass cannon, her decks bright with the red tunics of the forty regulars. Behind her followed ten big square-prowed bateaux crammed with 180 voyageurs, brilliant in their sashes, silk kerchiefs, and capotes. Slipping in and out of the flotilla were seventy painted birchbark canoes containing close to three hundred tribesmen—Dickson, in Indian dress, with fifty feathered Sioux; their one-time enemies, the Chippewa, with coal black faces, shaved heads, and bodies daubed with pipe clay; two dozen Winnebago, including the celebrated one-eyed chief, Big Canoe; forty Menomenee under their head chief, Tomah; and thirty Ottawa led by Amable Chevalier, the half-white trader whom they recognized as leader.

Ahead lay the island of Michilimackinac. Shaped like an Aboriginal arrowhead, it was almost entirely surrounded by 150-foot (45-m) cliffs of soft grey limestone. The British had abandoned it grudgingly following the Revolution, though they realized its strategic importance. Control of

Mackinac meant control of the western fur trade. No wonder Roberts had no trouble conscripting Canadian voyageurs.

They were pulling on their oars like madmen, for they had to reach their objective, some fifty miles (80 km) to the southwest, well before dawn. Around midnight, about fifteen miles (24 km) from the island, they spotted a birchbark canoe. Its passenger was an old crony from Mackinac, a Pennsylvania fur trader named Michael Dousman. He was sent by Porter Hanks, the American commander, to try to find out what was taking place north of the border.

Dousman, in spite of the fact that he was an American militia commander, was first and foremost a fur trader, and an old colleague and occasional partner of the leaders of the voyageurs and Indians. He greeted Dickson and the others as old friends, and cheerfully told Roberts everything he needed to know: the strength of the American garrison, its armament (or lack of it), and—most important of all—the fact that no one on the island had been told that America was at war.

Dousman's and Roberts's concerns were identical. In the event of a struggle they wanted to protect the civilians on the island from the wrath of the Indians. Dousman agreed to wake the village quietly and herd everybody into the old distillery at the end of town where they could be guarded by the detachment of regulars. He promised not to warn the garrison.

CHAPTER FOUR

Bloodless Victory

AT MACKINAC THE AMERICANS SLEPT. THE LAKE WAS SILENT IN THOSE SMALL HOURS — SILENT SAVE FOR THE WHISPER OF WAVES LAPPING THE SHORELINE. IN THE STARLIGHT, THE ISLAND'S CLIFFS STOOD OUT DARKLY AGAINST THE SURROUNDING FLATLAND. IN THE FORT ABOVE THE VILLAGE, AT THE SOUTHERN TIP, THE AMERICAN COMMANDER, LIEUTENANT HANKS, LAY ASLEEP, IGNORANT OF A WAR THAT WOULD TRAGICALLY AFFECT HIS FUTURE. IT WAS NINE MONTHS SINCE HE HAD HEARD FROM WASHINGTON. FOR ALL HE KNEW OF THE CIVILIZED WORLD HE MIGHT AS WELL BE ON THE MOON.

The civilized world ended at the Detroit River, some 350 miles (560 km) to the southeast. Mackinac Island was its outpost, lying in the narrows between Lakes Huron and Michigan. Whoever controlled it controlled the routes to the fur country—the domain of the Nor'Westers, beyond Superior and the no man's land of the Upper Missouri and Mississippi. It was a prize worth fighting for.

Hanks slumbered on, oblivious of the quiet bustling in the village directly below—of low knockings, whispers, small children's cries quickly hushed, rustlings, soft footsteps, the creak of cartwheels on grass—slumbered fitfully, his dreams troubled by a growing uneasiness, until the drum roll of reveille woke him.

At three that morning the British had landed on a small beach facing the only break in the escarpment at the north end of the island. With the help of Dousman's ox team, the voyageurs managed to drag the two six-pounders (3-kg) over the boulders and through thickets up to the 300-foot (90-m) crest that overlooked the fort at the southern tip. Meanwhile, Dousman had tiptoed from door to door waking the inhabitants, silently herding them to safety.

When Hanks woke, he peered over the palisades at the fort and gazed down at the village below, a crescent of whitewashed houses, following the curve of a pebbled beach. He saw at once that something was wrong because the village was not sleeping; it was dead. No curl of smoke rose above the cedarbark roofs; no human cry echoed across the waters of the lake; no movement ruffled the weeds that edged the roadway.

What was going on? He ordered his second-in-command, Lieutenant Archibald Darragh, to find out, but he did not need to wait for Darragh's report. Clambering up a slope was the surgeon's mate, Sylvester Day, who preferred to live in the village. Dr. Day's breathless report was blunt: British redcoats and Indians had landed. The villagers had been herded into an old distillery at the west end of town. Three of the most prominent citizens were under guard as hostages.

He saw at once that something was wrong because the village was not sleeping; it was dead. No curl of smoke rose above the cedarbark roofs; no human cry echoed across the waters of the lake; no movement ruffled the weeds that edged the roadway.

Hanks reacted instantly. He mustered his men, stocked his blockhouses with ammunition, charged his field pieces, and followed the book. He must have known that he was merely playing soldier, for he had fewer than sixty effective troops under his command—men made stale by their frontier exile. Presently he became aware of a British six-pounder (3-kg) on the forested bluff above pointing directly into his bastion. Through the spring foliage he could see the flash of British scarlet and—the ultimate horror—the dark forms of their Native allies. A single word formed in his mind, a truly terrible word for anyone with frontier experience: *massacre*—visions of mutilated bodies, decapitated children, disembowelled housewives, scalps bloodying the pickets.

Hanks could fight to the last man and become a hero—after his death. If it were merely the aging troops of St. Joseph's that faced him, he might be prepared to do just that, but to the last woman? To the last child? Against an enemy whose savagery was said to be without limits?

A white flag fluttered before him. Under its protection a British truce party marched into the fort, accompanied by the three civilian hostages.

The parley was brief and to the point. Hanks must surrender. The accompanying phrase "or else" hung unspoken in the air. The hostages urged him to accept, but it is doubtful whether he needed their counsel. He agreed to everything. The fort and island would become British. The Americans would have to take the oath of allegiance to the King or leave. The troops were to be paroled to their homes. That meant that they promised to take no further part in the war until exchanged with prisoners from the other side.

The war? *What* war? The date was July 17. A full month had passed since the United States declared war on Great Britain but this was the first Hanks had heard of it. Nobody in Washington seemed to have seen the urgency of a speedy warning to the western flank on the American frontier. It was typical of this senseless and tragic conflict that it should begin in this topsy-turvy fashion, with the invaders invaded in a trackless wilderness hundreds of kilometres from the nerve centre of command.

For that oversight the American government would pay dearly. This bloodless battle was also one of the most significant. The news of the capture of Mackinac Island touched off a chain of events that frustrated the Americans in their attempt to seize British North America.

And so the first objective in Isaac Brock's carefully programmed campaign to frustrate invasion had been taken without firing a shot. "It is a circumstance I believe without precedent," Roberts reported to Brock. And for the Indians' white leaders he had special praise. Their influence with the tribes was such "that as soon as they heard capitulation was signed they all returned to the Canoes, not one drop either of Man's or Animal's blood was Spilt ..." Hanks's bloodless surrender had prevented a massacre.

Dickson's Indians felt cheated out of a fight. They complained to the Red-Haired Man, who kept them firmly under control, explaining that Americans could not be killed once they surrendered. To placate them he turned loose a number of cattle which were chased around the island, their flanks bristling with arrows until they hurled themselves into the water. They were further appeased by a distribution of blankets, provisions, and guns taken from the American military stores. There, they also found tonnes of pork and flour, a vast quantity of vinegar, soap, candles, and— to the delight of everybody—357 gallons (1,600 L) of high wines and 253 gallons (630 L) of whisky, enough to get every man, white and red, so drunk that had an enemy of force appeared on the lake it might easily have recaptured the island.

In addition to these spoils a treasure of government-owned furs brought the total of captured goods to ten thousand pounds sterling, all of it to be distributed according to custom among the regulars and volunteers who captured the fort. Every private soldier eventually received ten pounds as his share of the prize money, the officers considerably more.

The message to the Indians was clear: America was a weak nation and rewards could be gained in fighting for the British. The fall of Mackinac gave the British the entire control of the tribes of the Old Northwest.

Porter Hanks and his men were sent off to Detroit under parole. They gave their word not to take any further part in the war until they were exchanged for British or Canadian soldiers of equivalent rank captured by the Americans. This method was used throughout the conflict to eliminate the need for large camps of prisoners to be fed and clothed at the enemy's expense. The Americans who stayed on the island were obliged to take an oath of allegiance to the Crown; otherwise, they must return to American territory. Most found it easy to switch sides, since they had done it before. A good many were originally British until the island changed hands in 1796.

CHAPTER FIVE

Prisoners of the British

LIKE PORTER HANKS, GENERAL WILLIAM HULL'S TATTERED ARMY DID NOT
KNOW THAT WAR HAD BEEN DECLARED AS THEY TRUDGED DOGGEDLY TOWARD
DETROIT. AT THE FOOT OF THE MAUMEE RAPIDS, HULL WAS ABLE TO RELIEVE
HIS EXHAUSTED TEAMS BY LOADING THE SCHOONER *CUYAHOGA* WITH ALL HIS
EXCESS MILITARY STORES — UNIFORMS, BAND INSTRUMENTS, ENTRENCHING
TOOLS, PERSONAL LUGGAGE — AND SOME THIRTY-SIX OFFICERS AND MEN,
TOGETHER WITH THREE WOMEN WHO HAD SOMEHOW MANAGED TO KEEP UP
WITH THEIR HUSBANDS THROUGH THE LONG TREK NORTH.

That was foolish. War was clearly imminent even though Hull, marching on to Detroit, had no word about it. His own officers pointed out that
the *Cuyahoga* would have to pass under the British guns at Fort
Amherstburg—guns that were guarding the narrow river boundary—
before she could reach Detroit. But their commander, sublimely unaware of
his country's declaration, remained confident that the vessel would get to
Detroit before the British army.

Hull's assistant quartermaster-general, an observant soldier named
William K. Beall, stretched out on the deck admiring the view of Lake Erie.
Beall was the kind of man who notes everything and writes it all down. It's
from men and women like him that we can gain a picture of the past. He
was a prosperous Kentucky plantation owner who had never beheld so
much fresh water stretching beyond the horizon. The only water he had
seen since leaving home had flowed sluggishly in saffron streams veining
the dreadful swamps through which the army had just toiled.

As the schooner approached Amherstburg, the little town nestled outside the British fort, Beall was charmed by the view of sunny wheat fields

rippling in the breeze. This southern fringe of orchards was the garden of Upper Canada, but most of the province beyond remained a wilderness, its great forests of pine and oak, maple and basswood broken here and there by small patches of pioneer civilization, like worn spots on a rug. Today Amherstburg is a flourishing town—almost a suburb of Windsor.

Vast swamps, dark and terrifying, smothered the land. Roads were few and, in some seasons, impassable. Sensible travellers moved by water, and it was along the margins of the lake and the banks of the larger river that the main communities such as Amherstburg had sprung up. Between these villages lay smaller settlements. Plots of winter wheat, oats, and rye, fields of corn and vegetables blurred the edges of the forest. Here, along the Detroit River, fruit trees had been bearing for a decade and cider had become a staple drink.

To Beall everything appeared to wear "the cheering smiles of peace and plenty." In the distance he spotted a picturesque Indian canoe. But, as the canoe came closer, it was transformed into a Canadian longboat commanded by an officer of the provincial marine, Lieutenant Frederic Rolette, with six seamen, armed with cutlasses and pistols, pulling on the oars.

Rolette called to *Cuyahoga*'s captain, Luther Chapin, to lower his mainsails. Chapin was open mouthed. He'd expected a friendly hail, but now he saw six muskets raised against him. Before he could act, Rolette fired his pistol in the air. Chapin struggled with a sail. Beall and his fellow passengers were in confusion. What was happening? Beall ordered the captain to hoist the sail and press on, but Chapin replied that was not possible.

Rolette now pointed his pistol directly at young George Gooding, a second lieutenant in charge of the soldiers and baggage.

"Douse your mainsails!" Rolette ordered. Gooding hesitated.

"I have no command here, sir!" he shouted. Rolette fired directly at the schooner, the ball whistling past Beall's head. Captain Chapin pleaded for instructions.

"Do as you please," answered the rattled Gooding, whose wife was also on deck. As the mainsails tumbled, Rolette boarded the packet.

He was astonished to find the decks jammed with American soldiers. They weren't aware the war had started, but Rolette couldn't be sure of that. Nor did he know that all but three were ill, their muskets and ammunition out of reach in the hold. He did know, however, that he was outnumbered five to one.

That did not dismay him. He was a seasoned seaman accustomed to acts of boldness and decision. At the age of twenty-nine, this French-speaking Quebecker had a record any officer might envy. He had fought in the two greatest sea battles of the era—the Nile and Trafalgar—under the finest commander of his time, Horatio Nelson. He had been wounded five times, and before this newest contest was over he would be wounded again. Now he informed the astonished American soldiers that the war was on.

After the schooner had docked, the British realized the importance of their prize. For here they discovered two trunks belonging to General Hull containing documents of extraordinary value.

Losing no time, he ordered everybody below decks and posted sentries at the hatches and arms chests with orders to shoot any man who approached them. He told the helmsman to steer the ship under the cannons of Amherstburg and the band to play "God Save the King."

After the schooner had docked, the British realized the importance of their prize. For here they discovered two trunks belonging to General Hull containing documents of extraordinary value. Hull's aide-de-camp—his son Abraham—had foolishly packed the general's personal papers with his baggage. The astonished British found that they now possessed all the details of the army that was opposing them: field states, complete statistics of the troops, names and strengths of their regiments, an incomplete draft of Hull's strategy, all his correspondence to and from the American secretary of war. It was a find equal to the breaking of an enemy code. The entire package was sent to Brock at York who grasped its significance at once and laid his own plans.

But no one was quite certain how to behave. Had war actually come? Even the British were reluctant to believe it, and William Beall, now a prisoner, doubted it. He was sure his captors were wrongly informed and that, when Hull demanded his return, he and his companions would be permitted to go on to Detroit.

The British were polite, even hospitable. Beall's opposite number in the

British quartermaster department, Lieutenant Edward Dewar, urged the Americans not to think of themselves as prisoners, but merely detainees. It was all very unpleasant, Dewar murmured. He hoped the report of the war might prove incorrect. He hoped the Americans would be able to spend their time in detention as agreeably as possible. If there was any service he and his fellow officers could render, he would be pleased to do so. He wished the schooner had been allowed by without interruption. And if they got authentic information that the war had not been declared, the prisoners would be released at once.

Having accepted the parole of the Americans (that they wouldn't try to escape), Dewar invited them to his home where there was wine, cider, and biscuits. The lieutenant remarked that it would be improper to invite the Americans to dine with them, but he took them to Boyle's Inn and Public House for dinner. Then the men left the inn and strolled through the streets through crowds of Indians. Every white man bowed politely to the strangers, and one even invited them into his house and poured them several glasses of wine.

Many of the citizens of Amherstburg were new arrivals in Upper Canada who had little interest in politics or war. They formed part of a clear but powerless majority in a province of sixty thousand, having been shut out of all public office by the élite group of British and Loyalist administrators who controlled the government. That didn't concern them because they were prospering on their free acreages. Democracy might be virtually non-existent in Upper Canada, but so were taxes since the province was financed by the British treasury. As for the prospect of the war, they dismissed that. Everyone echoed that sentiment.

The captured American women, being non-combatants, were sent to the American side; the men remained aboard a British ship, the *Thames*. Beall estimated that there were at least five hundred Indians in Amherstburg. On July 4, as the sounds of the Independence Day cannonades echoed across the water from Detroit, two hundred Sauk warriors arrived—the largest and best-formed men that Beall had ever seen. On the following day, the sound of Hull's bugler blowing reveille revealed that the Army of the Northwest had reached the village of Brownstown directly across the river, less than a day's march from Detroit.

By nightfall Amherstburg was in a panic. Women and children ran crying toward the vessels at the dockside, loading the decks with trunks and valuables. Indians dashed about the streets shouting. Consternation and dismay prevailed as the call to arms was sounded. The enemy, in short, was in striking distance of the thinly guarded fort, the sole British bastion on the Detroit frontier. If Hull could seize it in one lightning move, then his army could sweep up the valley of the Thames and capture most if not all of Upper Canada.

Beall viewed all that with mixed feelings. He was a sensitive and compassionate man, and he was already starting to pine for his wife, Melinda, back in Kentucky. He felt "sensibly for those on both sides who might loose [*sic*] their lives." His British hosts had been decent to the point of chivalry, and it was difficult to look at them as enemies. On the other hand, he was convinced that his day of deliverance was at hand. Surely General Hull would cross the river, crush all resistance at Amherstburg, free him from further service, and if the campaign was as decisive as everyone expected, then he would return swiftly to Melinda's arms.

CHAPTER SIX

Invasion!

MEANWHILE, ON THE AMERICAN SIDE ALL WAS CONFUSION. THE CRUCIAL DISPATCH FROM WASHINGTON TO GENERAL HULL ANNOUNCING THE DECLARATION OF WAR WAS HIDDEN SOMEWHERE IN THE CLEVELAND MAIL. THE POSTMASTER HAD WRITTEN ORDERS TO FORWARD IT AT ONCE, BUT NOBODY COULD FIND IT. (IN THOSE DAYS, TOO, THEY HAD PROBLEMS WITH THE MAIL!) EVERYBODY COULD GUESS WHAT IT CONTAINED BECAUSE THE NEWS HAD ALREADY REACHED CLEVELAND.

A young Cleveland lawyer, Charles Shaler, stood ready to gallop through swamp and forest to the rapids of the Maumee and on to Detroit if necessary once the missing document was found. Apparently nobody thought to send him off at once with a verbal message while the others rummaged for the official one. Finally someone suggested the dispatch might be in the Detroit mail, so reluctantly the postmaster broke the law, opened the bags, and found it.

Off when Shaler, swimming the unbridged rivers, plunging through the wilderness, vainly seeking a relay steed to replace his gasping horse. Some eighty hours later, on the evening of July 1, he reached the rapids to discover the army had decamped, and galloped on after it. He reached it at two the following morning.

General Hull, half dressed, read the dispatch, registered alarm, ordered Shaler to keep quiet, called a council of officers, and ordered a boat to take after the *Cuyahoga.* He was too late, of course. The army moved on, Shaler riding with the troops. When he reached Detroit his horse dropped dead of exhaustion as a result of the frantic journey.

The army arrived at Detroit on July 5 after thirty-five days of struggle through Ohio's swampy wilderness. Today, it is one of the largest cities in the United States—"Motown" to many. But the soldiers found a primitive settlement of only twelve hundred straggling on the outskirts of a log fort. Like their neighbours on both sides of the river, most were French-speaking, descendants of families that settled on the land a century before and whose strip farms with their narrow river frontage showed their Quebecois background. Some of their descendants remain there today—on both sides of the river. Hull thought they were "miserable farmers"—people with no agricultural tradition. They raised apples for cider and gigantic pears for pickling, but they paid little attention to other forms of agriculture, depending principally on hunting, fishing, and trading with the Indians. In short, they couldn't provision his troops.

That was Hull's dilemma. His supply line was two hundred miles (320 km) long, stretching south along the makeshift trail his men had hacked out of the forests. To secure his position he would have to have two months' provisions. An express rider took the news to the governor of Ohio, who immediately raised a company of citizen volunteers and sent them north to escort a brigade of pack horses loaded with flour and provisions, and a drove of beef cattle. But to reach Hull's army they would have to follow the road that hugged the southwestern shore of Lake Erie and the Detroit River. That would be dangerous because the British controlled the water.

Meanwhile, Hull was concerned about the fate of the baggage captured aboard the *Cuyahoga*. Had the British actually rifled through his personal possessions and discovered his official correspondence? He sent a polite and studiedly casual letter to the commander at Fort Amherstburg, Lieutenant-Colonel Thomas Bligh St. George, who told him in equally polite words to go to hell.

But St. George was a badly rattled commander. He was an old campaigner with forty years of service in the British army, much of it spent in active warfare in the Mediterranean. He had been a staff officer for the last ten years, and clearly he had difficulty coping with the present crisis. He commanded a lightly garrisoned fort that needed repairs and reinforcements. Across the river an army of two thousand sat poised for invasion. Scrambling about in a fever of preparation, he was "so harassed for these five days and nights, I can scarcely write." Brock, who got his letter, was dismayed to discover that St. George had let three days slip by before bothering to tell him that the American army had reached Detroit.

Meanwhile Fort Amherstburg was still in chaos. Indians were coming and going, eating up the supplies. Nobody could guess how many of them there were from day to day. The same was true of the militia. St. George had no real idea of how many men he commanded or whether he had the resources to feed them. His accounts were in disarray. And he didn't have enough officers to organize the militia. Many were leaving for home or trying to leave. There weren't enough arms to supply them, and he didn't know how he could pay them.

The little village of Sandwich lay directly across the river from Detroit. That, St. George realized, would be Hull's invasion point. He stationed some militia units at Sandwich, but he had little hope they would be effective. In order to study their movements he sent a detachment of regulars. To supply the wants of this confused and amateur army, he had to make use of everything that fell in his way. That included a brigade of eleven bateaux loaded with supplies that the North West Company had sent from Montreal to Fort William at the lakehead. St. George seized these and impressed the seventy voyageurs.

St. George had no real idea of how many men he commanded or whether he had the resources to feed them. His accounts were in disarray. And he didn't have enough officers to organize the militia.

On the docks and the streets the Indians performed war dances, leaping and capering before the doors of the inhabitants who gave them presents of whisky. William Beall, still captive aboard the *Thames*, noted in his diary that he had seen "the great Tecumseh," whom he described as "a very plane [*sic*] man, rather above middle-size, stout built, a noble set of features and an admirable eye. He is always accompanied by Six great chiefs who never go before him. The women and men all fear that in the event of General Hull's crossing and proving successful, that the Indians being naturally treacherous will turn against them to murder and destroy them."

To the whites, the Indians were "murdering savages." To the Indians, the whites were just as bad. Certainly the frontiersmen of Ohio, Kentucky, and Tennessee were as savage as any Native. Memories of the Battle of Tippecanoe, in 1811, still rankled among Tecumseh's mixed band of followers. His village, at the junction of the Tippecanoe and Wabash Rivers, had been destroyed by a force of regulars and militiamen under a future U.S. president, William Henry Harrison. Harrison, then governor of Indiana Territory, was greedy for Indian land and determined to shatter Tecumseh's dream of an Indian confederacy stretching from Florida to Lake Erie. And so the Shawnee war chief, with several hundred Natives from half a dozen American tribes, had gone over to the British in the vain hope that they would help him achieve his goal.

"Here is a chance presented to us," he said, "—a chance such as will never occur again for us Indians of North America to form themselves into one great combination and cast our lot with the British in this war."

Tecumseh's followers had shadowed Hull's army all the way through Michigan Territory, warned by their leader to take no overt action before war was declared and he could bring his federation into alliance with Great Britain. Hull had done his best to neutralize them, sending messages to a council at Fort Wayne, promising protection and friendship if the Indians would stay out of the white man's war.

But Tecumseh refused: "I have taken sides with the King, my father, and I will suffer my bones to bleach upon this shore before I recross that stream to join in any council of neutrality."

Upriver at Detroit, Hull prepared to invade Canada by landing his army at Sandwich. He tried to move on July 10 but, to his dismay, discovered that hundreds of militiamen, urged on in some cases by their officers, invoked their constitutional right and refused to cross the river to fight on foreign soil.

Hull tried again the following day. Two companies refused to enter the boats. One finally gave in, but the other stood firm. Hull threw around words like "coward" and "traitor" but to no avail. The crossing was again aborted.

At Sandwich across the river (now a suburb of present-day Windsor), an equally reluctant body of citizen soldiers—the militia of Kent and Essex counties, only recently called to service—all sat and waited. They had little if any training, militia service being mainly an excuse for carousing. They weren't eager to fight, especially in midsummer with the winter wheat ripening in the fields. Patriotism had no meaning for most of them; that was the exclusive property of the Loyalists. Most were passively pro-American, having moved up from the border states. Isolated on the scattered farms, they had no sense of a larger community. They learned of the war through handbills. They didn't really care whether or not Upper Canada became another state of the American Union.

Lieutenant-Colonel St. George, convinced that they would flee to their homes at the first shot, decided to get them out of the way before the attack was launched. Otherwise he knew their certain retreat would throw his force into a state of confusion. The only way to prevent them from melting away to their farms was to march the whole lot back to the fort and make the most of them. Maybe their backs could be stiffened by the example of the regular troops. But even that was doubtful. A good many former Americans said they wanted to join Hull as soon as he crossed into Canada.

At last, on July 12, a bright and lovely Sunday, Hull resolved to make the crossing even though two hundred of his men continued to stand on their constitutional rights. He feared further mutinies if he kept his troops inactive. He imagined Canadian settlers would feel themselves liberated from the British yoke once he landed and that they and the Indians would stay out of the war. His landing was unopposed.

Sandwich was a pleasant little garden village, almost every house set in a small orchard where peaches, grapes, and apples flourished. The conquering general seized the most imposing residence, belonging to Lieutenant-Colonel François Bâby. The Bâby family and the Hull family had been on intimate terms, but all Hull could say was that "circumstances are changed now."

Hull scarcely had landed when he insisted on issuing a proclamation intended to disperse the militia and frighten the inhabitants, many of whom were either terrified of his troops or secretly sympathetic to his cause. Most had fled. Those who remained welcomed the invaders as friends. They waved white handkerchiefs and flags from the windows and cried out, "We like the Americans." In spite of this, Hull couldn't resist issuing a bombastic proclamation that seemed designed to set the Canadians on edge.

… Separated by an immense ocean and an extensive Wilderness from Great Britain you have no participation in her counsels, no interest in her conduct. You have felt her Tyranny, you have seen her injustice, but I do not ask *you* to avenge the one or redress the other … I tender you the valuable blessings of Civil, Political, & Religious Liberty … In the name of my *Country* and by the authority of my Government I promise you protection … remain at your homes, Pursue your peaceful and customary avocations. Raise not your hands against your brethren … You will be emancipated from tyranny and oppression and restored to the dignified status of free men.

If the barbarous and Savage policy of Great Britain be pursued and the savages let loose to murder our Citizens and butcher our women and children, this war, will be a war of extermination … No white man found fighting by the Side of an Indian will be taken prisoner. Instant destruction will be his Lot … I doubt not your courage and firmness; I will not doubt your attachment to Liberty. If you tender your services voluntarily they will be accepted readily.

The United States offers you *Peace, Liberty* and *Security* your choice lies between these, & *War, Slavery,* and *Destruction,* Choose then, but choose wisely …

The general, who was afraid of the Indians, hoped that the document would force his opposite number at Fort Amherstburg to follow the lead of the United States and adopt a policy of Native neutrality. At the very minimum it ought to frighten the settlers and the militia into refusing to bear arms. That was its immediate effect. The Canadian militia was terrified. Within three days the force of newly recruited soldiers was reduced by half as the farm boys deserted to their homes.

But Hull had overstated his case. These were farmers he was addressing, not revolutionaries. Colonial politics touched very few. They didn't feel like slaves. They already had enough peace, liberty, and security to satisfy them.

This tax-free province was not America at the time of the Boston Tea Party. Why was Hull asking them to free themselves from tyranny? In the words of one, if they had been under real tyranny, "they could at any time have crossed the line to the United States."

Hull made another error. He threatened that anyone found fighting beside the Indians could expect no quarter. That rankled. *Everybody* would be fighting with the Indians; it wouldn't be a matter of choice. Some of the militiamen who had secretly hoped to go over to Hull in the confusion of battle had a change of heart. What was the point of deserting if the Americans intended to kill them on capture?

Hull's sudden action didn't fit the Upper Canadian mood. It was a pioneer society, not a frontier society. No Daniel Boones stalked the Canadian forests, ready to knock off an Injun with a Kentucky rifle or do battle over an imagined slight. The Methodist circuit riders kept the people law-abiding and temperate; prosperity kept them content. The Sabbath was looked on with reverence; card playing and horse racing were considered sinful diversions; the demon rum had yet to become a problem. There was little theft, less violence. Simple pastimes tied to the land—barn raisings, corn huskings, threshing bees—served as an outlet for the spirited. The new settlers wouldn't volunteer to fight; but most were prepared, if forced, to bear arms for their new country and to march when ordered. Hull's proclamation and his subsequent actions had the opposite effect from the one he intended. It helped turn the newcomers into patriotic Canadians.

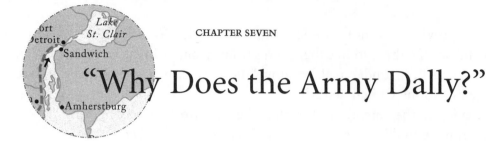

CHAPTER SEVEN

"Why Does the Army Dally?"

SITTING IN SANDWICH THAT JULY, HULL'S TROOPS BECAME RESTLESS. EVER SINCE THE DAY OF THE LANDING, THEY HAD EXPECTED THAT HULL WOULD SWEEP DOWN THE RIVER TO ATTACK THE BRITISH FORT AT AMHERSTBURG.

Why was the army dallying? That was a question that Robert Lucas, one of Hull's scouts, asked rhetorically in his diary. " … Had proper energy been used, we might have been in Malden [Amherstburg] now, we are tampering with them until they will be able to drive us back across the river."

As a scout, Lucas was used to acting on his own, swiftly and decisively, or with a small company of rangers. His job was to move silently ahead of the main force, protecting it from ambush and feeling out the lay of the land. Now he wanted to get on with it. Once Fort Amherstburg's guns were silenced, the way to Upper Canada lay wide open. The only other British forts on the western frontier were at the other end of Lake Erie and along the Niagara River. A second American army had been sent to attack those strong points. Its task was to cause a diversion, to pin down the defending British, and to prevent reinforcements from reaching Fort Amherstburg.

Lucas was one of many who thought that speed was essential. Amherstburg must be attacked and taken before Brock could divert more men to its defence. As a scout, he was used to swift, flexible movements. In Hull's mixed bag of raw recruits, untrained civilians, professional commanders, and elected leaders, he was a real mixture—general, captain, and private soldier rolled into one. This sprang out of his country's awkward military philosophy, which disdained the idea of a standing army and relied on volunteers for the nation's defence. For some time Robert Lucas had been a brigadier-general in the Ohio state militia. Eager to serve in the regular army, he applied in April of 1812 for a captain's commission. But a few days later, before it came through, McArthur ordered him to transmit from his brigade a proportion of the twelve hundred men required from the state in the coming war. What was he to do? Thirsty for action, Lucas set an example to his men by enlisting as a private in a volunteer company. To add to the confusion, the men elected his younger brother, John, as their captain.

Now, at Sandwich, Lucas was disgusted. Why indeed did the army dally? Hull wasn't short of supplies. He had sent his best regimental commander, Colonel Duncan McArthur, to raid the farms, the barns, and the fields up the Thames for food and equipment. McArthur, a former member of the Ohio legislature, had been voted colonel of the 1st Regiment of Ohio volunteers. It was said of him that he "looks more like a go-ahead soldier than any of his brother officers." But to a later English visitor, he was "dirty and butcher-like, very unlike a soldier in appearance, seeming half savage and dressed like a backwoodsman; generally considered being only fit for hard knocks and Indian warfare"—which, of course was exactly the kind of contest that was facing him.

McArthur lived up to his reputation. He and his men, moving without blankets and provisions, lived off the country and left a trail of devastation in their wake. They penetrated sixty miles (96 km) into the heart of Upper Canada: a land of stumps and snake fences; of cabins and shanties of basswood and cedar; of Dutch lofts and clay ovens; of grist mills, fanning mills, and windmills; of chicken hutches, corn cribs, hog pens, and cattle sheds; of pickled pork and pigeon pie and fresh milk kept cool in underground sheds; of oxen hitched in tandem, furrowing the glistening fields, and raw-boned men in homespun linsey-woolsey scything the tawny harvest of midsummer.

John McGregor, a trader and merchant, was one who lost everything. He had removed his goods to a neighbour's house on the Thames for safety—flour, merchandise, grain, livestock. He lost them all and almost lost his life as well, fleeing in haste when he learned that McArthur intended to shoot him on sight in the belief that he and his neighbour were rousing the Indians and the militia to resistance.

Farmers and townspeople were beggared by the raiders. Jean-Baptiste Beniteau's orchard of sixty fruit trees was destroyed, his fences and pickets reduced to ashes. His neighbour, Jean-Baptiste Ginac, was looted of all his livestock, pork, flour, oats, and corn. Another Jean-Baptiste, surnamed

Fourneau, lost 480 bushels (162 hL) of grain, all his cider, furniture, and his winter supplies of wood. A fourth, Jean-Baptiste Boismier, saw his entire fortune of 620 skins, together with his livestock, tools, utensils, and harvested corn, go to the enemy.

The raiding party returned in five days with two hundred barrels of flour, four hundred blankets, and wagons loaded with whisky, salt, cloth, guns, ammunition, household goods, tools—even boats. They destroyed green fields, ransacked homes, levelled orchards, trampled corn, and burned fences—actions that enraged the settlers and helped to turn them against their former comrades.

Hull's men made no allowance for old comrades. Lieutenant-Colonel François Bâby, whose house had become Hull's headquarters, had tried to save some of his chattels by hauling them off to a friend's home three miles (5 km) away. But Hull dispatched a party of dragoons with six wagons who took everything at gunpoint and then, emboldened, sliced up one of Bâby's finest coats with their sabres. Bâby's loss was staggering. He reckoned it at 2,678 pounds sterling.

Besieged by complaints, McArthur brushed them all aside and promised that everything would be paid for. Hull, he explained, had such footing in Canada that the British would never be able to drive him out.

Besieged by complaints, McArthur brushed them all aside and promised that everything would be paid for. Hull, he explained, had such footing in Canada that the British would never be able to drive him out. It certainly looked that way. At Fort Amherstburg the situation was deteriorating. Militia service was working a real hardship on those Canadian families who depended upon the able-bodied for their livelihood. Hundreds deserted. Those who remained loyal had no one to harvest their wheat and so lost it all to rot. St. George, the commander, was forced to release the oldest and least efficient to return to their farms. Others began to slip away. On July 8 he had 850 militiamen under his command; a week later the number had dropped to 471.

Meanwhile, Robert Lucas, who had seen more fighting than most of his followers in Hull's army, was back in action. On July 16, when Hull ordered two of his regimental commanders to search out the enemy country as far as the River Aux Canards, three miles (5 km) north of Amherstburg, Lucas offered to go along. The war would make his reputation, and he eventually rose to become governor of Ohio.

Once again, Lucas and the rangers were out in front of the main body. Colonel Lewis Cass of the 2nd Regiment, Ohio Volunteers, took charge. In spite of his lack of training, he outranked his fellow commander, Lieutenant-Colonel James Miller, a regular officer in command of the 4th Infantry Division. Cass was eager for glory and action. A stocky, coarse-featured lawyer of flaming ambition, he was U.S. Marshal for his state. Unlike Miller, a disciplined career officer, he didn't hesitate to bad-mouth Hull in public.

Cass decided to ford the river upstream and circle round the enemy, while Miller pinned down the sentries at the bridge, which was held by a small detachment of British regulars and Menomenee Indians.

Faced with an attack on their rear, the British retired. Cass couldn't pursue the chase because a stream blocked the way. But the British sentries on the bridge, John Dean and James Hancock, held their ground and became the first soldiers to shed their blood on Canadian soil.

And here, the Americans came up against the stubborn fighting qualities of the British regulars. Dean, with an arm broken by a musket ball, fought on with his bayonet until he was knocked to the ground and disarmed. Hancock, bleeding from at least two wounds and unable to support himself, continued to fight on his knees until he was captured. He died that night and was scalped by one of the Indians who sold the trophy to the British.

Now the Americans held the bridge—the bridge that could lead the army to Amherstburg. Cass and Miller both thought the entire force should move to within striking distance of the fort. But Hull dithered. He would not start an attack until his heavy artillery was ready. The fort could have been taken by an infantry assault, but Hull was convinced the slaughter would be appalling and so the bridge was abandoned.

Hull had other concerns. He did not know quite what was happening on the rest of the Niagara frontier. It was essential that an American army be in place along that river. Otherwise there was nothing to stop the British from concentrating their entire armies against him. He had been promised there would be diversions on the Niagara to support his invasion, but the communications were so bad that the general had no way of knowing whether that had been done.

Meanwhile, he was tormented by another problem. He was certain that Colonel Cass was trying to pressure him for reasons of personal ambition. He felt his authority slipping away. His officers' complaints were beginning to destroy his influence. He called council after council to quell their impatience, but it only eroded his command.

He was determined not to advance until he was absolutely certain of success. But how long would it take to prepare the cannon? Two days? Two weeks? After each meeting the time stretched. Hull feared defeat. Defeat would mean starvation for the troops and worse devastation by the Indians. The militia feared the Indians. And Dickson's Menomenee and Tecumseh's followers were terrifying the raw recruits, who on one occasion said "they would rather be killed by their own officers" who were trying to keep them in line "than by the damned Indians."

There was savagery on both sides. The first Indian scalp was taken during one skirmish by Captain William McCullough of the Rangers, who described in a letter to his wife how he tore it from the corpse's head with his teeth. William Beall and his fellow prisoners at Amherstburg heard of these skirmishes and hoped for his speedy deliverance. Hull's army was camped within reach. But instead of seeing American soldiers marching into town he was greeted by a more macabre spectacle.

Thomas McKee of the Canadian Indian Department arrived at the head of about fifty Indians, all naked except for their breech cloths. McKee, also dressed as a Native, halted opposite the gaping prisoners and hoisted a fresh scalp fastened to a long pole, which he shook exultantly, all the time taunting the captives with savage cries. It would, Beall wrote, "have chilled the blood of a Laplander … crimsoned the tawny cheek of an unrelenting Turk." Actually, the scalp was that of the unfortunate British sentry, Hancock—McKee's British ally.

Beall and his fellow prisoners couldn't understand what was keeping Hull from attacking. The optimism, good humour, and gallantry of those first days in captivity were gone. Beall no longer saw the British as gentlemen but as monsters. He was now totally disillusioned with Hull. The

British officers and soldiers were laughing at the American general, and as Beall wrote, "he is now the object of their jest and ridicule instead of being as he was formerly, their terror and greatest fear."

On July 26 Hull was shaken by an alarming piece of intelligence. A ship flying British colours was brought about by a shot from the shore. Aboard was a group of American citizens and soldiers led by Lieutenant Porter Hanks, the former commander at Mackinac who had been paroled. Now for the first time Hull learned of Mackinac's fall—a major disaster. Hull was convinced that "the northern hives of Indians" would shortly come "swarming down in every direction."

He felt himself surrounded by Indians. He figured there were perhaps two or three thousand advancing from Mackinac, not to mention the Iroquois of the Grand Valley who, though still neutral, might join the British at any time. And in front of them at Amherstburg lay another potent force—hundreds more Indians led by the great Tecumseh. Hull feared those more than he did the handful of British regulars.

By the end of July William Beall and the others had lost all hope of rescue from the fort. "I can hardly think that Genl. H. will be defeated," Beall wrote, "but appearances justify such a belief. I am confident that he will not take Malden though three hundred men could do it."

CHAPTER EIGHT

General Hull Backs Down

HULL KNEW THAT HE HAD TO CONTACT THE WAGON TRAIN OF SUPPLIES, WHICH HE DESPERATELY NEEDED TO FEED HIS ARMY. TO DO THAT HE SENT AN ARMED BODY OF TWO HUNDRED OHIO VOLUNTEERS ACROSS THE DETROIT RIVER TO INTERCEPT THE WAGONS BEFORE THEY COULD BE CAPTURED BY THE BRITISH. THE CATTLE AND PACK ANIMALS WERE MOVING ON TO THE RIVER RAISIN AFTER A GRUELLING TREK THROUGH DENSE THICKETS AND TREACHEROUS MIRE. NOW, UNABLE TO CONTINUE ON TO DETROIT UNDER THE GUNS OF FORT AMHERSTBURG, THEY WERE STALLED.

As usual, Robert Lucas was out ahead of the relief party. He and two fellow rangers lay in the bushes, watched by unseen eyes. Beside him was the ranger captain, McCullough—the same man who had the dubious distinction of being the only American thus far to take an Indian scalp. At first light McCullough and his scouts rose, mounted their horses, and made a wide sweep around the detachment. They scented trouble, noting tracks on the road and trails in the grass—evidence that a party of Indians had been watching them during the night. Out on the river, a faint *splish-splash* penetrated the shroud of mist that hung out over the water. Oars! The British were intent on capturing the supply line.

McCullough, Lucas, and the others rode on through the Wyandot village of Maguaga—deserted now, the houses empty. News of the victory at Mackinac had tipped the scales, and the Wyandot tribe wanted to be on the winning side.

The road forked around a cornfield. Lucas and a companion took the right fork; McCullough took the left and rode into an ambush. Lucas heard a volley of shots but before he could reach him, the scalper was himself scalped, tomahawked, riddled with musket balls. The rear guard was in a panic, but the Indians had already vanished into the tall corn.

Shaken, the detachment moved on, leaving three corpses under a cover of bark and ignoring a Frenchman's warning that a large force of Indians was waiting for them at Brownstown. The Americans didn't trust the French settlers, some of whom were pro-British and tried to confuse them with false reports.

The war party moved in double file. Between the files mounted men escorted the mail—a packet of personal letters written by Hull's soldiers to their families and friends, many of them critical of their general. More significantly, the mail contained Hull's dispatches to Washington, revealing both his plans and his pessimism.

Brownstown village lay ahead, but Brownstown Creek first had to be crossed. The only practical ford lay in a narrow opening with thick bushes on the right and fields of tall corn on the opposite bank and on the left—a perfect spot for an ambush. Lucas, the old hand, recognized the danger and rode along the right column, warning the men to see that their muskets were freshly primed.

At a range of no more than twenty-five yards (23 m), the Indians rose out of the corn, their high-pitched war cries mingling with the explosion of their weapons.

Tecumseh had recognized it too. He and his followers lay flat on their bellies directly ahead. As the Shawnee leader silently waited, the American files closed up to cross the creek. Then, at a range of no more than twenty-five yards (23 m), the Indians rose out of the corn, their high-pitched war cries mingling with the explosion of their weapons.

Lucas's horse was shot and toppled sideways against another wounded animal, pitching its rider onto the ground, his musket flying from his hand. Weaponless, Lucas tried with little success to rally his men. The odds were twenty to one in favour of the Americans, but the Indians were shouting so wildly that they believed themselves outnumbered.

It was not necessary to order a retreat—the Americans flung down their weapons, scattered the mail, and plunged headlong back the way they came, actually outrunning their pursuers, who followed them for three miles

(5 km) before giving up the chase. Lucas, covering their retreat as best he could, was the last man to escape.

The Battle of Brownstown, as it came to be called, represented a setback for Hull. The detachment had lost eighteen men killed and twenty wounded. Some seventy were missing, many hiding in the bushes. The following day most straggled back. Worse than the loss of seven officers was the abandoning of the mail. That raised Brock's spirits because here, in letters home, was strong evidence of the discontent and illness in the American ranks and of the lack of confidence in the leadership.

Even more important was Hull's letter of August 4 to the American secretary of war outlining the critical situation of his army, pleading for another two thousand men, and expressing his deep-seated fear of the Indians, who he believed would shortly be swarming down through Mackinac Island.

At Brownstown, meanwhile, a strong detachment of the British 41st—John Richardson's regiment—accompanied by militia and civilian volunteers had crossed the river. Too late to take part in the skirmish, they were prepared to frustrate any further attempt by Hull to open the supply lines. The British waited all night, unable to light a fire, shivering in the damp without blankets or provisions.

Now they were exposed to a spectacle calculated to make them shudder further. The Indians held a young American captive and were intent on killing him. Major Adam Muir, who headed the expedition, did his best to intervene. He even offered a barrel of rum and articles of clothing if the prisoner's life was spared. But then a series of piercing cries issued from the forest—the funeral convoy of a young chief, Blue Jacket, the only casualty among Tecumseh's followers. Four tribesmen carried in the body. Thomas Verchères de Boucherville, a citizen volunteer and experienced fur trader from Amherstburg, realized there was no hope for the American because the Indians were intent on avenging their chief, whose corpse was placed at the captive's feet.

The oldest Potawatomi chief raised his hatchet over the prisoner as a group of Indian women drew near. At the chief's signal, one plunged a butcher knife into the victim's head, a second stabbed him in the side, and the chief dispatched him with a tomahawk. Tecumseh, who would certainly have prevented the execution—for he did not believe in this kind of savagery—was not present.

Young de Boucherville would never shake the incident from his memory. "We all stood around overcome by an acute sense of shame," he wrote later. "We felt implicated in some way in this murder … and yet, under the circumstances what could we do? The life of that man undoubtedly belonged to the inhuman chief. The government had desperate need of these Indian allies. Our garrison was weak and these warriors were numerous enough to impose their will upon us. If we were to rebuke them in this crisis … they would withdraw from the conflict, and retire to their own country on the Missouri whence they had come to join us." De Boucherville was coming to realize what others would soon grasp, that the British were as much prisoners of the Indians as the young American whose tomahawked corpse lay stretched out before them.

Meanwhile, in his headquarters in François Bâby's unfinished mansion in Sandwich, Hull continued to waver. He had promised his impatient officers that he would attack the fort whether the artillery was ready or not, but now he had second thoughts. The British controlled the river. He could not float his artillery downriver in the teeth of their gunboats. But his enemies could cross the river at will and could harass the supply lines. He considered a retreat but backed off after a stormy meeting with Colonel McArthur. He brooded, changed his mind, called a council of his commanders, and finally agreed to adopt their plan of attacking the fort. He would move against it at the head of his troops "and in whatever manner the affair may terminate, it will never reflect on you, gentlemen."

At this dazzling news, Robert Lucas, back from the humiliation at Brownstown, was exultant. A wave of good cheer surged over the camp. Even the sick rose from their beds to seize their muskets. Orders were issued for five days' rations, and ammunition and whisky were loaded onto the wagons. All necessary tents, baggage, and boats were to be sent back to Detroit.

Then, on the afternoon of August 7, hard on the heels of news from Brownstown, came an express rider with dispatches for Hull from two American commanders on the Niagara frontier. Boats loaded with British troops had been seen crossing Lake Erie and headed for Amherstburg. More British regulars accompanied by Canadian militia and Indians were en route from Niagara by boat to the fort. Since the British controlled the lakes there was nothing the Americans could do to stop them.

At this point, both opposing generals were totally in the dark. Each believed his own position to be doubtful and his adversary's superior. Brock had decided on a risky move—to reduce his forces on the Niagara frontier to a minimum in order to bolster the defence of Amherstburg. Certainly he expected Hull to attack his weak garrison at any moment. He was desperate to reinforce it but despaired of holding it against great numbers.

But Hull was badly rattled. Isolated on Canadian soil and faced with alarming reports of more British soldiers arriving, he was convinced that Brock's combined force was not only stronger than his own, but growing at an alarming rate. Hull, unlike Brock, was no gambler. He felt doomed by bad luck—the supposedly friendly Indians turning against him, the blocking of his supply train, and now a fresh onslaught of fighting men. The general saw himself and his troops suddenly trapped in an unfriendly country, their backs to the river, their food running out, surrounded by Indians, facing Brock's regulars and Tecumseh's braves. Hull was convinced he must get his army back to American soil, with the barrier of the Detroit River between him and his enemies.

Hull, unlike Brock, was no gambler. He felt doomed by bad luck—the supposedly friendly Indians turning against him, the blocking of his supply train, and now a fresh onslaught of fighting men.

He broke the news to his officers. At that, the swarthy McArthur refused to give any further opinions as to the movement of the army. Hull suggested hesitantly that the army might withdraw as far as the Maumee. Cass told him that if he did that every man in the Ohio militia would leave him. That put an end to that. The army would withdraw to Detroit but no farther.

Lewis Cass was infuriated. To him, Hull's decision was fatal and unaccountable. This final about-face, he was convinced, had dispirited the troops and destroyed the last vestige of confidence they had in their commander.

He was undoubtedly right. It would have been far better if Hull had never crossed the river in the first place, at least until the supply lines were secure.

A sense of astonishment mingled with a feeling of disgrace rippled through the camp. Robert Lucas was one who felt it. The orders to recross the river under cover of darkness were, he thought, especially dastardly. But cross the army must, and when night fell the men slunk into their boats. By the following morning there was scarcely an American soldier left on Canadian soil.

Brock Takes the Offensive

ISAAC BROCK WAS HAVING TROUBLE WITH HIS LEGISLATURE IN LITTLE YORK. HE WAS CONVINCED THAT THE LEGISLATORS, EXPECTING AN AMERICAN VICTORY, WERE AFRAID TO TAKE ANY ACTION THAT MIGHT DISPLEASE THE CONQUERORS. THE MAJORITY OF CANADIANS, WHO HAD NO SAY IN THEIR OWN GOVERNMENT, WERE OBVIOUSLY UNWILLING TO FIGHT. BUT BROCK WAS DETERMINED TO RALLY THEM BY HARSH METHODS IF NEED BE. HE WANTED TO SUSPEND CIVIL RIGHTS AND ESTABLISH MARTIAL LAW, BUT THE LEGISLATURE WOULD NOT GO ALONG WITH HIM. PINNED DOWN AT YORK BY HIS CIVILIAN DUTIES, HE TOOK WHAT ACTION HE COULD TO STIFFEN THE DEFENCE AT FORT AMHERSTBURG BY SENDING A YOUNGER AND MORE EFFICIENT OFFICER, LIEUTENANT-COLONEL HENRY PROCTER, TO TAKE OVER FROM THE CONFUSED AND HARASSED ST. GEORGE.

Brock realized Amherstburg was vital. If Hull seized it—as he seemed likely to do—he could sweep up the Thames or turn eastward to attack the British rear at Fort George on the Niagara and link up with the second American army already forming along that gorge. Brock did not yet know that Hull had retreated across the river.

But Brock was weary of idle chatter in the legislature. He dismissed that body August 5 and, with the consent of his appointed council, declared martial law anyway. He decided on a mighty gamble. He would gather what troops he could, speed post-haste to Amherstburg at their head, and, if that fort had not fallen, provoke Hull into a fight and then try to move on to the Niagara frontier before the Americans attacked.

He was taking a long chance, but he had little choice. Off he went, moving swiftly southwest through the province calling for volunteers to accompany him to Amherstburg. Five hundred rushed to apply, many the sons of

British veterans. He could only take half that number. But the York Volunteers became Brock's favourite militia unit, including among its officers some of the finest names of the Upper Canada aristocracy. The war would entrench them into a tight little governing body soon to be known as "The Family Compact," so called because so many members of this élite group were related by blood or marriage.

Brock reached port at Dover on the north shore of Lake Erie on August 8. There, he hoped enough boats had been commandeered to move his entire force to Amherstburg. But at Dover, Brock found that not nearly enough boats had been provided, and most of those available were leaky, uncaulked, and dilapidated. It required a day to make ten of them ready, and these were in such bad shape that the men grew exhausted from constant bailing.

The flotilla could move no faster than the slowest vessel, the hundred-ton (90-t) schooner *Nancy*, which had to be manhandled over the narrow neck of the Long Point Peninsula—a back-breaking task that required the energy of all the boat crews.

The troops were held up by a thunderstorm but remained in good spirits. Brock wrote that "in no instance have I witnessed greater cheerfulness and constancy than were displayed by these Troops under the fatigue of a long journey in Boats and during extremely bad Weather." In Brock's words, "their conduct throughout excited my admiration."

That admiration was mutual. At one point Brock's own boat struck a sunken rock. His boat crew went to work with oars and poles. When they failed to push her free, the general, in full uniform, leapt over the side, waist deep in water. In an instant, the others followed and soon had the boat floating. Brock climbed back aboard, opened his liquor case, and gave every man a glass of spirits. The news of that act, spreading from boat to boat, animated the force.

The weather again turned capricious on August 11. The wind dropped. The men, wet and exhausted from lack of sleep, were forced to row in relays for hours. Then, a sudden squall forced the flotilla once more into the shore. That night the weather cleared, and the impatient general made another attempt to get underway, this time in the dark, his boat leading with a lantern in the stern.

They sailed all night, the boats too crowded for the men to lie down. The following morning they learned that Hull had retreated across the river to Detroit. At Point Pelee that afternoon, some of the men boiled their pork while others dropped exhausted onto the beach. Early next morning they set off again, and at eight in the forenoon, they straggled into Amherstburg, exhausted from rowing, their faces peeling from sunburn.

Brock was there before them. Unable to rest, the general and a vanguard of troops had left the previous afternoon and reached their objective shortly before midnight on August 13. Lieutenant-Colonel Procter and Matthew Elliott of the Indian Department were waiting on the quayside. Across the water came the rattle of musketry, which startled Brock. Elliott explained that Indians camped on Bois Blanc Island were expressing their joy at the arrival of reinforcements. Brock told them not to waste their ammunition. Midnight had passed by, but he could not sleep. First, he had to read the dispatches and mail captured at Brownstown. He sat in Elliott's study with his aide, Major J. B. Glegg, the yellow light from tallow candles flickering across the desk strewn with maps and papers.

Each man had taken the other's measure and both were impressed. According to Brock, "A more sagacious and gallant Warrior does not I believe exist. He was the admiration of everyone who conversed with him."

Suddenly the door opened, and Elliott stood before him accompanied by a tall Indian, dressed in a plain suit of tanned deerskin, fringed at the seams, and wearing leather moccasins heavily ornamented with porcupine quills. This was clearly a leader of stature. In his nose he wore three silver ornaments in the shape of coronets, and from his neck hung, on a string of coloured wampum, a large silver medallion of George III.

The Indian was beaming. Glegg got an instant impression of energy and decision. This must be Tecumseh.

Brock rose, hand outstretched. The contrast was striking: the British general—fair, large-limbed, blue-eyed, impeccable in his scarlet jacket, blue and white riding trousers, and Hessian boots—towered over the lithe figure of the Shawnee. Brief salutations followed. Brock explained about the waste of ammunition. Tecumseh agreed. Each man had taken the other's measure and both were impressed. According to Brock, "A more sagacious and gallant Warrior does not I believe exist. He was the admiration of everyone who conversed with him." Tecumseh's comment, delivered to his followers, was blunter. "This," he said, "is a *man*!"

Brock called a council of his officers and asked for a military assessment. Tecumseh urged an immediate attack on Detroit and unrolled a strip of elm bark. Then he pulled his scalping knife from his belt and proceeded to scratch out an accurate map of the fort and its surroundings.

It was clear the British and the Indians would be outnumbered. When Brock polled his officers, all but one advised against trying to cross the river.

Brock listened carefully to his subordinates' reservations and then spoke. Nothing, he said, could be gained by delay. "I have decided on crossing, and now, gentlemen, instead of any further advice, I entreat of you to give me your cordial and hearty support."

The following morning, standing beneath a great oak on the outskirts of the fort, he addressed several hundred Indians representing a dozen tribes on both sides of the border. He had come, said Brock, to battle the Long Knives who had invaded the country of the King, their father. The Long Knives were trying to force the British and Indians from their lands. If the Indians would make common cause with the British, the combined forces would soon drive the enemy back to the boundaries of Indian territory.

Tecumseh rose to reply. The hazel eyes flashed, and the oval face darkened as he conjured up the memory of the Battle of Tippecanoe:

"They suddenly came against us with a great force while I was absent, and destroyed our village and slew our warriors."

All the bitterness against the land hunger of the frontier settlements was revived:

"They came to us hungry and cut off the hands of our brothers who gave them corn. We gave them rivers of fish and they poisoned our fountains. We gave them forest-clad mountains and valleys full of game, and in return what did they give our warriors and women? Rum and trinkets and a grave!"

Brock had no intention of revealing the details of his attack plan to such a large assembly. But when the meeting was finished he invited

Tecumseh and a few older chiefs to meet him at Elliott's house. There, through interpreters, he explained his strategy. But he was concerned about alcohol. Could Tecumseh prevent his followers from drinking to excess? The Shawnee replied that his people had promised to abstain from all spirits until they had humbled the Long Knives. Brock had one further act of diplomacy. He issued a general order intending to heal the wounds caused by Hull's divisive proclamation—the one that threatened to "exterminate" anyone who fought beside the Indians. He was willing to believe, he said, that the conduct of the deserters proceeded "from an anxiety to get in their harvest and not from any predilection for the principles or government of the United States." That statement helped to unite the people behind him. Hull had deserted them. Brock, by implication, promised an amnesty. As he rode the same afternoon past the ripening apple trees to Sandwich, he knew he was passing through friendly country.

Brock's Ultimatum

MEANWHILE, IN DETROIT, ALL WAS NOT WELL WITH HULL'S ARMY. COLONEL
LEWIS CASS WAS SEETHING WITH FRUSTRATION OVER WHAT HE FELT WERE THE
FAILURES OF HIS COMMANDER. FROM THE OUTSET HE HAD THOUGHT OF HULL
AS A WEAK, OLD MAN. NOW, OTHER MORE SINISTER POSSIBILITIES BEGAN TO
FORM IN HIS MIND. CASS WAS CONTEMPLATING SOMETHING VERY CLOSE TO
TREASON, A WORD HE WOULD SHORTLY APPLY TO HIS COMMANDING OFFICER.

His disillusionment with Hull was shared by his fellow officers and soon
filtered down through the ranks. As the scout, Robert Lucas, wrote to a
friend: "Never was there a more Patriotic army … neither was there ever an
army that had it more completely in their power to accomplish every object
of their Desire than the Present, And must now be sunk into Disgrace for
want of a General at their head … "

The army was close to mutiny. A petition was circulating among the
troops urging that Hull be replaced by McArthur. The three militia generals, Cass, McArthur, and James Findlay, met with Lieutenant-Colonel Miller
and offered to depose Hull if he would take command. But Miller refused,
being a regular soldier. McArthur also refused, and all three turned to Cass,
who agreed to write secretly to Governor Meigs of Ohio, urging him to
march at once with two thousand men. Meigs, it was assumed, would
depose Hull. Cass wrote "that this army has been reduced to a critical and
alarming situation." He added, "believe all the bearer will tell you. Believe it,
however it may astonish you; as much as if told by one of us." He did not
care to put anything more detailed into writing.

By this time Hull knew of the incipient plot against him, but hesitated
to arrest the ringleaders, fearing perhaps a general uprising. However, he
had a perfect excuse for ridding himself temporarily of the leading malcon-

tents. Captain Henry Brush at the head of the supply train, still pinned down at the River Raisin, had discovered a backdoor route to Detroit. It was twice as long as the river road, but hidden from Fort Amherstburg. When he asked for an escort, Hull was only too pleased to dispatch both Cass and McArthur with 350 men for that task. They would leave Detroit at noon on August 14.

Of course, the general was weakening his own garrison, in spite of the strong evidence that the British were now at Sandwich, directly across the river, planning an attack. What was in Hull's mind? Had he already given up? He had in his possession a letter, intercepted from a British courier, written by Lieutenant-Colonel Procter to Captain Roberts at Mackinac, informing him that the British force facing Detroit was so strong that he need send no more than five thousand Indians to support it!

That was a sobering revelation. Brock and Tecumseh faced Hull across the river, but now at his rear he saw another horde of painted savages. He could not know the letter was a fake, purposely planted by Brock and Procter, who already had an insight into Hull's troubled state of mind through the captured documents. Actually, there were only a few hundred Indians at Mackinac, and on August 12 they were in no condition to go anywhere, being "as drunk as Ten Thousand Devils" in the words of one observer. Brock knew well that the threat of the Indians was just as valuable as their presence and a good deal less expensive.

Brock was also completing the secret construction of a battery directly across from Detroit—one long eighteen-pound (8-kg) gun, two long twelve-pounders (5-kg), and a couple of mortars—hidden for the moment behind a building in a screen of oak.

Lieutenant James Dalliba, Hull's gunnery officer, who had his own guns in the centre of Fort Detroit, asked Hull if he might open fire. "Sir, if you will give me permission, I will clear the enemy on the opposite shore from the lower batteries."

Dalliba would not soon forget Hull's reply.

"Mr. Dalliba, I will make an agreement with the enemy that if they will never fire on me, I will never fire on them," and off he rode, remarking that, "Those who live in glass houses must take care how they throw stones."

The following morning, to the army's astonishment, Hull had a large marquee, striped red and blue, pitched in the centre of camp, just south of the walls of the fort. Many in his army believed that Hull was in league with the British and the coloured tent was intended as a signal.

In a barrack room, a court of inquiry under Lieutenant-Colonel Miller was investigating Porter Hanks's surrender of Mackinac. Hanks had asked for the hearing to clear his name. But partway through the testimony, an officer looking out onto the river spotted a boat crossing from the opposite side under a white flag. Miller adjourned the hearing that would never be reopened.

Up the bank came Brock's two aides, Major Glegg and Lieutenant-Colonel John Macdonell, with a message for Hull. They were blindfolded and confined to a house in the town near the fort while Hull pondered Brock's ultimatum.

"The force at my disposal authorizes me to require of you the immediate surrender of Fort Detroit … "

The force at his disposal! Brock had, at the very most, thirteen hundred men; Hull had more than two thousand. Here was Brock proposing to attack a fortified position with an inferior force—an adventure that Hull, in giving up Amherstburg, had said would require odds of two to one.

He could not know the letter was a fake, purposely planted by Brock and Procter, who already had an insight into Hull's troubled state of mind through the captured documents.

But Brock had studied his man and knew his vulnerable spot. He wrote: "It is far from my intention to join in a war of extermination; but you must be aware that the numerous body of Indians who have attached themselves to my troops will be beyond my control the moment the contest commences … "

What Brock was threatening, of course, was a war of extermination—a bloody battle in which, if necessary, he was quite prepared to accept the slaughter of prisoners and of innocent civilians, including women and children. He was, in short, contemplating total war more than a century before that phrase came into common use. The war was starting to escalate, as all wars must. As impatience for victory clouded compassion, the end began to justify the means.

Like other commanders, Brock soothed his conscience with the excuse that he couldn't control his Native allies. Nonetheless, he was quite eager to use them. The conflict, which began so softly and civilly, was beginning to brutalize both sides. The same men who censured the Indians for dismembering non-combatants with tomahawks were quite prepared to blow the limbs off soldiers and civilians alike with twenty-four-pound (11-kg) cannonballs. Though it might offer some comfort to the attacker, the range of the weapons made little difference to the victim.

Hull mulled over Brock's extraordinary document for more than three hours. At last, he wrote: "I have no other reply, than to inform you, that I am prepared to meet any force which may be at your disposal, and any consequences which may result from any exertion that you may think proper to make."

Now the village of Detroit was alive with people running toward the fort carrying their family possessions or bearing their valuables. Across the river British troops were chopping down oaks and removing the buildings that masked the cannon. Hull immediately sent a messenger to recall the party under Cass and McArthur, who had become entangled in a swamp some twenty-five miles (40 km) away. The troops in Detroit, knowing their force to be superior, were astonished at what they considered the insolence of the British.

As soon as Brock's aides were safely across the river with a message for their general, the British cannonade commenced. Hundreds of kilograms of cast iron hurtled across the wide river, tearing into walls and trees and plunging through rooftops, but doing little damage. James Dalliba, with his battery of seven twenty-four-pound (11-kg) cannon, replied immediately to the first British volley. He stood on the ramparts until he saw the smoke and flash of the British cannon, then shouted, "Down!" allowing his men to drop behind the parapet before the shot struck. The British were aiming directly at his battery, attempting to put it out of action.

A large pear tree was blocking the guns and giving the British an aiming point. A young militia volunteer, John Miller, started to cut it down. As he was hacking away, a cannonball finished the job for him. Miller turned and shouted across the water: "Send us another, John Bull; you can cut faster than I can!"

The artillery duel continued until well after dark. The people scrambled after every burst, ducking behind doors, clinging to walls until they became used to the flash and roar. A mortar shell, its fuse burning brightly, fell into a house on Woodward Avenue. It tore its way through the roof, continued to the upper storey and into the dining room, around which the family were sitting. It ripped through the table, continued through the floor and into the cellar as the owners dashed for safety. They were no sooner clear than the shell exploded with such power that it tore the roof away.

Hull's brigade major, Thomas Jesup, reported that two British warships were anchored in midstream just opposite Spring Wells, two miles (3.2 km) from the fort. The British, he said, appeared to be collecting boats for an invasion. Hull sent an aide to report on these movements and was told that the British vessel, *Queen Charlotte*, was anchored in the river but could be dislodged by one of the fort's twenty-four-pounders (11-kg). But Hull shook his head and found reasons why the gun couldn't be moved. To Jesup the commander seemed pale and much confused.

At ten that evening the cannonade ceased. Quiet descended upon the American camp. The night was clear, the sky tinselled with stars, the river glittering in the moonlight. At eleven, General Hull, fully clothed, his boots still laced, slumped down in the barrack square and tried to sleep. Even as he slumbered, Tecumseh and his Indians were slipping into their canoes and silently crossing to the American side.

Surrender

THE BRITISH CROSSING BEGAN AT DAWN ON AUGUST 16. BROCK'S COURIERS HAD SCOURED THE COUNTRYSIDE AND ROUSED THE MILITIA FROM THE FARMS, EMPTYING THE MILLS AND HARVEST FIELDS. NOW THESE RAW TROOPS GATHERED ON THE SHORE AT McKEE'S POINT, FOUR HUNDRED STRONG, WAITING THEIR TURN TO ENTER THE BOATS AND CROSS TO THE ENEMY'S SIDE. BROCK AGAIN INTENDED TO DECEIVE HULL INTO BELIEVING THAT HIS ARMY WAS OUTNUMBERED BY BRITISH REGULARS. TO THAT END, HE ORDERED THAT THREE HUNDRED CIVILIANS COVER THEIR HOMESPUN WITH THE CAST-OFF CRIMSON TUNICS OF THE 41ST. IT WAS ONE OF SEVERAL DECEPTIONS THAT THE INGENIOUS GENERAL HAD DEVISED.

The Indians were already across, lurking in the forest, ready to attack Hull's flank and rear, should he resist the crossing.

The previous night they had executed their war dance—six hundred figures, leaping in the firelight, naked except for their breech cloths, some daubed in vermilion, others in blue clay, and still others tattooed with black and white from head to foot. But on this calm and beautiful Sunday morning, a different spectacle presented itself. A soft, August sun was just rising as the troops climbed into the boats and pushed out into the river, their crimson jackets almost perfectly reflected in the glassy waters. Behind them, the green meadows and ripening orchards were tinted with the dawn light. Ahead, in the lead boat, stood the glittering figure of their general. Already cannonballs and mortar bombs were screaming overhead.

On the far bank, pocked and riven by springs (hence the name Spring Wells), the figure of Tecumseh could be discerned, astride a white mustang, surrounded by his chiefs. The enemy was not in sight, and the troops landed without incident or opposition.

Brock's plan was to outwit Hull, to draw him out of his fort and do battle out in the open, where he believed his regulars could devastate the wavering American volunteers. Now, however, an Indian scout rode up with the word that enemy horsemen had been spotted three miles (5 km) to the rear. That was the detachment, 350 strong, that Hull had sent to the River Raisin and had recalled to reinforce Detroit. Suddenly Brock's position became precarious. His men were caught between the strong fortification and an advancing column in their rear. Without hesitation, the general changed his plans and decided on an immediate attack.

He drew up his troops in column and engaged in another deception. By doubling the distance between the sections he made his small force seem larger. His route to Detroit hugged the riverbank on his right, protected by the guns of the ships in the river and by the battery at Sandwich. On his left, slipping through the cornfields and woods, were Tecumseh's Indians.

At the town gate, the forward troops could spot two long guns, positioned so they could cover the road. A single round shot, properly placed, was capable of knocking down a file of twenty-five men like dominoes. American gunners stood behind their weapons, with matches burning.

Brock, at the head of the line, rode impassively forward, a brilliant target in his cocked hat and gold epaulettes. An old friend, Colonel Robert Nichol, trotted up to remonstrate with his commander; "Pardon me, general, but I cannot forbear entreating you not to expose yourself thus. If we lose you, we lose all; let me, pray you, to allow the troops to pass on, led by their own officers."

To which Brock replied; "Master Nichol, I duly appreciate the advice you give me, but I feel that in addition to their sense of loyalty and duty, many here follow me from a feeling of personal regard, and I will never ask them to go where I do not lead them."

But why had the Americans' gun not fired? After the fact, there was a host of explanations. One was that Hull refused to give the order for reasons of cowardice or treason. Another, more plausible, was that the British were still out of effective range, and the American artillery commander was waiting until they drew closer so that his grapeshot could slow down the columns.

If that was his plan, Brock outwitted him. Suddenly the British column wheeled to the left through an orchard and into a ravine where they were protected from the enemy guns. Fifteen-year-old John Richardson, marching with the 41st, breathed more easily. Brock commandeered a farmhouse as his headquarters and climbed up the bank to reconnoitre his position.

The town of Detroit, a huddle of some three hundred houses, lay before him. Its population, three-quarters French-speaking, was accustomed to siege and plunder, having been transferred three times by treaty, twice besieged by Indians, and burned to the ground only a few years previously. It was enclosed on three sides by a wooden stockade of fourteen-foot (4-m) pickets. Entrance could be gained only by three massive gates.

On the high ground to the northeast, covering three acres (1.2 ha), sprawled the fort. It was built originally by the British and repaired by the Americans. It had an eleven-foot (3.5-m) high earthen parapet, twelve feet thick (3.6 m). A ditch, six feet deep and twelve feet across (2 m x 3.6 m), together with a double row of pickets, each twice the height of a man, surrounded the whole. It was heavily armed with long guns, howitzers, and mortars. Most of the troops were quartered outside these walls.

> *William Hull appeared on the edge of nervous collapse. He had lost three of his battalion commanders. Cass and McArthur had not yet returned and Miller was too ill to stand up.*

The American position seemed impregnable but Brock had a secret weapon—psychology. Hull had already been led to believe that three hundred militiamen were regular troops. Now Tecumseh and his Indians were ordered to march in single file across an open space, out of range, but in full view of the fort. The spectacle had some of the quality of a vaudeville act. The Indians loped across the meadow, vanished into the forest, circled back and repeated the manoeuvre three times.

Hull's officers, who couldn't tell one Indian from another, thought they counted fifteen hundred painted savages, screeching and waving tomahawks. And so Hull was convinced he was outnumbered. Brock was still looking over his objective by himself some fifty yards (45 m) in front of his own troops when he spotted an American officer waving a white flag. The officer bore a note from his general. It appeared that Hull was on the verge of giving up without a fight.

In fact, at his post inside the palisade, William Hull appeared on the edge of nervous collapse. He had lost three of his battalion commanders. Cass and McArthur had not yet returned and Miller was too ill to stand up. A dozen Michigan volunteers on picket duty at the rear of the fort had allowed themselves to be captured by Tecumseh's Indians. Brush, in charge of the Michigan militia, believed that if an attack came his men would flee. The fort itself was jammed with soldiers, civilians, and cattle, all seeking refuge from the bombardment. It was difficult to manoeuvre.

The cannonade had unnerved Hull. He had seen plenty of blood in his revolutionary days, but now he was transfixed by a spectacle so horrifying it reduced him to jelly. Lieutenant Porter Hanks, relieved for the moment of appearing at his court of inquiry, had come into the fort to visit an old friend and was standing in the doorway of the officers' mess with several others, when a sixteen-pound (7-kg) cannonball came bouncing over the parapet and skipped across the open space. It struck Hanks in the midriff, cutting him in two, tore both legs off a second man, instantly killing him, and mangled a third. A second cannonball dispatched two more soldiers. Blood and brains spattered the walls and the gowns of two women who had sought refuge nearby. One fainted and the other began to scream.

Hull couldn't be sure from the distance who was dead, but a frightful thought crossed his mind: could it be his own daughter, Betsey? She and her child had taken refuge in the fort with most of her fellow citizens who lived in the vicinity.

Something very odd was happening to Hull. He was becoming catatonic. His brain, overloaded by too much information, refused to function. His brigade major, Thomas Jesup, found his commander half-seated, half-crouched on an old tent lying on the ground. His back was to the ramparts under the curtain of the fort that faced the enemy. Except for the movement of his jaws he seemed comatose. He was chewing tobacco at a furious rate, filling his mouth with it, absently adding quid after quid, sometimes removing a piece, rolling it between his fingers and then replacing it, so that his hands ran with spittle, while the brown juice dribbled from the corners of his mouth, staining his neck cloth, his beard, his cravat, and his vest. He chewed as though the fate of the army depended upon the movement of his jaws, rubbing the lower half of his face from time to time until it, too, was stained dark brown.

Jesup had reconnoitred the British position. He asked Hull for permission to move up some artillery and attack their flank. Hull nodded but he was clearly out of control. All he could say, as much to himself as to Jesup, was that a cannonball had killed four men.

It was the future as much as the present that rendered him numb. A procession of ghastly possibilities crowded his mind: his troops deserting pell-mell to the enemy; the women and children starving through a long siege; cannon fire dismembering more innocent bystanders; finally—the ultimate horror—the Indians released by Brock and Tecumseh, bent on revenge for Tippecanoe and all that came before it, ravaging, raping, burning, killing.

He saw his daughter scalped, his grandchild mutilated, his friends and neighbours butchered. He believed himself outnumbered and outmanoeuvred, his plea for reinforcements unheeded. He was convinced that defeat was inevitable. If he postponed it, the blood of innocent people would be on his hands. If he accepted it before the battle was joined, he could save hundreds of lives. He could, of course, fight on to the last man and go down in the history books as a hero. But could he live with himself, however briefly, if he took the hero's course?

There was another thought, too, a guilty thought, lurking like a vagrant in the darker recesses of that agitated mind. The memory of the notorious proclamation returned to haunt him. He himself had threatened no quarter to any of the enemy who fought beside the Indians. Could he or his charges, then, expect mercy in a prolonged struggle? Might the enemy not use his own words to justify their allies' revenge?

The shells continued to scream and explode above his head. Six men were now dead, several more were wounded, the fort in a turmoil. Hull determined to ask for a ceasefire at a parley with Brock, scrawled a note to his son, Abraham—his aide-de-camp—and asked him to get it across the river. Incredibly it didn't occur to him that Brock might be already outside the palisades with his troops.

At the same time Hull ordered a white tablecloth hung out of a window where the British artillery commander on the Canadian shore could see it. He had no intention of fighting to the last. In the future metropolis of Detroit there would be no Hull Boulevard, no Avenue of Martyrs.

Abraham Hull tied a handkerchief to a pike and gave it to Major Josiah

Snelling, Hull's aide. Snelling said he'd be damned if he'd disgrace his country by taking it out of the fort. Young Hull took it himself and crossed the river, only to discover that Brock was on the American side. When he got back, Snelling was persuaded to seek out the British general.

Outside the fort, Jesup, seeking to take command of the dragoons to meet Brock's expected attack, found the whole line breaking up and the men marching back toward the fort by platoons. Baffled, he asked what on earth was going on. An officer riding by told him: "Look to the fort!"

For the first time Jesup saw the white flag. He rode back, accosted Hull, and demanded to know if surrender was being considered. Hull's reply was unintelligible. Jesup urged Hull to hold out at least until McArthur and Cass returned, but all Hull could exclaim was, "My God, what shall I do with these women and children?"

Hull had already ordered the Ohio volunteers to retreat into the fort. Their commander, Colonel Findlay, rode up in a rage. "What the hell am I ordered here for?" he demanded. Hull replied in a trembling voice that several men had been killed and he believed he could obtain better terms from Brock if he capitulated now than if he were to wait for a storm or a siege.

"Terms!" shouted Findlay. "Damnation! We can beat them on the plain. I didn't come here to capitulate; I came here to fight!" He sought out Lieutenant-Colonel Miller and said, "The general talks of surrender, let us put him under arrest."

But Miller was a regular officer and no mutineer. "Colonel Findlay, I am a soldier. I shall obey my superior officer."

The shelling had ceased. Hidden in the ravine, Brock's men were enjoying breakfast provided by a British civilian who had refused to change allegiance when Detroit became an American community after the Revolution. The owner opened his doors to Brock's officers and the contents of pantry and cellar to his troops, who managed in this brief period to toss off twenty-four gallons (110 l) of brandy, fifteen gallons (68 l) of Madeira, and nine (41 l) of port.

In the midst of this unexpected revel, some of the men spotted Brock's two aides, Glegg and Macdonell, moving toward the fort with a flag of truce. Was it over so quickly?

Hull wanted a three-day respite. Brock gave him three hours. After that he said he'd attack. After this no-nonsense ultimatum it became clear that Hull was prepared for a full surrender. He would give up everything—the fort, its contents, all the ordnance, all supplies, all the troops, even those commanded by the absent colonels. *Everything.*

Hull tried to make some provision for those Canadian deserters who had come over to his side. Macdonell replied with a curt "totally inadmissible." Hull made no further objection and left the details of the surrender to his juniors.

Now, Brock rolled into the fort accompanied by a fife and drum corps. Fifteen-year-old John Richardson, chosen as a member of the advance guard, had never felt so proud than at this moment. But the guard had advanced a little too quickly. The articles of surrender stipulated the Americans must leave the fort before the British entered. A confused melee followed. The American soldiers were in turmoil, some crying openly, a few of the officers breaking their swords, and some of the soldiers breaking their muskets rather than surrender them. Others cried "treason!" and "treachery!" and heaped curses on their general's head. One of the Ohio volunteers tried to stab Macdonell before the advance guard moved back across the drawbridge.

Finally the tangle was straightened out. The Americans stacked their arms and moved out of the fort. The 4th Regiment of regulars, its members in despair and tears, gave up its colours sewn by a group of Boston ladies and carried through the battle of Tippecanoe.

Down came the Stars and Stripes. The Union Jack was hoisted high to the cheers of the troops. Young Richardson was one of those chosen to mount the first guard at the flagstaff. He strutted up and down at his post, peacock proud, casting his eyes down at the vanquished Americans on the esplanade below the fort.

Tecumseh knew many of the American prisoners and greeted them in Detroit without apparent rancour. Now in the aftermath of the bloodless victory more tales were added to his legend.

There was, for instance, the story of Father Gabriel Richard, the priest of Ste. Anne's parish who refused to take the oath of allegiance to the Crown because he said he had already sworn an oath to support the American Constitution. Procter imprisoned him at Sandwich and Tecumseh insisted on his release. Procter snubbed the Shawnee chief. Tecumseh swiftly assembled his followers and told Procter he would return to the Wabash River if the priest was not freed. The colonel gave in.

There are other tales. Tecumseh was speaking to his followers at the River Raisin when he felt a tug at his jacket and looked down and saw a small white girl. "Come to our house, there are bad Indians there," she said. He stopped his speech, seized his tomahawk, followed her, dropped the leader with one blow and, as the others moved to the attack, shouted out, "Dogs! I am Tecumseh!" When the Indians retreated, Tecumseh entered the house and found British officers present. "You are worse than dogs to break faith with your prisoners!" he cried. The British apologized for not having restrained the Indians. They offered to place a guard on the house, but the child's mother told them it wasn't necessary. So long as Tecumseh was near she felt safe.

For the British, if not for the Indians, Detroit's surrender was staggering. Upper Canada, badly supplied and even worse armed, now had an additional cache of 2,500 captured muskets, 39 heavy guns, 40 barrels of gunpowder, a 16-gun rig, a great many smaller craft, and a baggage train of 100 pack animals and 300 cattle, provisions and stores. The prize money to be distributed among the troops was reckoned at two hundred thousand dollars—an enormous sum considering that a private's net pay a month amounted to about four shillings—or one dollar a week.

Every soldier received prize money of more than four pounds—at least twenty weeks' net pay. The amount increased according to rank. Sergeants got eight pounds, captains forty pounds. Brock was due two hundred and sixteen pounds.

More significant was the fact that Brock had rolled back the entire frontier to the Ohio River, the line the Indians themselves claimed to be the border between white territories and their own lands. Most of Michigan Territory was now in British hands. Many Indians, such as the Mohawk of the Grand Valley, who had been reluctant to fight on either side, were now firmly and enthusiastically committed to the British cause. The same could be said for all the population of Upper Canada, once so lukewarm in defeat, now fired to enthusiasm by Brock's stunning victory. In Montreal, Quebec, the spectacle of Hull's tattered and ravaged followers invoked a wave of patriotic ardour.

In Canada, Isaac Brock was the man of the hour. In America, the very word "Hull" was used as a derogatory epithet. In their shame and despair, Americans of all political stripes lashed out blindly at the general who was universally considered to be a traitor and a coward.

But times and attitudes change. Today, one might ask, who was the real hero? Was it Isaac Brock, who was quite prepared, if forced, to let his Indian allies run wild through the fort, slaying men, women, and children. (Could Tecumseh have prevented a bloodbath?) Or was it Hull, the compassionate old soldier, who decided to surrender rather than see his people needlessly destroyed?

Hull was made the scapegoat for all of Washington's bumbling. When he was finally exchanged, he faced a court martial that was a travesty of a trial. His lawyer was not permitted to cross-examine those officers who came up against him or to examine other witnesses. The old general, untrained in the law, had to perform that task himself. Nor was he allowed to examine copies of his personal papers. The court was packed against him and he was eventually found guilty of cowardice.

Hull was sentenced to be shot, but the president took into account his revolutionary gallantry, and pardoned him. He spent the rest of his life attempting to vindicate his actions. It's an irony of war that had he refused to surrender, had he gone down to defeat, his fort and town shattered by cannon fire, his friends and neighbours ravaged by the misfortunes of battle, his soldiers dead to the last man, the civilians burned out, bombed out, and inevitably scalped, the tired old general would have been swept into the history books as a gallant martyr, his name enshrined on bridges, schools, main streets, and public buildings.

But for the rest of their lives, the very soldiers who, because of him, could now go back whole to the comfort of their homesteads, and the civilians, who were now able to pick up the strings of their existence, only briefly tangled, would loathe and curse the name of William Hull who, on his deathbed at the age of seventy-two, would continue to insist that he took the only proper, decent, and courageous course on that bright August Sunday in 1812.

INDEX

"The Death of Brock at Queenston Heights" (c. 1908)
by C. W. Jefferys. When Brock met his end at Queenston Heights,
the Canadian troops feared the worst.

THE DEATH OF ISAAC BROCK

CONTENTS

CHAPTER ONE

The Reluctant General

LIKE JOHN RICHARDSON, GEORGE STEPHEN BENJAMIN JARVIS WAS ONLY FIF-
TEEN YEARS OLD WHEN THE WAR OF 1812 BROKE OUT, BUT THAT DIDN'T STOP
HIM FROM RUSHING TO JOIN THE ARMY. HIS FAMILY WERE FIERCE LOYALISTS
WHO, AFTER THE AMERICAN REVOLUTION, HAD EXCHANGED THEIR COMFORT-
ABLE HOME IN DANBURY, CONNECTICUT, FOR THE WILDS OF NEW BRUNSWICK,
AND LATER THE MUDDY ROADWAYS OF LITTLE YORK, THE FUTURE SITE OF
TORONTO.

As Loyalists, the members of the sprawling Jarvis clan were eager to do
battle with their former compatriots. An older cousin, Samuel Peter Jarvis,
was a member of a militia unit, the 3rd York Volunteers, but young George
opted for the regular army and was accepted as a "gentleman volunteer" in
the British 49th. That was the favourite regiment of Canada's leading military figure, Major-General Isaac Brock, who had once been its colonel. As a
result, George Jarvis would shortly find himself in the thick of battle, splendid in the scarlet tunic and brass buttons of a professional warrior.

He was to take part in many memorable battles. Within two years, he
would be put in charge of a company of more than one hundred men, most
of them older than himself. But no moment would be quite as memorable
as his first engagement when, on a soft autumn day, he dashed up the slopes
of Queenston Heights right behind General Brock himself.

That battle, on October 13, 1812, was the most important ever fought
on Canadian soil. There, on a high cliff overlooking the Niagara River,
Canada successfully fought off an invasion by a formidable American army.
She also lost her most famous military figure, whose death is commemo-
rated by a marble pillar overlooking the battleground.

Tourists travel by the thousands each summer to gaze on Brock's Monument and to follow the battle itself, its course marked by signs and plaques. The slopes up which George Jarvis and his fellow soldiers toiled and struggled are no longer red with the blood of the participants. In October, the bright leaves of the sugar maple form an orange carpet, as they did on that day so long ago, when two neighbouring countries found themselves locked in combat.

The unnecessary war belongs to history; it never should have happened. But it did give history a nudge: it helped create a sense of community among the settlers north of the border, many of whom were new arrivals. In a very real sense, the victory at Queenston Heights, renowned now in song and story, marked the beginning of a new nationalism. Having forestalled a common enemy, the young volunteers and the newly arrived farmers began to think of themselves as Canadians.

The irony is that the general in charge of the American troops across the Niagara River didn't want to go to war. Stephen Van Rensselaer was an aristocratic landowner from upper New York State. An American militia man with no military experience, he was totally opposed to the whole idea of invading a neighbour. But in July of 1812, in one of the supreme ironies of a foolish and ironic conflict, he found himself a general, no less, in charge of an army of reluctant troops, ordered by his government to invade and seize Upper Canada. Thus it became for him a matter of honour that he prosecute the new war to the fullest, even at the risk of his own reputation.

His was one of two American armies that lay poised on the international border in the summer of 1812 with orders to strike at Canada. His men were camped at Lewiston, New York, on the Niagara River, directly across from the little village of Queenston. A second army, under General William Hull, was massed at Fort Detroit, directly across from the Upper Canadian village of Amherstburg.

In those days communications moved no faster than the speed of a trotting horse. Stephen Van Rensselaer had no way of knowing that General Hull's army had been decisively defeated on August 16 by a force of British and Canadians under General Isaac Brock and Indians under the great Shawnee war chief, Tecumseh. Terrified of an Indian massacre, Hull had surrendered Detroit and most of Michigan Territory without a fight. But nobody on the Niagara River or in the American capital of Washington was yet aware of this disaster.

And so, believing that Hull had been victorious and was now moving into Upper Canada, the Americans were urging Van Rensselaer to attack at once. They were under the impression that the Canadian stronghold at Fort Amherstburg had fallen and that the road to victory lay wide open. That was an illusion that Van Rensselaer himself did not share. But he had to follow orders.

He was supposed to be helping Hull by keeping the British and Canadians off balance. But that wasn't easy. The British controlled not only the far shore but also the Niagara River itself and two of the Great Lakes, Erie and Ontario. Van Rensselaer had fewer than a thousand men to guard a front of thirty-six miles (58 km). A third of that force was too ill to fight. None had been paid. His men lay in the open without tents or covering. Ammunition was low; there were scarcely ten rounds per soldier. There were no big guns, no gunners, no engineers, and scarcely any medical supplies.

Worse still, the state militia was refusing to fight on foreign soil—as was their right under the American Constitution. When the general planned a daring raid to capture a British gunboat, only sixty-six of his four hundred men agreed to join the expedition.

If the troops were reluctant, their militia leaders were inexperienced. Brigadier-General William Wadsworth of the New York State Militia knew so little of war that he pleaded to be released from the assignment. Stephen Van Rensselaer himself had no campaign experience. Nor did he look much like a soldier with his pert and amiable Dutch features and his shock of white hair curled in the style of the day. A Harvard graduate, a millionaire farmer, and a supporter of worthy causes, he was seen as a political threat by his rival, the Republican governor of New York, who gave him the post to get him out of the way. Not the best method of choosing an army commander whose men depended on him for their lives!

He accepted on the condition that his cousin, Solomon, be appointed his aide-de-camp, for Lieutenant-Colonel Solomon Van Rensselaer was a skilled military tactician—a regular soldier until the century's turn and then adjutant general for the State of New York.

Unlike the general, his handsome cousin was "all formed for war." The

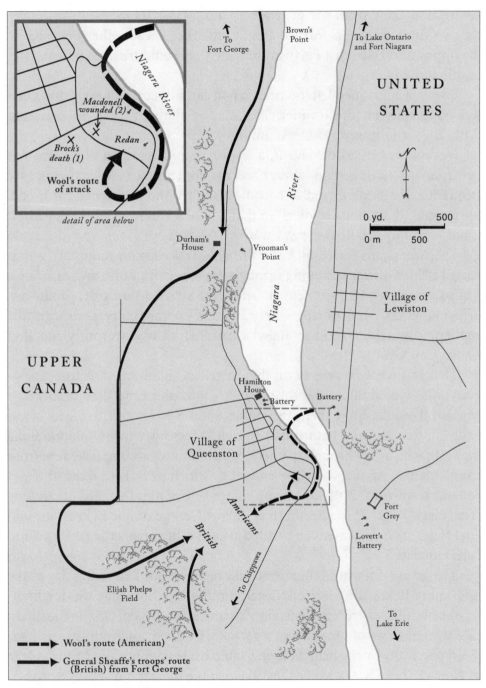

Battle of Queenston Heights

description came from the general's friend, Major John Lovett, who with the two Van Rensselaers formed a tight little trio. Because they belonged to the opposition Federalist Party in the state they could trust no other advice but their own.

Lovett, a confirmed letter writer, kept a careful record of everything that was happening on the frontier. The war, he thought, "was an Ominous Gathering of folly and madness." But he was prepared to fight.

He was a poet, a bon vivant, a lawyer by profession, and an amateur politician—a restless man, always seeking something new, changing jobs frequently. He didn't expect to become a soldier and he warned his friend, the general, "I am not a soldier." To that Stephen Van Rensselaer replied, "It is not your *sword*, but your *pen* I want."

The Americans feared an early British attack, but on August 16 a red-coated British officer, galloping through the American camp and carrying a flag of truce, brought excitement and then relief. More riders followed, bringing letters from Albany where Major-General Henry Dearborn, the supreme commander, had arranged a truce with the Governor General of Canada, Sir George Prevost.

That was what everybody on the American side wanted. A truce, however brief, would allow the Americans to buy the time they desperately needed. It would allow them to reinforce the Niagara frontier, which was badly undermanned. That frontier stretched thirty-six miles (58 km) along the river, which cut through the neck of the land separating Lake Erie from Lake Ontario. At the southern end, the British Fort Erie faced the two American towns of Buffalo, a lively village of five hundred, and its trading rival, Black Rock. At the northern end, Fort George on the British side and Fort Niagara on the American bristled at each other across the entrance into Lake Ontario.

The great falls, whose thunder could be heard for kilometres, lay at the mid-point. Below the gorge of Niagara on the American side was the hamlet of Lewiston, where Van Rensselaer's army was camped. On the Canadian side lay the village of Queenston, a partially fortified community overshadowed physically by the heights to the south and economically by the village of Newark (later Niagara-On-the-Lake) on the outskirts of Fort George.

At Lewiston the river was so narrow you could row across in ten minutes. A musket ball fired from one village to the other had the power to kill. For some time the Americans were convinced that the British would attack across the river. It was widely believed they had three thousand men in the field and another thousand on call. As is so often the case in war, both sides overestimated the forces opposite them.

General Isaac Brock had only four hundred regulars and eight hundred militia, most of whom had gone home to attend to the harvest. But New York State was totally unprepared for war. The arms were of varying calibres; no single cartridge would suit them. Few bayonets were available. There was only enough ammunition for one hour of fighting. The United States was not then the military machine it was to become in the twentieth century. Great Britain had the armed might.

Buffalo was in a state of panic. If Hull was beaten at Detroit, only a miracle could save Van Rensselaer's forces from ignoble defeat. Now, when least expected, the miracle had happened. The army had been given breathing space.

Lieutenant-Colonel Solomon Van Rensselaer, an old campaigner, immediately grasped the significance of the armistice. However, he faced a serious problem: all the heavy cannon and supplies he needed were far away at Oswego at the eastern end of Lake Ontario. The roads were bogs. Supplies could only be moved by water. The British controlled the lake and, under the terms of the truce, would not allow the Americans to use it. Solomon, however, was determined to force his enemies to give way. The security of the American army depended upon it.

He went straight to his cousin, the general. Something would have to be done, he said. "I shall make powerful effort to procure the use of the waters and I shall take such ground as will make it impossible for me to recede."

"Van, you may as well give up, you will not succeed," his friend Lovett told him.

"If I do not, it will not be my fault," retorted Solomon.

He put on full military dress and crossed to Fort George. There he met Brock's deputy, Major-General Roger Sheaffe. But when he proposed the use of all navigable waters as a common highway, Sheaffe rapped out one curt word. "Inadmissible!" he cried.

Now Solomon decided to engage in a Yankee bluff. "There can be no armistice," he said; "our negotiation is at an end. General Van Rensselaer will take the responsibility on himself to prevent your detaching troops from this district." The British officers leapt to their feet. Sheaffe gripped the handle of his sword.

"Sir," said he, "you take the high ground!" His opponent also rose to his feet and gripped his sword.

"I do, sir, and will maintain it."

There was silence. Sheaffe paced the room and finally he asked to be excused. Returning a few moments later after a discussion with his aides, he granted Solomon Van Rensselaer the use of the waters.

That was an enormous mistake, for it allowed the Americans to rearm themselves with the munitions stored at Oswego.

The truce could be cancelled by either side on four days' notice. It ended on September 8 with the Americans standing firm. Unless the British stopped their practice of seizing American ships and impressing American sailors, the Americans would continue the war. But by that time Van Rensselaer's army had been reinforced from Oswego with six regiments of regulars, five of militia, a battalion of riflemen—some six thousand men altogether—plus a great many heavy cannons and a quantity of pork and flour.

And so the balance of power on Lake Ontario had been tilted. General Van Rensselaer, taking advantage of the truce, shot off an express to Ogdensburg on the St. Lawrence to send nine ships to Sackets Harbor (near present-day Watertown, New York). This move would aid the American navy in their planned attack on the Upper Canadian capital of York the following year.

In spite of this, Solomon Van Rensselaer was not a happy man. He felt himself the plaything of remorseless fate—surrounded by political enemies, forced into a war he could not condone, nudged toward a battle he felt he could not win, separated from a loving wife at his estate, seven hundred miles (1,000 km) to the east. He knew communications were primitive, mail sporadic, dispatch riders scarce. Still, he fretted. Why had she not written? He had sent her a dozen letters and got no answer. He did not know—and wouldn't know until the affair at Queenston was over—that his wife, Harriet, was in the final stages of pregnancy and about to present him with a new son.

CHAPTER TWO

Brock's Frustration

ISAAC BROCK, RETURNING HOME ACROSS LAKE ONTARIO TO HIS CAPITAL AT YORK, WAS A NATIONAL HERO. HE COULD NOT CONTAIN HIS ECSTASY OVER HIS BLOODLESS VICTORY AT DETROIT, BUT EVEN HE WAS A LITTLE STUNNED BY THE WAVE OF ADULATION THAT SWEPT OVER THE COUNTRY — AT THE TWENTY-ONE-GUN SALUTES, THE POPULAR DEMONSTRATIONS, THE GUSHY NOTES OF CONGRATULATION. THEY WERE CALLING HIM THE SAVIOUR OF UPPER CANADA; BUT UPPER CANADA WAS STILL IN PERIL.

At forty-two, Brock was everybody's idea of a British warrior general—a handsome, strapping figure, standing six foot three (2 m), magnificent in his scarlet uniform and gold epaulettes. Equally at home in ballroom or barracks, unmarried but much sought after by his female admirers, he was nothing if not bold and impetuous.

Now he was eager to follow up his victory and keep up the momentum against the invading Americans. He was ready to roll up the entire New York frontier and hammer at them while they were still off balance and poorly supplied. He wanted a quick victory—one that would allow him to leave the stifling colonial atmosphere of Canada and get back to Europe to serve under the Duke of Wellington in the larger war against Napoleon.

But that was not to be. A message from Sir George Prevost informed him of the armistice the Governor General had concluded with the enemy. Prevost was hoping to conclude the war by a negotiated settlement without any more blood being spilled.

Brock had little patience with that. But his hands were tied and he could not conceal his bitterness. He was convinced that the sharp Yankees were using the armistice to buy time to reinforce their own position—and he was right. He must get back at once to Fort George on the Niagara frontier.

There he learned—from one of his officers who had been in Albany, New York, to arrange the armistice—that the Americans were convinced the British were weak. Certainly the Americans were stronger. He was dismayed to find how heavily they had been reinforced during the brief peace. He expected an immediate attack and sent at once to Amherstburg and Kingston for more troops.

There was one bright spot—the result, again, of the victory at Detroit. Three hundred Mohawk Indians were on the Niagara and another two hundred on their way under the controversial John Norton of the Indian Department. Born a Scotsman, now an adopted Mohawk chief, Norton saw himself as the successor to the great Joseph Brant.

Brock had mixed feelings about Norton's followers, who had cast aside their neutrality only as a result of British victories. To him any form of neutrality was little short of treason. He couldn't forgive the Mohawk. He couldn't understand why they didn't wish to fight for the British. He couldn't grasp the truth: that the quarrel was not really theirs and its outcome could not help them.

Brock wrote of "the disgrace into which they have fallen by their late conduct," but it is doubtful the Indians felt any sense of disgrace. They had simply been following a foreign policy of their own, which was to reap the benefits of fighting on the winning side.

Brock was eager to attack across the Niagara River and make himself master of upper New York State, but Prevost had reined him in. The Governor General still believed the path to peace lay in being as inoffensive as possible to the enemy. Even after the armistice ended he clung to the wistful fancy that the Americans would come to terms only if the British did nothing to annoy them. That was a foolish assumption. American honour had been stained; nothing would satisfy it but blood. It was psychologically impossible for the Americans to break off the war after the humiliation of Detroit.

Sir George Prevost made one telling point. Since the British were not interested in waging a campaign of conquest against the United States, but only in *containing* the war while battling the real enemy, Napoleon, it made sense to let the enemy take the offensive.

Brock had not been a soldier for the best part of three decades without learning to obey orders. Frustrated or not, he did as he was told. While he believed he could sweep everything before him from Fort Niagara to Buffalo, he was prepared to let the Americans make the first move.

Certainly they did not appear ready for that. Many of their soldiers, tired of the army, were deserting to Canada. More, Brock believed, would do so if the opportunity was offered. Those deserters who did not drown in the swirling Niagara River reported a poor state of morale on the American side. They complained of bad food, poor pay, and continual sickness. They were jealous of the militia, which they believed to be better fed and better treated. Brock was scornful of the American militia. He saw them as an undisciplined rabble of "enraged Democrats … who … die very fast."

Brock did not have the temperament for the kind of bloodless warfare that had been his lot since hostilities began. He was impatient for action. Since he couldn't start it, he hoped and expected the Americans would. He was convinced they would have to make a move soon to keep their restless and undisciplined militia in line—and he was again correct. To warn of attack he'd ordered a line of beacon signals along the frontier. Now he could only sit and wait.

Actually the war in Canada was only a minor fracas. Who in Europe could take it seriously? On September 9, the day after Prevost's armistice ended, Napoleon launched and won the Battle of Borodino, thus opening his way to Moscow. On that day the casualties exceeded eighty thousand— a figure greater than the entire population of Upper Canada. Meanwhile, on the Niagara frontier, two tiny, untrained armies faced each other across the boiling river, each afraid to make the first move, each expecting the other to launch an attack.

Brock was certain something decisive would happen before the end of September: "I say decisive because if I should be beaten, the province is inevitably gone; and should I be victorious, I do not imagine the gentry from the other side will be anxious to return to the charge."

In short, he would either be confirmed as the Saviour of Upper Canada or there would be no Upper Canada. Whatever happened, Brock was convinced this brief and not very bloody war would come to a swift conclusion. There were, of course, other possibilities, glorious and at the same time tragic, but these he did not consider.

CHAPTER THREE

Honour Must be Satisfied

IN LEWISTON, WHILE BROCK PLANNED A DEFENSIVE BATTLE, GENERAL STEPHEN VAN RENSSELAER FELT BOXED IN. HE FOUND HIMSELF PUSHED TO THE BRINK OF A CONFLICT FOR WHICH HE WAS INADEQUATELY PREPARED BY A SERIES OF CIRCUMSTANCES OVER WHICH HE HAD LITTLE CONTROL. EVENTS BEGAN TO PILE UP, ONE UPON THE OTHER, LIKE OCEAN BREAKERS, DRIVING HIM UNWITTINGLY TOWARD A FOREIGN SHORE.

On August 27, the camp was subjected to a dreadful spectacle. Across the river for more than a kilometre the men could see the remnants of Hull's defeated armies straggling along the opposite shore—ragged, shoeless, dispirited, the wounded groaning in open carts, the whole prodded onward by their British captors.

As Lovett put it in a letter to a friend: "The sensations this scene produced in our camp were inexpressible. Mortification, indignation, fearful apprehension, suspicion, jealousy, dismay, rage, madness." The effect on the American force was twofold: the militia was cowed by this demonstration of British power. But the hawks among the officers yearned for action.

"Alarm pervades the country and distrust among the troops," General Van Rensselaer wrote. Like Hull's beaten soldiers, many of his own had no shoes. All were clamouring for pay. "While we are thus growing daily weaker, our enemy is growing stronger." The British were reinforcing the high ground above Queenston, bringing men and guns and fortifying every prominent point from Fort Erie to Fort George.

The day before the armistice ended, Major Lovett came to the conclusion that "we must either fight or run." Yet nobody on the American side could guess Brock's intentions or even estimate the true strength of his force, because not a single man could be persuaded to risk his neck by acting as a spy on the Canadian shore. Van Rensselaer had to resort to the time-worn trick of sending officers across under flags of truce to deal with the enemy on various pretexts while peering at the fortifications.

Meanwhile, at Albany, Major-General Dearborn, Van Rensselaer's superior, felt his resolve wavering. He had expected to seize all of Upper Canada, and Montreal as well, before winter. Now, Hull's defeat had shaken him. He was an old man, indecisive, inexperienced, out of his depth, peevish, uninformed, and grossly overweight. The American military effort was in a state of confusion. Hampered by lack of supplies, men and money, he told the secretary of war that he had never found official duties "so unceasing, perplexing and fatiguing as at this place."

Political enmities created further distractions. The quartermaster-general of the army, Peter B. Porter, was a political rival of the Van Rensselaers. He was organizing a whispering campaign against them, insinuating that the general was a traitor who intended to surrender his army the moment it crossed the river.

> *The American military effort was in a state of confusion, hampered by lack of supplies, men, and money.*

The general, however, was convinced that the British were about to attack and was preparing for them. He decided to maintain Fort Niagara, opposite Fort George at the mouth of the river, decrepit though it was, by removing the roof from a stone building, mounting two twelve-pound (5-kg) cannon in its upper storey, and three big eighteen-pounders (8-kg) a kilometre upriver across from the British. He brought up an additional five hundred men stationed at Buffalo to strengthen his own force.

The British were also active. Gazing across the narrow river, Stephen Van Rensselaer could see the *Royal George* arrive with two hundred gunners. He had learned that one hundred smaller boats, loaded with stores for the British fort, had passed up the St. Lawrence together with two regiments of troops. The situation was critical. His plan was to hold out against what he thought to be superior strength until he was reinforced. There is no evidence that he contemplated an attack. It was the British who would attack—or so he believed.

But the British did not attack and the promised reinforcements did not arrive. In the American army of 2,000 on September 22, 149 were too sick to fight, including Solomon Van Rensselaer. The weather was dreadful. Raw winds and cold rains harassed the troops, soaking whatever blankets and tents were available.

In Albany, the capital of New York, General Dearborn continued to promise that money, men, and provisions would eventually be there. Troops were on their way from the western frontier to relieve Detroit, he said. But everything depended on what happened on the Niagara River: "*We must calculate on possessing Upper Canada before winter sets in,*" Dearborn wrote, underlining that passage as if, by a stroke of the pen, he could will his rag-tag army into victory.

To the relief of Van Rensselaer, the longed-for reinforcements arrived at the end of September. These included seventeen hundred soldiers under the command of one of the more curious specimens of American generalship, Brigadier-General Alexander Smyth. Pompous, self-important, and reluctant to follow orders, Smyth was a regular officer who disdained the militia. He had no intention of cooperating with his nominal commander, Van Rensselaer. Though he knew nothing of the country and had only just arrived, he advised the general that the best place for crossing the Niagara would be above the falls and not below them. As a result, he decided not to take his troops to Lewiston but to encamp them near Buffalo, thus splitting the American force. Nor did he report personally to Van Rensselaer. He claimed he was too busy.

By this time Van Rensselaer was determined to start operations himself, since the British showed no interest in attacking. Dearborn had demanded action. For better or for worse, Stephen Van Rensselaer was determined that he should have it.

On paper his chances of success were excellent. He now had eight thousand troops under his command, half of them regulars. Forty-two hundred were encamped at Lewiston. The rest were at Buffalo or Fort Niagara. To counter this force, Brock had about a thousand regular troops, some six hundred militiamen, and a reserve of perhaps six hundred militiamen and Indians strung out thinly from Fort Erie to Fort George.

But numbers didn't tell the whole story. Morale, sickness, discipline, determination—all these Van Rensselaer must consider carefully. By his own count he had only seventeen hundred *effective* militiamen with him at

Lewiston. The state of his army was such that he knew he would have to act swiftly if he acted at all:

> Our best troops are raw, many of them dejected by the distress their families suffer by their absence, and many have not necessary clothing. We are in a cold country, the season is far advanced, and unusually inclement; we are half deluged by rain. The blow must be struck soon or all the toil and expense of the campaign will go for nothing, and worse than nothing, for the whole will be tinged with dishonour.

The key word was "dishonour." It crept like a fog through the sodden tents of the army, blinding all to reality. It hung like a weight over the council chambers in Albany and Washington. Van Rensselaer felt its pressure spurring him to action, *any* action. No purpose now in disputing the war and its causes. No sense in further recrimination, or I-told-you-so's. Detroit must be avenged!

"The national character is degraded, and the disgrace will remain, corroding the public feeling and spirit until another campaign, unless it be instantly wiped out by a brilliant close of this." He knew that with his present force at Lewiston it would be rash to attempt an attack. But Smyth had arrived with an almost equal number, and that was enough.

Van Rensselaer planned a two-pronged attack: Smyth's regulars would cross the river near Newark (now Niagara-on-the-Lake) and storm Fort George from the rear. At the same time he would lead the militia from Lewiston to carry the heights above Queenston. That would divide the thinly spread British forces and cut their lines of communication, while driving their shipping out of the mouth of the Niagara River. It would provide the troops with warm and extensive winter quarters, act as a springboard for the following season's campaign, and—certainly not least—"wipe away part of the score of our past disgrace."

It was a workable scheme, but it depended upon Smyth's cooperation, and Smyth had no intention of cooperating. He acted almost as if Van Rensselaer didn't exist. When Van Rensselaer invited him to a council of officers to plan the attack, Smyth didn't reply. Even after Van Rensselaer wrote again, more explicitly, he didn't answer. Several days passed. Nothing. A fellow officer now informed Van Rensselaer that he had seen Smyth, who was unable to name the day when he could come to Lewiston for a council. The general thereupon sent a direct order to bring his command "with all possible dispatch." Silence.

This was a remarkable—almost unbelievable—state of affairs. In no other army would such defiance be tolerated, but the United States was not yet a military nation. The amiable Van Rensselaer didn't court-martial his disobedient underling. He simply proceeded without him. He had told Dearborn that it would be rash to attack Queenston with the militiamen under his command at Lewiston. And yet, in spite of the fact that Smyth's regulars were out of the picture, he determined to do just that.

He had very little choice, because at this point an incident occurred near Black Rock, close to Buffalo, that reduced his options.

There, on October 9, a combined force of about one hundred American seamen and soldiers managed to seize and put out of action two British gunboats, the *Detroit* and the *Caledonia*. They captured four cannon, two hundred muskets and so much pork that the British at Fort Amherstburg on the Detroit River were forced to live on half rations. They also captured a good many British soldiers.

This bold adventure represented the only American victory so far on the frontier. Its success goaded the Americans into premature attack. A thrill ran through the nation. At Lewiston, General Van Rensselaer was presented with an ultimatum from his troops, who were now hot for action—or claimed to be. The general was warned if he didn't take the offensive immediately they would all go home.

With Smyth sulking in Buffalo, Van Rensselaer decided to abandon his two-pronged attack and launch a single assault upon Queenston. A friend in Albany counselled caution, but the time was long past when he could accept such cool advice. The pressure on him was so great that he realized that "my refusal to act might involve me in suspicion and the service in disgrace." As John Lovett described it, "He was absolutely compelled to go to battle, or reap such consequences as no man could endure." It was not possible to wait, even though there was no proper plan of attack. Ready or not, he would have to strike the blow at once.

CHAPTER FOUR

The Attack Begins

ON THE EVENING OF OCTOBER 11, 1812, AT FORT GEORGE, BROCK RECEIVED AN ALARMING NOTE. CAPTAIN JAMES DENNIS, COMMANDING A COMPANY OF THE 49TH AT QUEENSTON, REPORTED THAT HIS TROOPS WERE IN A STATE OF MUTINY AND THAT THE MEN HAD THREATENED TO SHOOT THEIR OFFICERS.

Brock at once dispatched Major Thomas Evans to seize the mutineers. "I will make an example of them," he said, by which he meant that they would all be executed by a firing squad.

At the same time Brock told Evans to cross the river and offer Van Rensselaer an immediate exchange of prisoners taken on the *Detroit* and the *Caledonia* for an equal number of Americans he had released after the capture of Detroit.

And so, on the very eve of the most famous battle on Canadian soil, a British officer was able to enter and have a good look at the enemy camp.

Evans reached Queenston the following night to find the guardhouse gutted and Dennis in a state of alarm. Just as he was about to arrest the ringleaders for mutiny, he heard a scatter of musket fire from the American shore. Dennis told him that sporadic firing had been going on for some days, making it hazardous to use the door of the house on the river side of the building.

In spite of this hazard, Evans decided to cross the river at once and ordered Dennis to corral the prisoners for his return. Then, with shots still hurtling past his ears, he walked over to the home of a militia captain, Thomas Dickson, and asked his wife for a white handkerchief to use as a flag of truce while he and Dickson crossed the river. Mrs. Dickson protested. Others in the house joined her. They thought the venture far too dangerous.

The enemy was in a temper. Evans was told they would no longer respect the white flag.

At that, Evans seized Dickson by one hand, took the flag in the other, descended the steep steps to a canoe at the water's edge, and started off across the two-hundred-yard (180-m) stream in a shower of musket balls. The canoe became unmanageable and was about to sink, when the American fire suddenly stopped and the two men were able to reach the far shore.

As Evans was about to leap ashore, an American with a bayonet stopped him. He asked to see the adjutant general, Solomon Van Rensselaer, but was told that Solomon was too ill to receive him. He replied that he carried an important message from Brock. Eventually Major Lovett appeared and Evans presented his request about the prisoner exchange. Lovett's reply was abrupt and curiously evasive. He said nothing could be done "till the day after tomorrow."

This put Evans on the alert. What were the Americans planning for the next day? When he pressed his case, Lovett remained evasive. It appeared to Evans that Lovett was trying to delay his return to the Canadian side—it was already past midday. Lovett didn't come back for two hours and then explained the prisoners had been sent on to Albany and couldn't quickly be brought back. But, he said, "all will be settled the day after tomorrow."

That constant harping on the morrow confirmed Evans's suspicions that the enemy was planning an immediate attack. He was anxious to get away and report to Brock. He had kept his eyes open. He noticed the Americans' numbers had been "prodigiously swelled by a horde of half-savage troops from Kentucky, Ohio, and Tennessee." Even more significant, he spotted about a dozen boats half-hidden along the riverbank and partially covered with brush. That convinced him that "an attack on our shores could not be prudently delayed for a single day."

He and Dickson paddled swiftly back to their own shore. Evans rushed to warn the regular companies and the militia stationed at Queenston. It was now past three o'clock. Fort George was six miles (10 km) away. Every man would be needed to defend the town, including the mutinous prisoners who Evans liberated, appealing to their loyalty and courage.

Then, after making sure a fresh supply of ammunition had been distributed, the harried brigade major set off at a gallop for Fort George, warning the various posts along the route of the coming danger. He reached the fort at six, having been exposed for thirteen hours to "wet feet and extreme heat without refreshment of any kind." He was so exhausted he couldn't speak. He took some food, recovered his breath, and was ushered into the dining room before Brock and his senior officers.

They didn't believe him at first. They offered to place bets against his prediction of an attack on the following day. Even Brock appeared doubtful, but he changed his mind as Evans talked on. With a grave face he asked Evans to follow him into his office, where he questioned him carefully on the day's events. At last he was convinced.

The two men came back to the dining room, where the general issued orders calling out all the militia in the neighbourhood that very evening. Others in outlying districts were told to report as swiftly as possible. He returned to his office to work late into the night. Evans toiled until eleven making all necessary preparations to meet the coming assault. Then he slumped onto a mattress. A few hours later his slumber was disturbed by the rumble of distant guns.

The attack began at three o'clock in the morning of October 13, but General Stephen Van Rensselaer's plan and his preparations for the assault were both faulty. He had already lost the advantage of surprise. Now he decided to make the first crossing with only a handful of bateaux—two large boats, each holding eighty men, and a dozen smaller ones, each holding twenty-five.

Now the general's lack of military experience worked against him. His initial attack force, which would cross in two waves, consisted of some six hundred men, half of them militia. A few kilometres upriver were more boats that could easily be floated down, but the general didn't take advantage of these. He believed that, once the boats were emptied on the opposite shore, they could quickly return for reinforcements. He thought that half a dozen trips would be able to ferry the entire force across the river. That was a serious miscalculation.

He didn't think either to make use of the seamen at Black Rock. These men were experienced boatmen. His own militia, of course, knew the river well. They'd been staring at it and sometimes navigating it under flags of truce for some six weeks, but those who had just joined his force from Buffalo, Black Rock, and Fort Niagara were strangers to the area.

There were other problems. Van Rensselaer had failed to distribute enough ammunition. He had not insisted strongly enough on the use of Smyth's regular forces at Buffalo. Nobody had thought to find boats large enough to transport heavy field pieces across the river. The bateaux couldn't handle cannon. Nor had the various commands been assigned to capture specific objectives. The orders were general and vague: get across, seize the village, gain the heights.

It was still dark when the first boats pushed off in the teeth of a chill, sleety drizzle. To oppose the landing, the British had fewer than three hundred men in and about Queenston. But the defenders were on the alert. John Lovett, who had been placed in charge of the American battery at Fort Grey, on the heights above Lewiston, noted that the Canadian shore was a constant blaze of musket fire.

It was still dark when the first boats pushed off in the teeth of a chill, sleety drizzle. To oppose the landing, the British had fewer than three hundred men in and about Queenston. But the defenders were on the alert.

He saw his friend Solomon Van Rensselaer land in what seemed to be a sheet of fire. His own eighteen-pound (8-kg) guns opened up to cover the attack, aided by two six-pounders (3-kg) and a mortar on the Lewiston shore. The cannonballs and shells whistled over the heads of the troops in the bateaux. But at the same moment, the British opened fire. Halfway up the heights in an arrow-shaped emplacement known as a *redan*, a single cannon began to lob eighteen-pound (8-kg) balls down on the boats. Darkness was banished as bombs burst and muskets flashed.

In one of the boats approaching the shore sat the oldest volunteer in the American army—an extraordinary Kentucky frontiersman named Samuel Stubbs, whose colourful turn of phrase enlivens his personal account of the battle. Sixty-two years old, scarcely five feet (1.5 m) in height, he gripped the rifle with which in just three months he had killed forty-five deer. Peering into gloom, illuminated now by the flash of cannon, Stubbs saw the opposite shore lined with redcoats "as thick as bees upon a sugar maple." In a few moments he was ashore under a heavy fire, "the damned redcoats cutting us up like slain venison," his companions dropping "like wild pigeons," while the musket balls whistled around him "like a northwest wind through a dry cane break."

Chaos reigned. Solomon's attack force had dwindled. Three of the boats, including the two largest containing almost two hundred men, had drifted downriver and turned back. On the bank above, Captain Dennis with forty-six British regulars and a handful of militiamen was keeping up a withering fire.

Solomon was no sooner out of his boat when a ball struck him in the right thigh. As he thrust forward, waving on his men, a second ball entered his thigh. The British were purposely firing low to inflict maximum damage. As the colonel continued to stumble forward, a third penetrated his calf and a fourth mangled his heel. Still he didn't stop. Two more struck him in the leg and thigh. Weak from loss of blood, his men pinned down by the killing fire, he tottered back with a remnant of his force to the shelter of the steep bank above the river and looked around weakly for his fellow commander.

Where was Lieutenant-Colonel John Chrystie? He was supposed to be in charge of the regulars. But Chrystie was nowhere to be seen.

Chrystie's boat had lost an oarlock and was drifting helplessly downstream while one of his officers attempted to hold an oar in place. None of these regulars was familiar with the river. They all depended upon a pilot to guide them. But as they came under musket fire from the Canadian bank, the pilot, groaning in terror, turned about and returned to the American side. Chrystie, wounded in the hand by grapeshot, struggled with him to no avail. The boat landed on the American side several hundred metres below the embarkation point, to which Chrystie and the others would have to return on foot.

That was probably the turning point of the battle. Chrystie's problems and the heavy fire from the opposite shore "damped the hitherto irrepressible ardour of the militia," in Solomon Van Rensselaer's later words. The very men who the previous day were so eager to do battle—hoping, perhaps, that a quick victory would allow them to return to their homes—now remembered that they were not required to fight on foreign soil. They seized on any excuse to give up. One militia major suddenly lost his zest for combat and discovered he was too ill to lead his detachment across the river.

Back at the embarkation point, Chrystie found chaos. No one, apparently, had been put in charge of directing the boats or the boatmen, most of whom had forsaken their duty. Some were already returning without orders or permission, landing wherever convenient and leaving the boats where they touched the shore. Others were leaping into bateaux of their own and crossing over, then abandoning the craft to drift downriver.

As Chrystie struggled to collect the missing bateaux, his fellow commander, Lieutenant-Colonel Fenwick, in charge of the second assault wave, arrived only to learn that he couldn't cross because there were no boats. Exposed to a spray of grape canister shot (grapeshot), he herded his men back into the shelter of the ravine until he managed to secure enough craft to move the second wave onto the river.

The crossing was a disaster. Lieutenant John Ball of the British 49th directed the fire of one of his little three-pounders (1.4-kg), known as "grasshoppers," against the bateaux. One was knocked out of the water with a loss of fifteen men. Three others, holding some eighty men, drifted into a hollow just below the stone house built by Robert Hamilton, the best-known trader on the frontier. All were slaughtered or taken prisoner, Fenwick among them. Terribly wounded in the eye, the right side, and the thigh, he counted nine additional bullet holes in his cloak.

None of the regular commanders had yet been able to cross the narrow Niagara. On the Canadian shore under the sheltering bank, Solomon Van Rensselaer, growing weaker from his wounds, attempted to rally his followers. They were still pinned down by cannon fire from the gun in the redan and the muskets of Captain Dennis's small force on the bank above.

But Captain John E. Wool, a young regular officer with the 13th Infantry, had a plan. He approached Solomon. Unless something was done and done quickly, he pointed out, all would be prisoners. The key to victory or defeat was the gun in redan. It *must* be seized. Its capture would signal a turning point in the battle that would relieve the attackers while the fire could be redirected, with dreadful effect, among the defenders.

But how could it be silenced? The heights were known to be unscalable from the river side. Or were they? Young Captain Wool had heard of a fisherman's path upriver, leading to the heights above the gun emplacement. He believed he could bring an attacking force up the slope and asked Solomon Van Rensselaer's permission to attempt the feat.

He was just twenty-three years old—a lithe, light youth of little experience but considerable ambition. One day he would be a general. The fact that he had been shot through the buttocks didn't dampen his enthusiasm. With his bleeding commander's permission, he set off with sixty men and officers, moving undetected through a screen of bushes below the riverbank. Solomon's last order to him was to shoot the first man in the company who tried to turn tail.

As Wool departed, the colonel slumped to the ground, among a pile of dead and wounded, a borrowed greatcoat concealing the seriousness of his injuries from his wet and shivering force. Shortly after that he was evacuated.

Meanwhile, Wool found the path and gazed up at the heights rising almost vertically more than three hundred feet (90 m) above him. Creased by gullies, blocked by projecting ledges of shale and sandstone, tangled with shrubs, vines, trees, and roots clinging to the clefts, they looked forbidding. But the Americans managed to claw their way to the top.

Wool, with his buttocks still smarting from his embarrassing wound, looked about him. Before him stretched an empty plateau, bordered by maples and basswood. But where were the British? Their shelters were deserted. Then, to his right, below, half-hidden by a screen of yellowing foliage, he saw a flash of scarlet and realized that the gun in the redan was guarded by the merest handful of regulars.

Brock had brought his men down to reinforce the village—an error that would cost him dearly. Wool's men, gazing down at the red-coated figures manning the big gun, could not fail to see the tall officer with the cocked hat in their midst. It was the general himself. A few minutes later, when all his men were assembled, their young commander gave the order to charge.

CHAPTER FIVE

"Revenge the General!"

AT FORT GEORGE, BROCK HAD BEEN AWAKENED IN THE DARK BY THE DISTANT BOOMING OF CANNON. WHAT WAS HAPPENING? WAS IT A FEINT NEAR QUEENSTON OR A MAJOR ATTACK? HE WAS INCLINED TO BELIEVE THE FIRST, FOR HE HAD ANTICIPATED VAN RENSSELAER'S ORIGINAL STRATEGY TO LAUNCH A TWO-PRONGED ATTACK AND DIDN'T KNOW ABOUT SMYTH'S OBSTINACY.

He was up in a moment, dressed, and on his grey horse, Alfred, dashing out the main gate, waiting for no one, not even for his two aides, who were hurriedly pulling on their boots. On this dark morning, with the wind gusting sleet into his face and the southern sky lit by flashes of cannon, he did not intend to stop for anybody.

As he hurried through the mud toward Queenston, he met young Samuel Jarvis, a subaltern in his favourite militia unit, the York Volunteers. Jarvis, cousin of George, was galloping so fast in the opposite direction that he could not stop in time. But he finally reigned in his horse, wheeled about, and told the general the enemy had landed in force at the main Queenston dock. Jarvis's mission shouldn't have been necessary because of Brock's system of signal fires, but in the heat of battle nobody had remembered to light them.

On Brock galloped in the pre-dawn murk, past harvested grain fields, soft meadows, and luxuriant orchards, the trees still heavy with fruit. The York Volunteers, stationed at Brown's Point, were already moving toward Queenston. Brock dashed by, waving them on. A few minutes later his two aides also galloped by.

Dawn was breaking, a few red streaks tinting the sullen storm clouds, a fog rising from the hissing river as Brock, spattered with mud from boots to collar, galloped through Queenston to the cheers of the men of his old regiment, the 49th, including young George Jarvis. The village consisted of about twenty scattered houses separated by orchards, small gardens, stone walls, and snake fences. Above hung the brooding escarpment, the shore of a prehistoric glacial lake. Brock did not slacken his pace but spurred Alfred up the incline to the redan, where eight gunners were sweating over their eighteen-pounder (8-kg).

From this vantage point the general had an overview of the engagement. Below him stretched the panorama of Niagara—one of the world's natural wonders, now half-obscured by the black smoke of musket and cannon. Directly below him he could see Captain Dennis's small force pinning down the Americans crouching under the riverbank at the landing dock. Enemy shells were pouring into the village from John Lovett's battery on the Lewiston heights, but Dennis was holding. A company of light infantry occupied the crest directly above the redan.

Unable to see Wool's men scaling the cliffs, Brock ordered the infantry down into the village to reinforce Dennis. Across the swirling river, at the rear of the village of Lewiston, he glimpsed battalion upon battalion of American troops in reserve. On the American shore several regiments were preparing to embark. At last Brock realized that this was no feint.

He instantly sent messages to Fort George and to Chippawa asking for reinforcements. Some of the shells from the eighteen-pounder (8-kg) in the redan were exploding short of their targets and he told one of the gunners to use a longer fuse. And then as he did so, the general heard a ragged cheer from the unguarded crest above, and looking up, saw Wool's men charging down upon him, bayonets glittering in the wan light of dawn.

He and the gunners had time for one swift action: they hammered a ramrod into the touch-hole of the eighteen-pounder (8-kg) and broke it off, thus effectively spiking it. Then, leading Alfred by the neck reins—for he had no time to remount—the commander-in-chief and the administrator of Upper Canada scuttled ingloriously down the hillside with his men.

In an instant the odds had changed. Until Wool's surprise attack, the British were in charge of the battle. Dennis had taken 150 prisoners. The gun in the redan was playing havoc with the enemy. Brock's forces controlled the heights. But now Dennis was retreating to the village and Wool's band was being reinforced by a steady stream of Americans.

Brock took shelter at the far end of the town in the garden of the

Hamilton house. It would have been prudent, no doubt, to wait for rein-forcements—but Brock was not prudent. As he saw it, hesitation would lose the battle. Once the Americans consolidated their position in the village and on the heights, they would be impossible to dislodge.

It was that that spurred him on to renewed action—the conviction that he must counterattack while the enemy was still off balance. Brock believed that whoever controlled the heights controlled Upper Canada. They could dominate the river and turn it into an American waterway. Possession of the high ground and the village would slice the thin British forces in two, give the Americans warm winter quarters, and allow them to build up their invading army for the spring campaign. In short, if Queenston Heights was lost, then the province was lost.

> *Brock managed to rally some two hundred men from the 49th and the militia. "Follow me, boys," he cried as he wheeled his horse back toward the foot of the ridge. He reached a stone wall and took cover behind it.*

Brock managed to rally some two hundred men from the 49th and the militia. "Follow me, boys," he cried as he wheeled his horse back toward the foot of the ridge. He reached a stone wall and took cover behind it. Young George Jarvis, standing a few metres away, watched him dismount.

"Take a breath, boys," he said. "You will need it in a few moments." Jarvis and the others cheered.

He had stripped the village of its defenders, including Captain Dennis, bleeding from several wounds, but still on his feet. He sent some men under Captain John Williams to attack Wool's left. Then he vaulted the stone fence and leading Albert by the bridle, headed up the slope at a fast pace, intent on taking the gun in the redan.

Jarvis and the others, struggling to keep up, slid and stumbled on the slippery footing of wet leaves. Above them, through the trees, Wool's men could be seen reinforcing the gun emplacement. A confused skirmish fol-lowed.

The battle see-sawed. The Americans were driven almost to the lip of the precipice and somebody started to wave a white handkerchief. At that, Wool tore it away and ordered a charge. The British were beaten back.

The sun, emerging from the clouds, glistened on the crimson maples, on the Persian carpet of yellow leaves, on the epaulettes of the tall general, sword in hand, rallying his men for a final charge. It made a gallant spectacle: the Saviour of Upper Canada, brilliant in his scarlet coat, buttons gleaming, plumed hat, marking him unmistakably as a leader, a gap opening up between him and his gasping followers.

Did he realize he was a target? No doubt he did. He had already been shot in the hand. But that was a matter of indifference. Leaders in Brock's army were supposed to lead. The spectacle of England's greatest hero, Horatio Nelson, standing boldly on deck in full dress uniform, was still green in British memory. Both officers by their actions were marked for spectacular death; in fact they seemed to court it. Brock's nemesis stepped out from behind a clump of bushes and when the general was thirty paces from him, drew a bead with his long border rifle, and buried a bullet in his chest, the hole equidistant from the two rows of gilt buttons on the crimson tunic.

Fifteen-year-old George Jarvis, only a few feet behind, ran up. "Are you much hurt, sir?" he asked. There was no reply. Brock placed his hand on his breast and slowly sank down lifeless. A grisly spectacle followed as a cannonball sliced another soldier in two and the severed corpse fell upon the stricken commander.

The gallant charge had been futile. Brock's men retreated down the hill carrying their general's body, finding shelter at last under the stone wall of the Hamilton garden at the far end of the village. Here they were joined by two companies of York Volunteers—the same men whom Brock had passed on his gallop to Queenston.

Arriving on a dead run, these soldiers caught their breath as American cannon fire poured down upon them from the artillery post on the opposite heights. A cannonball sliced off one man's leg, and skipped on, crippling another in the calf. Then, led by Lieutenant-Colonel John Macdonell, the dead general's young aide, the enlarged force made one more attempt to recapture the heights.

Impulsively, Macdonell decided to follow his late commander's example. Possessed of a brilliant legal mind, he had little experience in soldiering. He called for a second frontal attack on the redan and seventy volunteers followed him up the heights to join the remainder of the 49th under Captain John Williams taking cover in the woods. Together the two officers formed up their men and prepared to attack.

"Charge them home and they cannot stand you!" cried Williams.

The men of the 49th, shouting, "Revenge the general!" swept forward. Wool, reinforced by several more men, was waiting for them.

As Macdonell on horseback waved his men on, his steed was struck by a musket ball, reared and wheeled about. Another ball struck Macdonell in the back, and he tumbled to the ground fatally wounded. Williams, on the right flank, also fell, half-scalped by a bullet. As Captain Cameron rushed forward to assist his fallen colonel, a ball struck him in the elbow and he, too, dropped.

In terrible pain, Macdonell crawled toward his closest friend, Lieutenant Archibald McLean of the York Volunteers, crying, "Help me!" McLean attempted to lead him away and was hit by a ball in the thigh. Dismayed by these losses, the men fell back, bringing their wounded with them. Dennis was bleeding from five wounds. Williams, horribly mangled, survived. But Macdonell was doomed.

Everything that Brock feared had happened. The Americans now occupied both the village and the heights and were sending over reinforcements, now that they had unopposed possession of the river. The British had retreated again to the outskirts of the village. All of the big guns, except for the one downstream at Vrooman's Point, had been silenced. At ten o'clock on this dark October morning, Upper Canada lay in peril.

At that point all the American forces should have been across the river, but so many boats had been destroyed or abandoned that General Van Rensselaer was finding it difficult to reinforce his bridgehead. Actually he had no more than a thousand men on the Canadian side and of these, two hundred were useless. Stunned by their first experience of warfare, the untrained militiamen cowered beneath the bank. No power, it seemed, no exhortation to glory or country, no threat of punishment could move them.

The general crossed at noon with his captain of engineers, whose job it was to help the troops on the heights. Unfortunately all the entrenching tools had been left at Lewiston. They never did arrive. So the general sent Lieutenant-Colonel Winfield Scott, a regular officer, to the top of the ridge to take over from the wounded Wool. Then he prepared to return to the American shore. As he did so, a rabble of American militiamen leaped into the boat with him.

Scott worked furiously with the engineers to prepare a defence of the high ground. He knew that British reinforcements were on their way from Chippawa and Fort George—an American-born militiaman had deserted with that information. Scott would like to attack the Chippawa force, cutting it off from the main army, but he didn't have enough men for the job and his little force was diminishing. Whole squads of militiamen were slinking away into the woods and the brush of the bluffs.

He realized his danger. Ammunition was running out. He had managed to get a six-pound (3-kg) gun across the river in a larger boat, but there were only a few rounds available for it. In the distance he could see a long column of red-coated regulars marching up the road from Fort George under Brock's successor, Major-General Roger Sheaffe.

He desperately needed to get the eighteen-pound (8-kg) cannon at the redan into action to protect his rear and cover the landing of the reinforcements his general had promised him. But Brock had spiked it so well that Scott's men couldn't drive or drill the ramrod out. Scott scrambled down the hillside to help, but as he did so a terrifying sound pierced the air—it was the screaming war whoop of the Mohawks. They came swooping out of the woods and hurtling across the fields, brandishing their tomahawks, driving in Scott's advance guard and forcing the trembling troops back. Only Scott's presence and voice prevented a general rout. The cries of the Indians carried across the river and sent a chill through the militiamen on the far side.

At about the same time, two British guns opened up in the garden of the Hamilton house, effectively preventing the river crossing. Now Scott realized his chance of getting reinforcements before the final battle were slim. He could see the men he needed—hundreds of them, even thousands—lined up on the far shore like spectators at a prize fight. But for all the good they could do him, they might as well have been back on their farms, where most of them fervently wished they were.

General Van Rensselaer was helpless. He had promised reinforcements and ammunition to the defenders on the heights, but could supply neither. He had sent to Brigadier-General Smyth asking for more men, but Smyth had again refused. He couldn't budge the troops at the embarkation point. They had been milling about for some hours in the drizzle watching the boats return with terribly wounded men and sometimes with deserters, watching other boats founder in the frothing stream. Now, with the screams of the Indians echoing down from the heights, they had no stomach for battle.

Unable to budge them, Van Rensselaer sent a note to the heights: "I have passed through my camp; not a regiment, not a company is willing to join you. Save yourselves by a retreat if you can. Boats will be sent to receive you."

That promise was hollow. For the terrified boatmen refused to recross the river.

CHAPTER SIX

Victory

EARLIER THAT MORNING AT NEWARK, CAPTAIN JAMES CROOKS OF THE 1ST LINCOLN MILITIA, NOTING THE WEATHER WAS BAD, DECIDED TO TURN OVER AND GO BACK TO SLEEP AND LET HIS SUBORDINATE HANDLE THE PARADE. BUT, JUST AS HE STARTED TO DOZE OFF, A KNOCK CAME AT THE WINDOW AND A GUARD REPORTED THE YANKEES HAD CROSSED THE RIVER AT QUEENSTON.

Crooks leaped from his bed, pulled on his uniform, and ordered his men to form up. At the fort's gate he ran into the artillery commander, Captain William Holcroft, who told him he was about to open fire on Fort Niagara across the river but was short of men. Crooks supplied him with several, including Solomon Vrooman, who was sent to man the twenty-four-pounder (11-kg) on a point almost two kilometres away. That big gun was never out of action and did incalculable damage. Indeed it was one of the reasons the American militia was refusing to cross the river.

A deafening artillery battery followed. The Americans heated their cannonballs until they glowed red and fired them into the village and the fort. They burned the courthouse, the jail, and fifteen other buildings before their batteries were reduced by the British cannon.

Meanwhile, Brock's express had arrived from Queenston with orders for 130 militiamen to march immediately to the relief of the heights. Crooks assembled men from five companies, formed them into a reinforcement detachment, and marched them toward the scene of the battle. A kilometre out of Newark he was told of Brock's death. He tried in vain to keep the news from his men, but was surprised to find it had little immediate effect.

At Brown's Point, he passed one of the York Volunteers, who asked him where he was going. "To Queenston," he said. The officer told him he was mad. He said if he went any farther all his people would be taken prisoner.

The general was dead. His force was completely routed. His aide was mortally wounded. Four hundred Yankees were on his flank, moving through the woods to attack Newark. Crooks dismissed all this, replying that he had his orders and would keep going. He told his men to load their muskets and marched on. Shortly after that he encountered a second officer who repeated almost word for word what he had heard a few minutes before. Again, Crooks ignored him.

About a kilometre from town he halted his men at a farmhouse. It was filled with American and British wounded, including the dying Macdonell. The troops were hungry, having missed their breakfast. Crooks sent them foraging in a nearby garden to dig potatoes. Soon every pot and kettle in the house was bubbling on the fire, but before the potatoes could be eaten General Sheaffe arrived with the remainder of the 41st Regiment and ordered them to fall in. Off they marched to battle, still hungry.

Sheaffe was a cautious commander. He had no intention of repeating Brock's frontal assault. He planned instead a wide flanking movement to reach the plateau above the village, where Wool's Americans were preparing for battle. His force would veer off to the right, away from the river, before entering the village, make a half-circle around the heights, and climb under cover of the forest by way of an old road two miles (3.2 km) west of Queenston.

Here Sheaffe expected to be joined by the second detachment that Brock had ordered from Chippawa. In this way he could keep his line of march out of range of the American guns on the heights above Lewiston. At the same time, the Indians who had preceded him would act as a screen to prevent the enemy patrols from intercepting him as he formed up for battle.

Meanwhile, Captain Holcroft of the Royal Artillery had at great risk managed to trundle two light guns through the village, across the ravine, and into the garden of the Hamilton house. He was guided by Alexander Hamilton himself, a local merchant, son of the original owner, who knew every corner of the ground. It was these guns that Winfield Scott heard, effectively blocking the river passage, as John Norton and his Mohawks harassed his forward positions.

The Indians, screening Sheaffe's force, continued to harry the Americans. They poured out of the woods, whooping and firing their muskets. Then they vanished into the trees, preventing Scott from consolidating his position and driving in the advance guard and flank patrols to prevent contact with the advancing British. Bit by bit they were forcing the Americans into a tighter position on the heights.

Their nominal chief was John Brant, the eighteen-year-old son of the late Joseph Brant, the greatest of the Mohawk chieftains. But the real leader was the theatrical Norton, a strapping six-foot (2-m) Scot who thought of himself as an Indian and had ambitions to succeed his late mentor. He was more Indian than most Indians and had convinced many British leaders that he was a Cherokee. He wore his black hair in a long tail held in place by a scarlet handkerchief into which he had stuck an ostrich feather. Now, brandishing a tomahawk, his face painted for battle, he whooped his way through the woods, terrifying the American militia and confusing the regulars.

Directly behind the woods on the brow of the heights, hidden by the scarlet foliage and protected by the Mohawks, Roger Sheaffe formed up his troops. He was in no hurry. He controlled the road to Chippawa and was waiting for Captain Richard Bullock to join him with another 150 men from the south.

Captain Dennis of the 49th had already joined his company, his body caked with blood. Exhausted and wounded as a result of the battle at the river's edge, he refused to leave the field until the day was won. Now he stood with others, waiting for the order to advance, while the American gunners poured down fire from across the river. For the unblooded militia, the next hour was the longest they had known as a rain of eighteen-pound (8-kg) balls and smaller shot dropped about them.

At about four o'clock, just as Bullock came up on the right flank, Sheaffe ordered his men to advance in line. He now had about a thousand men. The enemy had almost the same number. But many of the American militiamen, with the war cries of the Indians echoing in their ears, had fled into the woods or down the cliff and toward the river.

When Scott counted his dwindling band, he was shocked to discover that it numbered fewer than three hundred. In the distance he saw the scarlet line of British regulars, marching in perfect order, Indians in one flank, the militia slightly behind, two three-pound (1.4-kg) grasshopper guns firing. He had just received Van Rensselaer's despairing note that reinforcements were not possible. The Americans called a hurried council and agreed to a planned withdrawal.

Now the battle was joined. James Crooks, advancing with his militia detachment, had been in many hailstorms but none, he thought wryly, where the stones flew as thick as bullets on this October afternoon. Little scenes illuminated the battle and remained with him for the rest of his days: the sight of an Indian tomahawking a York militiaman in the belief that he was one of the enemy; the sight of the Americans' lone six-pounder (3-kg), abandoned; the bizarre spectacle of Captain Robert Runchey's platoon of black troops—escaped slaves—advancing beside the Indians; the sight of a companion, his knuckles disabled by a musket ball at the very moment of pulling the trigger.

Scott's regulars were attempting to cover the American withdrawal. The colonel himself leaped on a fallen tree and literally made a stump speech, calling on his men to die with their muskets in their hands to redeem the shame of Hull's surrender. But the British advance continued with all the precision of a parade-ground manoeuvre, which, of course, it was. The Americans were trapped between the cliff edge on their left and the cannon fire from Holcroft's gun in the village below them on their right.

The Indians whooped forward once more. The British and Canadian militia advanced behind with fixed bayonets. The American line wavered, then broke. The troops rushed toward the cliffs, some tumbling down the hill, clinging to bushes and outcroppings, others, crazed with fear, leaping to their deaths on the rocks below. Scores crowded the beaches under the shoulder of the mountain, waiting for boats that would never come. Others, badly mangled, drowned in the roaring river.

Winfield Scott, Wadsworth, and their fellow officers realized now that only a quick surrender would save their force from being butchered by the Indians. But the problem was how to get a truce party across to the British lines. Two couriers, each carrying a white flag, had tried. The Indians had killed them both. So Scott decided to go by himself.

There were no white handkerchiefs left. But the engineering officer had a white cravat, which Scott tied to his sword point. He would rely on his height and his splendid uniform to suggest authority. But these attributes were of little value because he was immediately attacked and seized by young Brant and another Indian who sprang from a covert and struggled with him. Scott's life was saved by the timely appearance of John Beverley Robinson and his friend, Samuel Jarvis of the York Volunteers, who freed him and escorted him to Sheaffe.

There the British general accepted Scott's surrender and called his bugle to sound the ceasefire. The Mohawks paid no attention. Enraged at the death of two of their chiefs, they were intent on exterminating all the Americans huddled under the cliff. Scott hotly demanded to be returned to share their fate, but Sheaffe persuaded him to have patience. He was himself appalled at the slaughter. After the battle was over, some of his men would remember their general flinging off his hat, plunging his sword into the ground in a fury, and demanding that his men halt the bloodshed or he, Sheaffe, would immediately give up his command and go home. A few minutes later the firing ceased, and the battle was over. It was half past four. The struggle had raged for more than twelve hours.

The American line wavered, then broke. The troops rushed toward the cliffs, some tumbling down the hill, clinging to bushes and outcroppings, others, crazed with fear, leaping to their deaths on the rocks below.

Now, to Winfield Scott's humiliation and despair, some five hundred militiamen appeared from hiding places in the crevices along the cliffs and raised their hands in surrender. The British had taken 925 prisoners, including a brigadier-general, five lieutenant-colonels, and sixty-seven other officers. They let one man go free—the little sexagenarian, Samuel Stubbs of Boonsboro, Kentucky. Stubbs had expected to be killed and scalped. Now he discovered that the British looked on him as an oddity—as if he had been born with two heads. A British officer took one look at him and let him go. "Old daddy," he said, "your age and odd appearance induce me to set you at liberty, return to your home and think no more of invading us!"

Stubbs promised cheerfully to give up fighting but he didn't mean it. "I was determined I wouldn't give up the chase so, but at 'um again." And so he was, all the way from the attack on Fort York to the bloody battle of New

Orleans where, in his sixty-sixth year, he was responsible for the deaths of several British officers.

The Americans suffered some 250 casualties, including the mangled Solomon Van Rensselaer, who would eventually recover, and John Lovett, who was incapacitated for life. What began as a lark for him ended as tragedy. For Lovett, the conversationalist and wit, the world went silent. Placed in charge of the big guns on the heights above Lewiston, he was rendered permanently deaf.

By contrast the British casualties were light. They had lost only fourteen killed and seventy-seven wounded. But there was one loss that could not be measured and by its nature evened the score at the Battle of Queenston Heights. Isaac Brock was gone, and there was no one to fill his shoes.

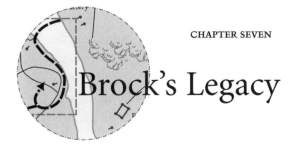

Brock's Legacy

ALL OF CANADA WAS STUNNED BY BROCK'S LOSS. HIS OWN SOLDIERS OF THE 49TH WHO WERE WITH HIM IN HOLLAND AND AT COPENHAGEN WERE PROSTRATED BY THE NEWS. OF ALL THE SCENES OF SORROW AND DESPAIR THAT DAY, THE MOST EMOTIONAL IS THE ONE REPORTED BY LIEUTENANT-COLONEL DRISCOLL OF THE 100TH REGIMENT WHO HAD COME UP FROM FORT ERIE TO HELP DIRECT ARTILLERY FIRE AGAINST THE AMERICAN BATTERY AT BLACK ROCK.

At two that afternoon Driscoll looked up to see a provincial dragoon gallop up, dishevelled, without a sword or helmet, his horse bathed in foam, his own body spattered with mud.

One of Brock's veterans, a man named Clibborn, spoke up: "Horse and man jaded, sir; depend upon it, he brings bad news."

Driscoll sent the veteran across to discover what message the dragoon had brought. The soldier doubled over to the rider but returned at a funereal pace, and Driscoll realized something dreadful had occurred. He called out, "What news, Clibborn? What news, man? Speak out."

Clibborn walked slowly toward the battery, which was still maintaining a brisk fire at the Americans across the river. Musket balls ploughed into the ground around him. He didn't seem to see them. He couldn't speak, could only shake his head. At last, he slumped down on the gun platform, his features dead white, his face a mask of sorrow.

Driscoll couldn't stand the silence and shook Clibborn by the shoulder. "For heaven's sake, tell us what you know!"

Clibborn answered at last, almost choking, "The general is killed; the enemy has possession of Queenston Heights."

With those words, every man in the battery became paralyzed. Guns ceased firing. These men of the 49th, all of whom had served under Brock in Europe, were shattered by the news. Some wept openly, others mourned in silence, several began to curse in frustration. The sound of enemy cheers, drifting across the river, roused them to their duty. In a helpless rage over the death of their general, they became demonic, loading, traversing, firing the heavy guns as if they were light field pieces, flinging round after round across the river in an attempt to avenge their former chief.

All over the province, similar expressions of grief were manifest. Major Glegg, Brock's military aide, called it "a public calamity." Young George Ridout of the York Volunteers wrote his brother: "Were it not for the death of General Brock and Macdonell our victory would have been glorious … but in losing our man … is an irreparable loss." Like many others, young Ridout was convinced that Brock was the only man capable of leading the divided province. Samuel Jarvis crossed the lake to bring the news of the tragedy where "the thrill of dismay … was something indescribable."

Sir George Prevost, when he learned of his general's death, was so badly shaken he could scarcely hold a pen with which to report the tragedy to his superiors.

Meanwhile, Sheaffe concluded an immediate armistice with the Americans, "the most ruinous policy that ever was or could have been adopted for the country," to quote a nineteen-year-old subaltern, William Hamilton Merritt, the future builder of the Welland Canal. Certainly had Brock lived, he would have pursued Van Rensselaer's badly shaken force across the river to attack Fort Niagara and seize the northern half of New York State. But Sheaffe was a more cautious commander.

Brock's body, brought back to Newark, lay in state for three days. His funeral, in George Ridout's words, was "the grandest and most solemn that I have ever witnessed or that has been seen in Upper Canada." Guns boomed every moment during the funeral procession while across the river at both Niagara and Lewiston the Americans fired a salute to their old enemy.

Upper Canada was numb, its people drawn closer by a common tragedy that few outsiders could comprehend. In the United States, attention was quickly diverted by another naval skirmish in which the American frigate *Wasp*, having disabled the captured British sloop of war *Frolic*, was herself taken by the enemy.

Europe was far more interested in the fate of Moscow under attack by Napoleon, who at that very moment was preparing to withdraw his army from the charred and deserted Russian capital. That bitter decision, still unknown to most of the world, marked the beginning of the end of the war with France. Had President Madison foreseen it, the invasion of Canada by the Americans, still scarcely underway, would never have been attempted.

The picture of Brock, storming the heights at Queenston, urging on the brave York Volunteers and saving Canada in the process, is one that would become part of an imperishable legend for the fledgling nation. He was the first Canadian war hero, an Englishman who hated the provincial confines of the Canadas, who looked with disdain on the civilian leaders, who despised democracy, the militia, and the Indians, and who could hardly wait to shake the Canadian mud from his boots. None of that mattered. His monument stands today, dominating the ridge, not far from where he fell.

Here is where the myth of Isaac Brock began. By Confederation it had grown to the point that the battlefield had become, in the phrase of the *Canadian Monthly*, "one of Canada's sacred places." Yet, with Brock dead, Upper Canada—and Lower Canada, too—would need more saviours. The war was not over—nor would it be for another two years.

Brock's splendid pillar has become a mecca for tourists, reinforcing the myth of Brock that began to grow within moments of his death. He is remembered less for his real contribution to the country: his military foresight, his careful preparation for war during the years of peace, his astonishing bloodless capture of Fort Detroit, an American stronghold. Today when Canadians hear his name, the picture that still forms in their minds is of that final impetuous dash, splendidly heroic but tragically foolish, up the slippery heights of Queenston on a gloomy October morning.

INDEX

"A Seneca Chief" by F. W. Greenough, 1836.
Aboriginal peoples played a major role in the battles of the
War of 1812. With bitterness against American policy and the
Battle of Tippecanoe, there was a confluence of Native forces
that worked with the Canadians and the British.

REVENGE OF THE TRIBES

CONTENTS

CHAPTER ONE

The Shawnee Brothers

THIS IS A STORY OF REVENGE AND RETALIATION. IT IS THE STORY OF HOW A FORCE OF WHITE MEN LED BY A FUTURE PRESIDENT OF THE UNITED STATES SAVAGELY ATTACKED AND DESTROYED AN INDIAN VILLAGE. IT IS THE STORY OF HOW, IN THE WAR THAT FOLLOWED, THE INDIANS CLAIMED A TERRIBLE PRICE FROM THE AMERICAN SOLDIERS SENT TO HUNT THEM DOWN.

Although they received precious little credit for it, the Indians played a key role in defeating the American armies who tried to invade Canada in 1812 and 1813. Indeed, it's possible that without the Indians' help, the British and Canadians who took credit for winning the war might have lost it. For that, the country owed a great deal to the remarkable Shawnee war chief, Tecumseh, whose hatred of the Americans caused him to side with the British.

Tecumseh's relentless enemy was William Henry Harrison, the ambitious governor of the Indiana territory south of Lake Michigan. Harrison wanted to swallow three million acres (1.2 million ha) of Native hunting grounds that had never been given up by the Indians. For that he had the official agreement of the president himself, James Madison.

In 1809 Harrison got it—or thought he did—for a pittance. At a mere two dollars an acre, it cost him only about fifty thousand dollars; it was worth six million. In short it was a barefaced steal. Harrison had the agreement of the major tribes—Miami, Delaware, Eel, and Potawatomi—but he forgot the Shawnee. They were thought of as intruders, having been driven north from their original hunting grounds in Kentucky. Ignoring them was Harrison's mistake.

Into Harrison's capital of Vincennes in August of 1810 rode Tecumseh with a delegation of warriors to bargain with the governor. The meeting was to be held at his estate in the shade of a canopy not far from Harrison's great brick mansion. Here were assembled the town's leading citizens, guarded by a platoon of soldiers, all craning their necks to see the Shawnee chief who had the impertinence to keep their governor waiting for several days. Now, at last he arrived, accompanied by thirty warriors, their faces smeared with vermilion paint, and all armed with tomahawks and clubs.

The Americans saw a handsome figure, tall for his tribe—at least five foot ten (1.75 m)—with an oval rather than an angular face, his complexion light copper, his nose handsome and straight. Everyone who met him noticed his eyes, which were clear, bright hazel under dark brows, and his teeth, which were white and even.

He was naked to the waist, his head shaved save for a scalp lock. He walked with a brisk, elastic step in spite of a bent leg fractured and poorly set after a youthful fall from a pony. There were some who thought him the finest specimen of a man they had ever seen, but no authentic likeness exists on paper or canvas because he refused to have his portrait painted by a white man.

He would not join the white delegation seated under the canopy. He intended to speak as in a council circle, which puts every man on the same level. "Houses," he said, "are made for white men to hold councils in. Indians hold theirs in the open air."

"Your father requests you sit by his side," said Harrison's interpreter.

Tecumseh raised an arm and pointed to the sky.

"My father! The Great Spirit is my father! The earth is my mother—and on her bosom I will recline."

Such was the man that the frustrated Harrison was forced to deal with in his attempt to seize the Indian hunting grounds. When the Shawnee chief spoke, the governor had to listen—for this half-naked man in the deerskin leggings was one of the greatest orators of his time. His reputation had preceded him. He was known as a supreme performer who could rouse his audience to tears, laughter, fury, and action. Even those who couldn't understand his words were said to be held by the power of his voice.

As the council proceeded, Tecumseh made it quite clear that he intended to prevent the land sold by the other tribes from falling into the hands of the whites. Harrison had no choice but to stop the surveys. He knew now that he would never get his land at two dollars per acre until the power of Tecumseh and his mysterious brother, known as the Prophet, was broken forever.

The two didn't look like brothers. Tecumseh was almost too handsome to be true. His younger brother, however, was ugly, awkward, and one-eyed. The Prophet was elusive and unpredictable. Tecumseh was a clear-eyed military genius. Yet the two were a team, their personalities and philosophies interlocking like pieces of a jigsaw puzzle.

Tecumseh dreamed the ancient dream of an Indian confederacy stretching from Florida to Lake Erie — an alliance strong enough to resist white pressure.

Unlike the Prophet, Tecumseh was a warrior—but a warrior of a different breed. The ritual tortures that were part of the culture of many tribes sickened him. He did not believe that it made a man braver to eat the heart of a bold but defeated enemy. He would not allow his followers to kill or rape women and children—a practice that had until recently been normal in many European armies.

Tecumseh dreamed the ancient dream of an Indian confederacy stretching from Florida to Lake Erie—an alliance strong enough to resist white pressure. To achieve that end, he was prepared to travel astonishing distances preaching to the various tribes. Already the nucleus of a new alliance was forming at the junction of the Tippecanoe River and the Wabash. More than a thousand members of half a dozen tribes had flocked there in answer to the call of Tecumseh's brother. The settlement was known as Prophet's Town.

Harrison felt the time was ripe for a preventive war. He wanted to smash the power of the Shawnee brothers, put his surveyors back on the Indian hunting grounds, and head off an Indian alliance with the British to the north.

He chose to launch the military campaign in August of 1811. Tecumseh was in the south rallying the tribes. Harrison meant to attack and destroy Prophet's Town before the Shawnee war chief returned.

Tecumseh had already warned his brother that he must not, on any account, be prodded into battle. But Harrison meant to prod him. He marched to the edge of the disputed territories, built a fort (which was named "Fort Harrison"), and then invaded the Indian territory at the head of a thousand men.

On November 6, about a dozen miles (20 km) from his objective, he drew up his forces in battle order. A delegation of Indians arrived on a peace mission. Harrison assured them that all he sought was a proper camping ground. They agreed to meet and talk the following day; but there was no meeting.

We don't know what the Indians were thinking because the only accounts of the battle come from white men. But some things are fairly certain. The Indians didn't trust Harrison; they expected him to attack and were determined to attack first. In that they were correct. But the battle, when it came, was started by accident. A nervous sentry fired his weapon at an unseen enemy, and chaos followed.

Harrison was pulling on his boots at four the following morning when he heard yells and gunfire. The struggle that followed was bitter. Harrison escaped being killed only because his grey horse went missing and he was forced to mount a different one. The Indians failed to recognize it and instead shot one of his colonels, mounted on a similar horse.

But they could not overcome a superior force, including 250 well-trained soldiers from the 4th U.S. infantry. Harrison rode from point to point trying to control the battle. The Indians were acting in a most un-Indian fashion, responding with considerable discipline to signals made by the rattling of deer horns. They would fire a volley, then retreat out of range, reload, and advance again.

By daybreak the entire line of soldiers was engaged. As the Indians began to falter at last, Harrison determined on a charge from the flanks. That was the climax of the battle. The level of the sound became unbearable—an ear-splitting mixture of savage yells, shrieks of despair, the roar of musketry, agonizing screams, victorious shouts, and dying cries mingling in a continuous terrifying uproar that would ring in the ears of survivors long after the last wound was healed.

Harrison's charge succeeded. Out of ammunition and arrows, the Indians retired across the marshy prairie where horses could not follow. The Americans uttered prayers of thanks, bound up their wounds, scalped all the dead Indians, and killed one who was wounded—for white soldiers could be just as savage as the so-called "savages."

Two days later they swept through Prophet's Town—empty save for one aged Indian woman—on a mission of revenge and plunder. They destroyed everything, including all the beans and corn that they themselves could not eat—some three thousand bushels (110,000 l) stored for the winter. They found British weapons in some of the houses, which confirmed their suspicion that British agents had been encouraging the Indians to attack. Then they burned all the houses and sheds and left. Thus ended the Battle of Tippecanoe, which has sometimes been called the first battle in the War of 1812.

More than any other incident, it was this vicious attack on a peaceful Indian community that helped create the horror that followed. For the Indians the land was sacred; in their view, nobody owned it—the hunting grounds were open to all. But now they were being swindled of their birthright, and that swindle was achieved by bloodshed and brutality. In the events that followed, one might well ask: who were the real savages—the Indians fighting for their heritage, or Harrison and his soldiers intent on taking it by force?

The battle was celebrated as a great victory for Harrison, who eventually used Tippecanoe as a rallying cry in his successful attempt to win the U.S. presidency in 1840. But he lost almost one-fifth of his force and he failed to break up Tecumseh's confederacy or diminish the Prophet's power.

The raids on the white settlements continued. Settlers and soldiers were ambushed. Whole families were scalped and mutilated by tribesmen driven into a rage by Harrison's attack. Farmers were forced to abandon their fields and cabins. Some fled the territory.

Tecumseh returned at last to Prophet's Town and later he spoke of his experience: "I stood upon the ashes of my own home, where my own wigwam had sent up its fire to the Great Spirit, and there I summoned the spirits of the braves who had fallen in their vain attempts to protect their homes from the grasping invader, and as I snuffed up the smell of their blood from the ground I swore once more eternal hatred—the hatred of an avenger."

Harrison's boast that he had shattered the alliance was hollow. By May of 1812, Tecumseh had six hundred men under his command making bows and arrows. In Washington, war fever rose, fuelled by tales of frontier violence and the legend of Tippecanoe. Tecumseh waited and held his men back for the right moment. For a while he would pretend to be neutral, but when the moment came he was determined to lead the forces of his confederacy across the border to fight beside the British against the common enemy.

CHAPTER TWO

Scorching the Earth

ON JUNE 18, 1812, WHEN THE AMERICANS DECLARED WAR AGAINST GREAT BRITAIN, GOVERNOR HARRISON'S FOLLY IN MAKING AN ENEMY OF TECUMSEH BECAME APPARENT. ON BOTH SIDES OF THE BORDER, THE VARIOUS TRIBES FLOCKED TO SUPPORT THE BRITISH AND THE CANADIANS.

It was Tecumseh at the head of his own braves who helped the British win the first battle, seizing Fort Detroit and most of Michigan Territory.

Later, at a battle at Queenston Heights, the British were again victorious, again helped by the Indians, this time the Mohawks under William Norton.

With Detroit in ruins, with hundreds of Americans now held prisoner, and the British controlling both sides of the northern border, the United States made plans for another expedition. Governor Harrison was called into service to lead an army of Kentuckians to regain Detroit for the United States.

Every able-bodied man in Kentucky seemed to want to fight. By the end of the year, more than eleven thousand Kentuckians were in the army. In many ways they were like their traditional enemies, the Indians. They were hardy, adventurous men—romantic, touchy, proud, bold, courageous, and often very cruel. The state of Kentucky itself lay on the old Indian frontier. Memories remained of bloody Indian wars. Youths were raised on tales of British and Indian raiders killing, scalping, and ravaging during the Revolution (though killing and scalping weren't confined to one side). The Battle of Tippecanoe had revived the fear and hatred. The reports of British weapons found at Prophet's Town confirmed to the people of the state that John Bull—as they called the British—was again behind the Indian troubles.

Harrison, newly appointed commander-in-chief of the Army of the Northwest, received the dreadful news of the fall of Detroit on August 26, two days before he reached Cincinnati. He had twenty-one hundred men under his command and an equal number on their way to join his force.

He faced a monumental task. He was short of almost everything—food, clothing, equipment, weapons, ammunition, flint, and swords. The only gun was an ancient cast-iron four-pounder (1.8-kg). Autumn was fast approaching with its chilling rain and sleet. He would have to hack new roads through forest and swamp, and build blockhouses and magazines. And all the time he would be watched and harassed by the Indians.

He was determined to crush all Indian resistance without mercy. Columns of cavalry fanned out to destroy every Indian village within sixty miles (100 km). Some of these excursions cost the Americans dearly. One officer, Colonel John Scott, insisted on leading an attack on Elkheart River in Indiana Territory even though his fellow officers urged him not to go. Scott mounted his horse, crying out, "As long as I am able to mount you, none but myself shall lead my regiment …" That was the death of him. Exhausted after a march of three days and nights, he was barely able to return to camp, and shortly after he died.

Harrison's policy was to search and destroy. He saw no difference between neutral and hostile tribes. His intention was to turn the frontier country into a no man's land, denying both shelter and food to the Indians. Mounted troops burned several hundred houses, ravaged the cornfields, destroyed crops of beans, pumpkins, potatoes, and melons, ransacked the graves and scattered the bones. The Potawatomi and Miami fled to the British for protection and waited for revenge.

Harrison planned to move his army to the foot of the rapids of the Maumee in three columns. One force on his left would march from the recently built Fort Winchester along the route of the Maumee River. The central force of twelve hundred would follow the road to the same rendezvous. A division on their right would proceed to Wooster, Ohio, by way of the Upper Sandusky River.

But one force was soon pinned down on the Maumee because the promised supplies were not forthcoming. A second mounted brigade was ordered to dash to the foot of the rapids of the Maumee to harvest several

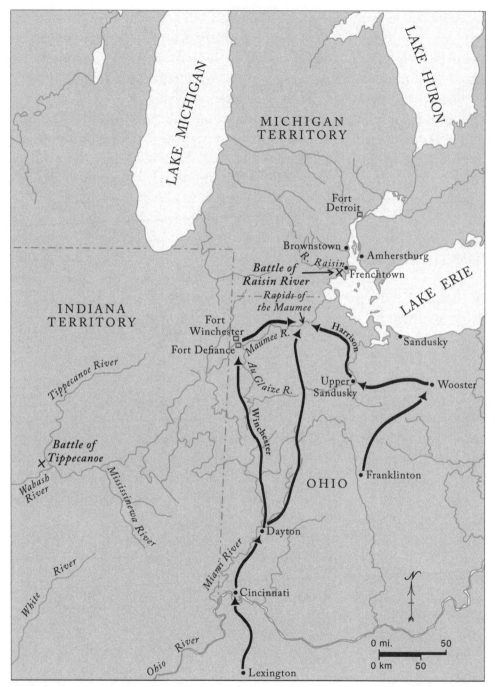

Harrison's three-column drive

hundred hectares of corn for the famished troops. But the scalping of a ranger less than two hundred yards (180 m) from the camp caused such a panic that the mission had to be abandoned. Rations remained scarce, in spite of Harrison's promises. There was little flour, almost no salt, and the beef—what there was of it—was deplorable.

Ignoring strict orders, the men wandered out of camp, wasting their ammunition in search of game. Many were barefoot, their clothes in rags. They slept on frozen ground, some without blankets. More than two hundred were sick at one time. By November they began to die from typhus.

And Detroit, as well as most of Michigan Territory, was still in British hands.

Harrison's fellow governor, Isaac Shelby of Kentucky, was determined to retake Detroit before winter, and therefore ordered more attacks on the Indians. Two thousand mounted volunteers, enlisted for only thirty days, were ordered to march against the tribes in both Indiana and Illinois Territories. Shelby believed he could succeed if the weather remained dry. But if it rained, he would be stuck at the rapids of the Maumee until the lake was sufficiently frozen to bear the weight of the army and its baggage.

Then came appalling news from the Niagara frontier. A second American army had tried to invade Canada at Queenston and had been hurled back from the heights by a combined force of British regulars, Canadian volunteers, and Mohawk Indians. Coming on the heels of the disaster at Detroit, this was a major blow to American morale.

By October 22, Harrison found he could not set a firm date for the recapture of Detroit. He would need a million rations at the rapids of the Maumee before he could mount an attack. But the driving rain that everyone feared now came. The roads were in desperate condition. The horses, attempting to struggle through the swamps, were dying by the hundreds. He couldn't move his supplies or his guns.

With his left flank wide open to Indian attack, Harrison decided to prevent further Indian raids by striking at the Miami villages along the Mississinewa, a tributary of the Wabash. On November 25 Lieutenant-Colonel John Campbell and six hundred cavalry and infantry set out to do the job. The results were disastrous.

In spite of Campbell's attempts at secrecy, the Miami knew of the plan ahead of time. They left their villages, waited until the troops were exhausted, and then launched a night attack, destroying a hundred horses, killing eight men, and wounding forty-eight.

A false rumour spread, that the dreaded Tecumseh was on his way at the head of a large force. Campbell's dejected band beat a hasty retreat. His men were now in a bad way. The weather turned bitterly cold. Their food was almost gone. The wounded were dying from gangrene. The remainder suffered from frostbite. A relief party finally got them into Greenville, where it was found that three hundred men—half of Campbell's force—were disabled. Harrison had lost the core of his cavalry while the Indians had escaped untouched.

Meanwhile, his left column, under General James Winchester, was still pinned down near the junction of the Maumee and the Au Glaize River waiting for supplies. It was impossible to get them through the Black Swamp that lay between the Sandusky and the Maumee. The troops were out of flour, existing on bad beef, pork, and hickory nuts. Sickness and death had reduced the force to eleven hundred. Winchester's forces numbered eighteen hundred at the beginning of October. Daily funerals cast a pall over the camps. The growing realization that there was no chance of invading Canada that year contributed to the loss of morale.

On Christmas Day, Winchester got orders to move to the rapids as soon as he received two days' rations. There he would be joined by the right wing of the army. Two days later the supplies arrived, and on December 29 the troops set off for the rapids. Few armies have presented such a ragtag appearance. In spite of the midwinter weather, scarcely one man possessed a greatcoat or cloak. Only a lucky few had woollen garments. The remainder were dressed in the clothes they wore when they left Kentucky, their cotton shirts torn, patched, and ragged, hanging to their knees, their trousers also cotton. Their matted hair fell uncombed over their cheeks. Their slouch hats had long since been worn bare. Those who owned blankets wrapped them about their bodies as protection from the blizzards, holding them in place by broad belts of leather into which were jammed axes and knives. The officers were scarcely distinguishable from the men. They carried swords or rifles instead of long guns, and daggers in place of knives.

Now these men were forced to become beasts of burden because the horses were not fit to pull the weight. Harnessed five to a sleigh, they hauled their equipment through snow and water for eleven days. The sleighs were badly made—too light to carry the loads, not large enough to cross the half-frozen streams. Provisions and men were soon soaked through. The days were bad but the nights were a horror. Knee-deep snow had to be cleared away before a camp could be made. Fire had to be struck from flint on steel. The wet wood often refused to burn. It was so cold they couldn't prepare beds for themselves. The Kentuckians simply toppled down on piles of brush before the smoky fires and slept in their steaming garments.

Then, on the third day, a frantic message from Harrison arrived: *turn back!* The general had picked up another rumour that the formidable Tecumseh and several hundred Indians were in the area. With the Indians at his rear and with no certainty of provisions at the rapids, any further movement toward Canada this winter would be foolhardy.

But Winchester was in no mood to retreat. He was a man who had suddenly been released from three months of dreadful frustration. Now at last he was on the move. It must have seemed to him like some sort of progress. It was action of a kind and at the end, who knew? More action, even glory, beckoned. He had no stomach to turn in his tracks and return to "that loathsome place," nor did his men. And so they moved on to tragedy.

CHAPTER THREE

A Hunger for Glory

As Winchester's forces staggered on toward the rapids of the Maumee, ignoring Harrison's warning, Lieutenant-Colonel Henry Procter at Fort Amherstburg, across the river from the captured Detroit, came to the wrong conclusion. He was convinced that the Americans had gone into winter quarters. His Indian spies had observed no movement around the Winchester camp for several weeks. He was convinced that Harrison had decided to hold up any attempt to recapture Detroit till spring. That was just as well, because Procter had only a skeleton force of soldiers and a handful of Indians to fight the Americans.

The Indians concerned him. He couldn't control them. He really didn't like them. Although they fought on the British side, their loyalty wasn't really to the British or to the Americans but to their own kind. They would support the British, but only as long as they believed it suited their own purposes.

From the British point of view the Indians didn't observe the so-called rules of warfare, which were, of course, white European rules. Tecumseh was the only chief who could restrain his followers from killing and torturing prisoners and ravaging women and children. But Tecumseh had headed south to try to draw the Creek and the Choctaws to his confederacy, and his brother, the Prophet, had returned to the Wabash.

Procter needed to keep the Indians active. He had attempted to capture Fort Wayne, but that attempt failed though it slowed Harrison's advance. Now he was under orders from the higher-ups to avoid all offensive warfare. His only task was to defend against the invader.

He had to be careful. The Indians' loyalty depended on a show of British resolution. The only way their confidence and goodwill could be preserved was to attack the Americans and kill as many as possible and let the braves have their way with the rest.

Thus his strategy was to let the Americans keep the tribes in a fury—which was what they were doing. Harrison's attempt to subdue the Indians of the northwestern frontier had delayed his advance until midwinter and caused widespread anger among the various bands. Some six thousand had been left homeless, nineteen villages had been ravaged, seven hundred lodges burned, thousands of kilograms of corn destroyed.

Savagery increased on both sides. The Kentuckians took scalps whenever they could. Nor were women and children safe from the army. In one unprovoked attack on an Indian village near Mansfield, south of Lake Erie, the Ohio militiamen had burned all the houses and shot several of the inhabitants.

The worst attacks the previous fall had been against the Indian villages on the Peoria lakes southwest of Lake Michigan. These were destroyed by a force of American rangers and volunteers under Governor Ninian Edwards of Illinois Territory. One raid would not soon be forgotten. A mounted party under a captain named Judy came upon an Indian couple on the open prairie. When the man tried to surrender, Judy shot him through the body. Chanting his death song, the Indian killed one of Judy's men and was in turn riddled with bullets. A little later the same group captured and killed a starving Indian child.

In their rage, Edwards' followers scalped and mutilated the bodies of the fallen, and ransacked the Indian graves for plunder. Small wonder, then, that the Potawatomi chief, Black Bird, cried out in fury to a Canadian: "The way they treat our killed and remains of those that are in their graves to the west make our people mad when they meet the Big Knives. Whenever they get any of our people into their hands they cut them like meat into small pieces."

All that fall the Indians continued to concern Procter. They devoured his provisions at an alarming rate and Tecumseh's restraining hand was absent. Procter solved part of his supply problem by sending most of the Indians to the rapids of the Maumee, where several hundred hectares of corn were waiting to be harvested—the same corn that Harrison had been trying to seize.

Harrison's scorched earth policy backfired—to the gain of the British. Indian spies infiltrated Ohio and reported that Winchester was again advancing. The British sent couriers to the villages of the Ottawa and the Potawatomi in Michigan Territory and to the Miami in Indiana. Within a month the Native force had increased from three hundred to almost eight hundred braves, all stirred to a fever by Harrison's army.

On January 11, Winchester's army reached the rapids of the Maumee. Two days later Procter got the news and quickly called out the militia and assembled the Indians.

Procter planned to ravage the Detroit frontier in order to deny the Americans provisions and shelter. On January 14, he sent Major Ebenezer Reynolds of the Essex militia with two companies and a band of Potawatomi to the little village of French-town on the River Raisin. Reynolds's orders were to destroy the village and all its supplies and to remove the French-speaking settlers to Canadian soil.

> *Their town, a simple row of some twenty houses, squatted on the north bank three miles (5 km) from the mouth. It was not designed as a fort. Its only protection was a fence of split pickets.*

That would not be a pleasant task. Nobody wanted his home destroyed, his property removed, or his cattle driven off and killed by Indians. The settlers had worked hard to improve their farms, which lay on both sides of the narrow, low-banked river. Their town, a simple row of some twenty houses, squatted on the north bank three miles (5 km) from the mouth. It was not designed as a fort. Its only protection was a fence of split pickets to secure the yards and gardens.

The villagers were in a panic. As Reynolds and his men moved in, a delegation slipped away heading for the rapids of the Maumee to plead with Winchester for help. They carried a note for Harrison informing him that "five hundred true and brave Americans can secure the District of Erie—A timely approach of our armies will secure us from being forced to prison and the whole place from being burned by savage fury."

Winchester knew that if he was to save this settlement he must act at once. On January 17 he and his senior officers sat in council. Should they go to the relief of Frenchtown? For almost four days word had been coming back of Indian outrages and British high-handedness.

Everything was being moved from the village—cattle, sleighs, grain, and foodstuffs. Winchester's information was that the British force was ridiculously small. But it was building rapidly. If the Americans moved quickly, they could acquire food for themselves at Frenchtown by taking three thousand barrels of flour and much grain. That prospect must have seemed as tempting as the relief of the villagers.

Lieutenant-Colonel John Allen rose. He was a graceful, commanding presence, perhaps the most popular man in Winchester's army and certainly the most distinguished and most eloquent. A handsome Kentuckian, tall, sandy-haired, blue-eyed, he was one of the state's great orators—a leading lawyer, a state senator, and once a candidate for governor. When he spoke all would listen because he commanded as much respect as, if not more than, his general.

He was fed up with inactivity—weary of slow movements that got him nowhere. He hungered for action and now he saw his chance. The army could go to the aid of the defenceless inhabitants of Frenchtown, obtain the desperately needed food at the settlement, and strike a decisive blow against the British. That would open the road to Detroit some thirty miles (50 km) to the northwest. At last they could cover themselves with glory.

The council didn't need much convincing, nor did Winchester. Why wait for Harrison, who was sixty-five miles (105 km) away? A victory over the British—*any* victory—could make Winchester a national hero. His men were as eager to move as he. The term of the six-month volunteers would end in February and they had refused to re-enlist. All wanted one brief taste of glory before returning home.

They had just received a welcome shipment of woollen underwear. Their morale, reduced by long weeks of inactivity and hunger, had risen again. And there was *food* at Frenchtown! Winchester, who had already asked for more reinforcements, now sent a second letter to Harrison announcing his intention to send a force to relieve Frenchtown and hold it.

One of Harrison's many frustrations during this exhausting fall and winter had been the collapse of communications. His letter to Winchester urging him to abandon his march to the rapids came too late. Winchester's reply that he would move ahead anyway didn't reach him until the force was actually at its destination. It was carried by an eighteen-year-old Kentucky volunteer named Leslie Combs, who, with a single guide, crossed one hundred miles (160 km) of trackless forest through snow so deep that the two men dared not lie down for fear of suffocating and were forced to sleep standing up. Exhausted, ill, and starving, the two reached Fort McArthur on January 9. Two days later, Harrison, at Upper Sandusky, got Winchester's letter.

Five days went by during which time Harrison had no idea of Winchester's position or plans. Then, on the night of January 16, he learned that Winchester had reached the rapids and wanted reinforcements. Apparently he was contemplating an attack. That news alarmed Harrison. If it was in his power he would call Winchester off!

He set off at once for Lower Sandusky, travelling so swiftly that his aide's horse dropped dead of exhaustion. There he immediately dispatched a troop of artillery, guarded by three hundred infantrymen, to Winchester's aid. The camp at the rapids was only thirty-six miles (60 km) away; but the roads were choked with drifting snow, and the party moved slowly.

When, on January 18, he received confirmation of Winchester's plan to relieve Frenchtown, he was thoroughly alarmed. He ordered two more regiments to march to the rapids, and set off himself in a sleigh. Its slowness annoyed him. He seized his servant's horse and rode on alone. Darkness fell. The horse stumbled into a frozen swamp. The ice gave way. Harrison managed to free himself and pushed on through the night on foot. But he was too late.

CHAPTER FOUR

A Strange Weariness

WHILE HARRISON WAS DESPERATELY TRYING TO REACH WINCHESTER TO PRE-
VENT A DISASTER, WINCHESTER HAD ALREADY ORDERED LIEUTENANT-
COLONEL WILLIAM LEWIS AND 450 TROOPS TO ATTACK THE ENEMY AT
FRENCHTOWN ON THE RIVER RAISIN. OFF WENT LEWIS WITH THREE DAYS' PRO-
VISIONS, FOLLOWED A FEW HOURS LATER BY A SECOND FORCE OF ONE HUNDRED
KENTUCKIANS UNDER THE EAGER LIEUTENANT-COLONEL ALLEN.

The two forces met at Presqu'Isle, a French Canadian village on the
south side of the Maumee, twenty miles (32 km) from the rapids, eighteen
miles (29 km) from the Raisin. The soldiers were overwhelmed by their first
contact with anything remotely resembling civilization. A young soldier,
Elias Darnell, wrote in his journal that "the sight of this village filled each
heart with emotions of cheerfulness and joy, for we had nearly five months
in the wilderness, exposed to every inconvenience, and excluded from
everything that had the appearance of a civilized country."

The inhabitants poured out of their homes waving white flags and
shouting greetings. The troops were in high spirits. They knew that some
would be corpses by the next day, but with the eternal optimism of all soldiers each man clung to the conviction that he would survive. Nonetheless,
those who could write home sent letters to wives, parents, and friends.

Colonel James Price, commander of the Jessamine Blues, wrote to his
wife, Susan, in Kentucky, about their son. "Teach my son the habits of
industry ... industry leads to virtue ... not a day must be lost in teaching
him how to work ... it may be possible I may fall in battle and my only boy
must know that his father, next to God, loves his country, and is now risk-
ing his life in defending that country against a barbarous and cruel enemy
... pray for me that you may be with me once more."

The following morning, January 18, as the Kentucky soldiers marched along the frozen surface of Lake Erie toward their objective, they met refugees from Frenchtown. They wanted to know what kind of artillery the British troops had. "Two pieces large enough to kill a mouse" came the reply.

From Frenchtown came word that the British were waiting. Lewis formed his troops up on the ice. As they came in sight of the settlement the lone British howitzer opened up. "Fire away with your mouse cannon!" some of the men cried. Then, as the long drum roll sounded the charge, they crossed the slippery river, clambered up the bank, leaped over the village pickets, and drove the British back toward the forest.

The battle raged from 3 PM to dark. When dusk fell, the British had been driven two miles (3 km) from the village, and the Americans were in firm control. Now the soldiers at both Frenchtown and the rapids felt they were unbeatable—that they could roll right on to Detroit, cross the river, and capture Amherstburg.

The troops on the Raisin were dangerously exposed. Yet their eagerness for battle was such that Winchester would have found it difficult to withdraw them even if he had wanted to. But Winchester did not want to. Caught up in the ecstasy of victory, seeing himself and his army as saviours of his country's honour, he took what troops he could spare—fewer than three hundred—and marched off to Frenchtown.

There was another force drawing him and his men toward the village—an attraction quite as powerful as the prospect of fame and glory. Frenchtown, at that moment, was close to paradise. Here on the vine-clad banks of *la Rivière au Raisin* was luxury: fresh apples, cider by the barrel, sugar, butter, whisky, and more—houses with roofs, warm beds, hearth sides with crackling fires, and the soft presence of women.

When Winchester arrived late on the twentieth, Lewis's men had already sampled these delights. There was some vague talk of reinforcing their position but that was only talk. The men were weary from fighting, unruly from drink, and in no mood to take orders.

The village was surrounded on three sides by a palisade constructed of eight-foot (2.4-m) logs, split and sharpened at the ends. These pickets, which did not come all the way down to the riverbank, enclosed a compact community of log and shingle houses, interspersed with orchards, gardens, barns, and outbuildings. The whole space formed a rectangle two hundred yards (180 m) along the river and three hundred yards (275 m) deep.

On the right of the village, down the river, lay an open meadow with a number of detached houses. There, Lieutenant-Colonel Samuel Wells encamped his regulars. Winchester didn't like that. He thought that the regulars would be better placed within the palisade, but Wells insisted, pointing out that the regular soldiers should *always* be on the right of the militia. Winchester didn't argue. Wells's men were exposed, but he expected to find a better campground on the following day.

Leaving Wells in charge of the main camp, the general and his staff, including his teenaged son, took up quarters on the south side of the river in the home of Colonel Francis Navarre, a local trader. This was a handsome building, the logs covered with clapboard, the whole shaded by pear trees originally brought from Normandy. Winchester was given a spacious guest room at the front of the house warmed by a fireplace.

It was now Wells's turn to object. He believed the general and his officers should be as close as possible to the troops on the far side of the river in case of sudden attack.

But James Winchester had made up his mind. For twenty years as a wealthy plantation owner he had enjoyed the creature comforts of a relaxed life. For five months without complaint he had slept out, exposed to the weather, enduring hardships with his troops, existing on dreadful food—when there was food at all—drinking sometimes stagnant water scooped out of wagon tracks. Later he would argue that there was no house in Frenchtown—that he would have had to move some of the wounded. But that was clearly false.

The general and his troops were overcome with fatigue. The sudden victory, the almost magical appearance of food, drink, warmth, and shelter—the stuff of their dreams for these past weeks—gave them a dreamlike confidence. There was talk of moving the camp to a better position, and on the following day the general and some of his officers rode out to look over the ground. Nothing came of that. Apparently it didn't occur to them that it might be a good idea to put the river between themselves and the British.

Wells left camp that morning, claiming he had baggage to collect at the rapids. Winchester thought Wells had lost faith in him. He sent a note to Harrison saying he didn't believe any attack would take place for several days. He learned later that Harrison had arrived at the Maumee rapids and that reinforcements were on their way. That added to the general air of self-satisfaction.

It is a rule of war that from time to time even the best generals suffer from a common failing—a refusal to believe their own intelligence reports. Mental blinkers narrow their vision. They reject any evidence that fails to support the truth as they see it. Winchester seemed deaf to all suggestions that the British were massing for attack.

Navarre's son, Peter, had scouted along the mouth of the Detroit River and returned to report that the British, with a large body of Indians, would be at the Raisin some time after dark. But even after a second scout confirmed the story, Winchester remained deaf to the warnings. Later in the evening one of Lewis's ensigns learned from a tavernkeeper that he had been talking to two British officers about an impending attack. But Lewis did not take that report seriously.

Some of Winchester's field officers expected that a council would be called that night. But there was no word from the general. Although Winchester had issued vague orders about strengthening the camp, little had been done. Nor did he issue ammunition, stored at Navarre's house—even though Wells's troops were down to ten rounds per man.

It was bitterly cold. The snow lay deep. Nobody had the heart to send pickets out onto the road leading into the settlement. One soldier, twenty-one-year-old William Atherton, noticed that most of the men acted as if they were perfectly safe, some wandering about town until late into the night. Atherton himself felt little anxiety, though he had reason to believe the situation was perilous. He slept soundly until awakened by the cry, "To arms! To arms!" the thundering of cannon, the roar of muskets, and the discordant yells of the attacking Indians.

CHAPTER FIVE

The Battle of Frenchtown

AT AMHERSTBURG LONG PAST MIDNIGHT ON JANUARY 19, THE YOUNG PEOPLE OF THE TOWN AND THE OFFICERS OF THE GARRISON HAD GATHERED TO HOLD A BALL TO CELEBRATE THE BIRTHDAY OF QUEEN CHARLOTTE, THE WIFE OF GEORGE III, THE MAD OLD KING OF ENGLAND. SUDDENLY IN DRAPER'S TAVERN THE MUSIC STOPPED AND IN WALKED PROCTER'S DEPUTY, LIEUTENANT-COLONEL ST. GEORGE, DRESSED FOR THE FIELD. HIS VOICE, LONG ACCUSTOMED TO COMMAND, DROWNED THE CHATTER.

"My boys," said the colonel, "you must prepare to dance to a different tune; the enemy is upon us and we are going to surprise them. We shall take the route about four in the morning, so get ready at once."

Procter had just learned of the British defeat at the Raisin. He realized the Americans were in an exposed position and their numbers not large. He determined to scrape up as many men as he could and counterattack at once.

Procter planned swiftly. He sent a detachment to defend Detroit. He left Fort Amherstburg virtually defenceless, manned only by the sick and least effective members of the militia. The remainder—every possible man who could be called into service, including provincial seamen from the gunboats—were sent across the river. He counted 597 able men and more than five hundred Indians—Potawatomi displaced from their homes by Harrison, with bitter memories of Tippecanoe; Miami, victims of the recent attacks at Mississinewa; and the Wyandot, under Chief Roundhead, formerly of Brownstown.

The first detachment left immediately, dragging three three-pound (1.4-kg) cannon and three small howitzers on sleighs. Fifteen-year-old John Richardson was young enough to find the scene romantic—the troops moving in a thin line across the frozen river under cliffs of rugged ice, their weapons, polished to a high gloss, glittering in the winter sunlight.

The following day the rest of the force crossed the river, spent the night at Brownstown, and prepared to move early in the morning. As darkness fell, John Richardson's favourite brother, Robert, aged just fourteen, a midshipman in the Provincial Marine, sneaked into camp. His father, an army surgeon, had given him strict orders to stay out of trouble on the Canadian side, but he longed to see action and joined one of the gun crews.

In the morning, Procter moved his force of one thousand to Rocky River, twelve miles (20 km) from Brownstown and six miles (10 km) from Frenchtown. Two hours before dawn on the following day, they rose, marched the intervening distance, and silently descended upon the enemy.

The camp at Frenchtown was asleep, the drum roll just sounding reveille. This, surely, was the moment for attack, while the men were still in their blankets, but Procter went by the book, which insisted that an infantry charge be supported by cannon.

Precious moments slipped by, and the army's momentum slowed as

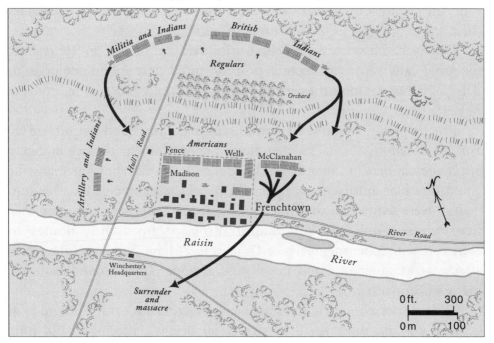

The Battle of Frenchtown

Procter placed his pieces. A sharp-eyed Kentucky guard spotted the movement. A rifle exploded. The leading grenadier of the 41st dropped dead. A bullet had literally gone in one ear and out the other. Surprise was lost as the battle began. Procter's caution would cost the lives of scores of good men.

It was still dark. The British and Canadians could see flashes of musket fire several hundred metres to the front but nothing else. Slowly, in the predawn murk, a blurred line of figures took shape, standing out in front of the village. They fired a volley at this welcome target but the line stood fast. They fired again without effect. Who were these supermen who did not fall when the muskets roared? Dawn provided the answer. They had been aiming, not at their enemies, but at a line of wooden pickets that protected the village.

A second problem frustrated them. Procter had placed one of his three-pounders (1.4-kg) directly in front of his centre. The American fire—aimed at the gun—played upon the men behind it, while the gunners themselves were in the line of fire of their own men in their rear.

The fire grew hotter. Behind the palisades, the Americans could easily pick out targets against the lightening sky. When the British abandoned the three-pounder (1.4-kg) twenty yards (18 m) from the fence, the Kentuckians leaped over the fence and captured it. At that, a young British seaman seized the drag rope and hauled it back to the British line just as a musket ball shredded his heel.

Private Shadrach Byfield was fighting in Adam Muir's company of the 41st when the man on his left fell dead. It was light enough now to see the enemy and he spotted a Kentuckian coming through the palisades. "There's a man!" cried Byfield to a friend. "I'll have a shot at him." As he pulled the trigger, a ball struck him under the left ear. He toppled to the ground, cutting his friend's leg with his bayonet in the process.

Byfield was only twenty-three—a Wiltshire man who had joined the British army at eighteen. He was the third in his family to enlist, which had caused his poor mother to fall into a speechless fit from which she never recovered. Now he believed his last moment had come.

"Byfield is dead!" his friend cried out. Shadrach Byfield replied, in some wonder, "I believe I be." An age-old question flashed across his mind, a question that must occur to every soldier the instant he falls in battle. "Is this death?" he asked himself. "Is this how men die?"

But he wasn't dead. He raised his head and began to creep off on his hands and knees.

"Byfield," called a sergeant, "shall I take you to the doctor?"

But Shadrach Byfield, at twenty-three, was an old soldier.

"Never mind me, go and help the men," he said and made his way to a barn to have his wounds dressed. There he encountered a sight so disturbing that he could never forget it—a young midshipman wounded in the knee, crying in pain for his mother, convinced he was going to die.

At the palisade, John Richardson felt as if he was sleepwalking. The early call and the six-mile (10-km) march had exhausted him. Even as the balls began to whistle above his head, he continued to feel drowsy. He tried to fire his musket but found it wouldn't respond. Someone the night before had stolen his flintlock and replaced it with a damaged part.

The infantry manual listed twelve separate drill movements for firing a Brown Bess musket and Richardson went through all of them without success. All he got was a flash in the pan. He found a bit of wire, tried to fix his weapon, fired again, got another flash. He felt more frustration and then fear at being fired on by an unseen foe and not being able to shoot back. Later he came to realize that he had fired fifty rounds and that not one had any effect on the pickets and probably not on the enemy either. The musket was a wretchedly inaccurate weapon.

To his horror, Richardson noted that the American sharpshooters were picking off the wounded British and Canadians as they tried to crawl to safety and some were making use of the tomahawk and scalping knife. He struggled valiantly with his useless weapon when he heard his name called. Somebody shouted that his brother had been wounded—young Robert's right leg was shattered as he applied a match to a gun. Now in great pain, Robert begged to be carried off, not to the staff section where his father was caring for the wounded, but to another part of the field so that he might escape his parent's wrath. And there, Shadrach Byfield witnessed his suffering.

On the left of the British line, Richardson could hear the war whoops of the Indians who, with the help of the Canadian militia, were driving directly through the open fields in which Lieutenant-Colonel Wells insisted on placing the regulars of the 17th U.S. Infantry. Wells was still at the Maumee. The second-in-command, Major McClanahan, could not hold his unprotected position. The troops retreated to the frozen river.

Now the Americans were in full flight across the river with Lieutenant-Colonel William Caldwell and a band of Indians under Roundhead, Split Log, and Walk-in-the-Water in hot pursuit. One of the Wyandots overtook an American officer and was about to tomahawk him when Caldwell interceded, made him a prisoner, and took him to the rear. The Kentuckian, catching him off guard, drew his knife and slit Caldwell's throat from ear to ear. But the wound was shallow and Caldwell, who was as tough as his Indian followers, caught his attacker's arm, pulled the dagger from his throat, and plunged it again and again into his prisoner's body until he was dead. Caldwell survived.

But where, when all this was going on, was the general? Winchester had awakened to the sound of musket fire and howitzer bombs exploding. He ran to the barn, borrowed a horse from his host, and dashed to action. His two battalion commanders, William Lewis and John Allen, joined him, and the three attempted to gather the fleeing men together under the bank of the Raisin. It was too late. The troops, pursued by the Indians, were in a panic. Lewis sent two companies to the right flank to reinforce the regulars, but these too were in retreat.

The three officers withdrew across the river and attempted a second rally behind the fences on the south side. It was hopeless. The men dashed past into a narrow lane leading to the main road. That was suicide, because the Indians were ahead of them and behind them on both sides of the lane. One hundred men were shot, tomahawked, and scalped. Winchester attempted a third rally in an orchard about a mile and a half (2.5 km) from the village. It also failed.

The right flank was now in full retreat, the men throwing away their weapons in panic. John Allen, shot in the thigh during his attempts to stall the retreat, limped on for two miles (3 km) until he could go no further. Exhausted and in pain, he slumped onto a log, resigned to his fate. One of the Potawatomi chiefs, seeing his officer's uniform, decided to capture and ransom him. But just as he showed his intention a second Indian moved in.

Allen killed him with a swipe of his sword. The other shot the colonel dead and scalped him.

Winchester and Lewis were more fortunate. They fell into the hands of Roundhead, the principal chief of the Wyandot. Roundhead, after stripping the general of his cocked hat, coat, and epaulettes, took the two officers and Winchester's seventeen-year-old son by a roundabout route back behind the British lines. The battle for the village was still raging, but Winchester, noting Procter's artillery, dazed by the rout, and despairing of any reinforcements from Harrison, gave up hope. As the Indians returned, each with as many as eight or nine scalps hanging from his belt, Winchester asked to see Procter. The British commander was blunt.

Procter warned that if there was no surrender he would have to set the town on fire. If he was forced to attack, he could not be responsible for the conduct of the Indians or the lives of the Americans.

"Some of your troops, sir, are defending themselves from the fort in a state of desperation—had you not better surrender them?"

"I have no authority to do so," replied Winchester, shivering in his silk shirt. "My command has devolved upon the senior officer in the fort, as you are pleased to call it."

Procter warned that if there was no surrender he would have to set the town on fire. If he was forced to attack, he could not be responsible for the conduct of the Indians or the lives of the Americans. If Winchester would surrender, he would be responsible for both. Winchester repeated that he was no longer in command but would recommend surrender to his people.

The command of the American force still fighting in the palisade had devolved on Major George Madison, a forty-nine-year-old veteran of the Revolution. At this moment he was concerned about the possession of an empty barn 150 yards (135 m) from the palisade. If the enemy seized that building, they would hold a commanding position overlooking the defenders. Madison called for a volunteer to set fire to the barn. A young ensign, William O. Butler, stepped forward, seized a blazing stick of firewood, vaulted the fence, and dashed toward the barn under direct fire from the British and Indians on both sides.

Butler reached the barn, flung the burning brand into a pile of hay, and raced back through a hail of musket balls. He had almost reached the safe-ty of his own lines when he realized the hay had not caught. Back he went again, re-entered the barn, fanned the hay into a roaring blaze, and outran the Indians trying to head him off. With his clothes ripped by passing mus-ket balls, he tumbled across the pickets and came to a full stop, standing upright trying to catch his breath. It was then that a musket ball struck him full in the chest. Fortunately, it had lost its force. Butler survived. Like his commander, George Madison, he would one day run for governor of Kentucky.

Now came a lull in the fighting. Of the sixteen British gunners, thirteen were casualties. The remainder were too numb with cold to fire their weapons. Their ammunition was low. Procter had withdrawn his forces into the woods, waiting for the Indians to return from the chase before resum-ing the attack. The defenders seized this interlude to devour some breakfast. That was the moment when Winchester agreed to attempt a surrender.

The Americans, seeing a flag of truce, thought that Procter was asking for time to bury his dead. It did not occur to any that surrender was being proposed. When he learned the truth, George Madison was mortified. And yet he knew his position was hopeless, for he had only a third of a keg of cartridges left. The reserve supply remained at the Navarre house across the river.

However, Madison insisted on conditions: "It has been customary for the Indians to massacre the wounded prisoners after a surrender," he reminded Procter. "I shall therefore not agree to any capitulation which General Winchester may direct, unless the safety and protection of all the prisoners shall be stipulated."

Procter stamped his foot: "Sir, do *you* mean to dictate for *me?*"

"I mean to dictate for myself," Madison coolly replied. "We prefer to sell our lives as dearly as possible rather than be massacred in cold blood."

Procter agreed, but not in writing. Private property, he promised, would be respected. Sleighs would be sent the following morning for the American sick and wounded. The disabled would be protected by a proper guard.

Thus the battle ended. Some of the troops pleaded with their officers not to surrender, saying they would rather die in action. But the general feeling was one of despair. To Thomas P. Dudley, another Lexington volunteer, "the mortification of the thought of surrender, the Spartan band who fought like heroes, the tears shed, the wringing of hands, the swelling of hearts, indeed, the scene beggars description."

Only thirty-three men had managed to escape. McClanahan, Wells's second-in-command, was one. Private John J. Brice was another. He got away by pulling off his shoes and running through the snow in his stocking feet in order to leave tracks resembling those of an Indian in moccasins. Thus he became the first man to report the defeat and surrender to Harrison.

Winchester's loss was appalling Two hundred Kentuckians were dead or wounded. Another seven hundred were prisoners of the British. But the worst was yet to come. The blow to American morale, already bruised by the losses at Detroit and Queenston, was overwhelming. As for Harrison, the Battle of Frenchtown had already wrecked his plans. His left wing had been shattered. His advance on Detroit was halted indefinitely. He had to withdraw to the Maumee out of reach of the enemy. Largely because of the Indians, the idea of a swift victory over Canada was gone forever.

CHAPTER SIX

Massacre

IN FRENCHTOWN, ON JANUARY 23, YOUNG WILLIAM ATHERTON WOKE AT DAWN TO FEEL THE WOUND IN HIS SHOULDER THROBBING. HE COULD NOT ESCAPE A FEELING OF DREAD THAT HAD TORMENTED HIS SLEEP. AN OMINOUS STILLNESS HAD COME OVER THE VILLAGE WHERE THE AMERICAN WOUNDED WERE STILL HELD. PROCTER, FEARING AN EARLY ATTACK FROM HARRISON, HAD LONG SINCE DRAGGED HIS OWN WOUNDED OFF ON SLEDS. SINCE THERE WERE NOT ENOUGH OF THESE FOR THE AMERICANS, HE HAD PROMISED TO RETURN EARLY IN THE MORNING TO TAKE THEM ALL TO AMHERSTBURG.

But the promise made no sense. If Procter was afraid of Harrison, why would he then return for the wounded? If he didn't fear him, why had he taken everybody with him except one officer, Major Reynolds, and three interpreters?

Actually, Harrison, learning of the disaster, had withdrawn his relief force. In the course of the criticism that followed, nobody bothered to ask why. With Procter's forces off balance and Fort Amherstburg virtually defenceless, Harrison might easily have snatched victory from defeat. But he contented himself with putting all the blame on Winchester.

The camp at Frenchtown was uneasy. Some time in the dark hours of the night, Reynolds and the interpreters had slipped away. Atherton's fears were further aroused by an Indian, apparently a chief, who spoke fluent English and came into his quarters the evening before, apparently trying to get information about Harrison's movements. But just as he left, the Indian made an oddly chilling remark: "I am afraid some of the mischievous boys will do some mischief before morning," he said.

The sun had been up for more than an hour when Atherton's fears were realized. Without warning the door of the house in which he and some of the wounded were being cared for was forced open. An Indian, his face smeared with red and black paint, appeared waving a tomahawk, followed by several others. Their purpose was loot. They began to strip the clothing and the blankets from the wounded men, groaning on the floor.

Atherton, near the door, managed to slip out of the room, only to come face to face with one of the most savage-looking Indians he had ever seen. His face was painted jet black. Half a bushel of feathers was fastened to his scalp lock. An immense tomahawk gleamed in his right hand. A scalping knife hung from his belt. He seized Atherton by the collar, propelled him out the front door, led him through the gate and down the river for a hundred yards (90 m) to the home of Jean-Baptiste Jerome, where several wounded officers had spent the night. The building had also done duty as a tavern, and the Indians were ransacking the cellars for whisky.

In front of the house, Atherton saw a scarecrow figure, bleeding, barefoot, and clad only in a shirt and drawers. This was Captain Nathaniel Hart, commander of the Lexington Light Infantry, inspector of the Northwest Army. He was the messenger whom Harrison sent to Winchester the night before the battle. He was twenty-eight and wealthy, having made a fortune in hemp. Now he was pleading for his life.

The previous night, Hart, badly wounded in the knee, was visited by an old friend, a Canadian militia captain, William Elliott, who had once been cared for in the Hart home in Lexington during a bout of illness. Hart had Elliott's promise that he would send his personal sleigh for him in the morning and bring him back to Amherstburg. In fact Elliott had assured all the wounded and injured in Jerome's house that they were in no danger. That promise was hollow. They were all in deadly peril. Some were already dying under the tomahawk blows of the Indians.

Hart turned to an Indian he recognized—the same English-speaking chief who Atherton had encountered the evening before. He reminded him of Elliott's promise.

"Elliott has deceived you, he does not intend to fulfil his promise," the Indian replied.

"If you will agree to take me, I'll give you a horse or a hundred dollars," Hart declared. "You shall have it on our arrival at Malden."

"I cannot take you."

"Why?"

"You are too badly wounded."

"Then," asked Captain Hart, "what do you intend to do with us?"

"Boys," said the Indian, "you are all to be killed."

Hart kept his composure and said a brief prayer. Atherton expected at any moment to feel the blow of a tomahawk. A scene of pure horror followed. Captain Paschal Hickman emerged from Jerome's house, dragged by an Indian who threw him face down into the snow. Hickman had already been tomahawked. He died as Atherton watched in terror. Then, taking advantage of the confusion, Atherton began to edge away slowly, hoping not to be seen.

Albert Ammerman, another unwilling witness, crouched on a log, guarded by his Indian captor. A private in the 1st Regiment of Kentucky Volunteers, he had been wounded in the thigh but had been doing his best to conceal his injury, for he knew it was the Indians' practice to kill all who could not walk. He watched helplessly while the Indians looted the houses, stripped the clothes from the wounded, tomahawked and scalped their prey, and set fire to the buildings. Some, still alive, forced their heads out of the windows, half-enveloped in smoke and flames, seeking rescue. But there was no rescue.

Ammerman was marched off at last toward Brownstown with some other prisoners. After limping about half a mile (800 m), they were overtaken. One Indian had Captain Hart in custody and was having a violent argument with another, apparently over the reward that Hart had offered for their safe conduct. As Ammerman watched, the two took aim at each other as if to end the quarrel. But they did not fire. Instead they turned upon their prisoner, pulled him from his horse, knocked him down with a war club, tomahawked him, scalped him, and stripped him of his remaining clothes, money, and belongings.

Ammerman, who was later ransomed in Detroit, noted that Hart during these final moments refrained from making any pleas. He appeared to the end to be perfectly calm. The news of his death, when it finally reached Lexington three months later, would cause a particular shiver of despair and fury in Kentucky. For this mangled and naked corpse, thrown like carrion onto the side of the road, was once the brother-in-law of Henry Clay, a famous American politician.

Back at Frenchtown, little William Atherton—he was only five foot five (1.65 m)—was trying to reach a small log building some distance from the scene of horror. He edged toward it and was a few steps from it when a Potawatomi seized him and asked where he was wounded. Atherton placed his hand on his shoulder. The Indian felt it and found it was not serious. He decided that Atherton would be his prize for later ransom. He wrapped him in a blanket, gave him a hat, took him to the back door of one of the houses, and put him in charge of all his plunder.

It was some time before Atherton realized that his enemies did not intend to kill or ransom him. On the contrary, they were determined to turn him into an Indian and almost succeeded.

Atherton was flabbergasted. For the best part of an hour he had expected certain death. Now he lived in the faint hope that his life might be spared. He experienced "one of those sudden transitions of mind impossible to either conceive or express, except by those whose unhappy lot it has been, to be placed in like circumstances."

As the house blazed behind him, Atherton watched his fellow prisoners being dragged away to Brownstown. For the first time perhaps, he had been aware of the value a man places on his own life. He saw members of his own company, old acquaintances, so badly wounded they could hardly be moved from their beds, suddenly leap up, hearing that the Indians would tomahawk all who could not leave on foot. They hobbled past him on sticks. Unable to keep up, they were soon butchered.

After two hours, Atherton's captor returned with an army pack horse and a great deal of plunder. The Potawatomi handed his prisoner the bridle and the two set off on the road to Brownstown, bordered now by a ghastly hedgerow of mutilated corpses.

They halted for the night at Sandy Creek, where a number of Potawatomi were encamped. Here, around a roaring fire of fence rails, the Indians fed their captives gruel. And here another grisly scene took place. An Indian walked up to Private Charles Searls and proposed to exchange his moccasins for the soldier's shoes. Following the exchange, a brief conversation took place with the Indian asking how many men Harrison had with him. The name of the hero of Tippecanoe drove him into a sudden rage. With his anger rising, he called Searls a "Madison," raised his tomahawk, and struck him a deep blow on the shoulder. Searls, bleeding profusely, clutched the weapon embedded in his flesh and tried to resist. A surgeon's mate, Gustavus Bower, told him his fate was inevitable. Searls closed his eyes as the fatal blow fell. Not long after that, three more men were murdered at random.

When Atherton asked his captor if the Indians intended to kill all the prisoners, the Indian nodded. Atherton tried to eat, but he had no stomach for it even though he had had little food for three days. Then he realized his captor didn't understand English, and so a vestige of hope returned.

The march resumed with many alarms. Atherton was in daily fear of his life. He slept with a kerchief tied around his neck in the belief that the Indians would want to steal it before tomahawking him in his sleep, thus giving him some warning. But they did not kill him. His captor, whose brother had been killed at the River Raisin, had other plans.

It was the custom of the Potawatomi, among others, to adopt healthy captives into the families of those who had lost sons in the same engagement. It was some time before Atherton realized that his enemies did not intend to kill or ransom him. On the contrary, they were determined to turn him into an Indian and almost succeeded.

Dr. John Todd, a surgeon with the Kentucky Volunteers, was taken to the British camp where he again met Captain William Elliott. He urged Elliott to send a sleigh back to pick up some of the badly wounded, but Elliott knew it was too late and said so. When Todd pressed his case, Elliott said that charity began at home, and that the British and Canadians must be cared for first. He added, in some exasperation, that it was impossible to restrain the Indians and tried to explain that they were simply seeking revenge for their own losses. The Battle of Tippecanoe was only fourteen months in the past, the attacks along the Mississinewa less than two.

Along the frozen shores of the River Raisin a great stillness fell. The cold was numbing. Nothing moved. Those settlers who still remained in Frenchtown did not venture outside their doors.

In the little orchard across the river, along the narrow lane that led from the Navarre home and beside the Detroit River road, the bodies of the Americans lay, unburied. The Potawatomi had made it known that any white man who dared to touch the remains of any of the hated Harrison men would meet a similar fate.

The naked corpses lay strewn for many kilometres along the roadside in the grotesque attitude of men who, in a sudden flash, realize their last moment had come.

There, contorted in death, lay the flower of Kentucky: Captain Hart and Captain Hickman, Lieutenant-Colonel John Allen and Captain John Wollfolk, Winchester's aide-de-camp, who once offered a thousand dollars to anybody who would purchase him, but was tomahawked in spite of it. There was Captain John Simpson, a congressman, and Ensign Levi Wells, the son of Lieutenant-Colonel Sam Wells of the 4th Infantry, and Allen Darnell, whose brother looked on helplessly as he was scalped because he could not keep up with the others, and Ebenezer Blythe, a surgeon's mate, tomahawked in the act of offering ransom. And there, like a discarded doll, was the body of young Captain Price of the Jessamine Blues, whose last letter home gave instructions for the upbringing of his two-year-old son.

The war which had begun so gently turned ugly as all wars must. The mannerly days were over. New emotions—hatred, fury, a thirst for revenge, a nagging sense of guilt—distorted the tempers of the neighbours who once lived peacefully on both sides of the embattled border. And it was not over. Peace was still two years away. The blood had only begun to flow.

CHAPTER SEVEN

The Captive

IN APRIL 1813, LITTLE WILLIAM ATHERTON WAS STILL A CAPTIVE OF THE POTAWATOMI IN MICHIGAN TERRITORY. TO HIM, HOME SEEMED TO BE ON ANOTHER PLANET.

Adopted into a Potawatomi family to replace a son killed at Frenchtown, he now lived as an Indian, wore Indian buckskin, observed Indian customs. He hunted with bow and arrow, danced the corn dance, slept in a wigwam, ate boiled corn and bristly hog meat. He neither heard nor spoke English.

His only contact with white civilization was a tattered Lexington newspaper found among the Indians' effects. That was his sole comfort. He read and re-read it, clinging to the brittle pages as a reminder that somewhere beyond the brooding, snow-covered forests, there was really another world—a world that he once took for granted, but which came back to him now as if in a dream. Would he ever see it again? As winter gave way to spring, Atherton gave way to despair, stealing out of camp for moments of solitude when he could think of home and weep without being discovered.

In May, his captors headed for Detroit. On the way, they encountered another band which had just captured a young American surgeon in battle. What battle? Atherton had no way of knowing that the war was still continuing. The two men conversed eagerly in the first English that Atherton had heard in three months. Then the other departed, Atherton believed to his death.

They reached Amherstburg, but Atherton had no hope of escape. With his long, swarthy face and his matted brown hair, uncut for months, he was just another Indian to the British, who failed to notice his blue eyes. When the band moved across to Spring Wells, to draw rations at the British commissary, Atherton's Indian father learned with delight that his new son could write. He had him double the original number of family members on the chit, thus increasing the handout of provisions. Again, the British did not realize that Atherton was white.

He lost track of time. Crawling with vermin, half-starved, with no hope of escape from the family that nurtured but also guarded him, he threw himself on their mercy and pleaded to be ransomed. To his surprise, his Indian father agreed, though reluctantly. It was clear that Atherton had become part of the family, more a son than a captive. They could not refuse him, even though it meant losing him.

Eventually, in Detroit, they found a man who would give a pony for him. Atherton bid his Indian parents goodbye—not without sorrow, for they had, in their own fashion, been kind—and became a prisoner of war. All that summer he was lodged in a British guardhouse, almost naked, sleeping on the floor with a log for a pillow, wondering about the course of the war.

And the war went on. Of the triumphs and defeats of his own people, Atherton knew nothing. Only when his captors returned from the unsuccessful British siege at Fort Stevenson at Lower Sandusky, their faces peppered with small shot, did he have an inkling that beyond the quarter-house walls, all along the border men were still fighting and dying.

Summer gave way to fall. On September 10, 1813, Atherton and his fellow prisoners could hear the rumble of heavy guns across Lake Erie and knew that a naval battle was raging. At last, a private soldier whispered the truth: the Americans had defeated the British fleet and Erie had become an American lake. The victory touched off a major retreat. The British packed up hastily in the face of a new advancing army under Harrison. Atherton could hardly wait for the Kentucky forces to arrive and free him. But that was not to be. The prisoners were hurried across to the Canadian shore and herded up the Thames Valley, on to York, Kingston, and Montreal.

It seemed as if the entire city of Montreal turned out to stare at them— verminous, shaggy, half-starved after a journey of nine hundred miles (1,400 km). As Atherton trudged down the cobbled streets he noticed the doors and windows crammed with curious women. In the jail they were given a little "Yankee beef," taunted with the fact that it had been purchased by the British from Americans trading with the enemy.

Two weeks later they were sent on to Quebec City. The Kentuckians' reputation had preceded them. The Quebeckers thought of them as wild men—savage forest creatures, half-human, half-beast. They crowded to the jail, peering at the captives as they would at animals in a zoo, astonished, even disappointed, to find they did not live up to their billing. One man gazed at them for several minutes, and then delivered the general verdict: "Why, they look just like other people."

Beyond the prison the war raged on. Eventually Atherton was released and sent back across the border. In Pittsburgh he met a group of vaguely familiar men—British prisoners of war. Who were they? Where had he seen them before? Then he remembered. These were soldiers who were once his guards when he was a captive in Detroit. It all seemed a long time ago.

Atherton's story was not unique. Eighty or ninety Kentuckians were captured by the Potawatomi braves, and of these a good number were adopted into Indian families. Timothy Mallory had all his hair shaved off except for a scalp lock, his face painted half black, half red, his ears pierced for rings. John Davenport was painted, adorned with earrings, bracelets, and a silver band wound round his shaved skull.

"We make an Indian out of you," one of his captors promised, and "by'n by you have squaw, by'n by you have a gun and horse and go hunting."

Both these men lived as Indians for several months. Like Atherton, who preferred his treatment by Indians to that of the British (he found them "brave, generous, hospitable, kind and ... honest"), they were surprised to discover that their Indian families were generally fond of them. The women went out of their way to protect them when the braves indulged in drinking bouts. When at last they were ransomed, the Indians were clearly reluctant to part with them.

No one to this day knows exactly how many Kentucky Volunteers were held captive by the Natives, adopted into families that had lost sons in battle. No one knows exactly how many escaped or were ransomed. But it is possible, even probable, that as the war rolled on, there were still some Kentuckians who went entirely native, took Indian wives, and removed themselves from white society.

There was irony in this. But then it was a war of irony and paradox—a war fought over a cause that was removed before the fighting began; a war that everyone claimed to have won, except the real victors, who, being

Indians, were really losers; a war designed to seize by force a nation that could have been attacked by stealth.

And were there in the forests of Michigan among the Potawatomi—those veterans of Tippecanoe—certain warriors of lighter skin and alien background? If so, that was the final irony. Ever since the days of Thomas Jefferson, it had been official American policy to try to turn the Indians into white men. Who can blame the Indians if, in their last, desperate, doomed resistance, they should manage in some measure to turn the tables?

INDEX

"Meeting Between Laura Secord and
Lieutenant James FitzGibbon, June 1813"
by Lorne Kidd Smith. The journey of Laura Secord
is still a famous story of patriotism in Canada.
(Courtesy Library and Archives Canada, C-011053)

CANADA UNDER SIEGE

Contents

CHAPTER ONE

The Attack on Muddy York

THERE WAS A TIME, WHEN CANADA WAS YOUNG — AND STILL A COLONY OF
GREAT BRITAIN — WHEN AN INVADING ARMY FROM A FOREIGN LAND CROSSED
HER BORDERS, INTENT ON CONQUEST. THERE WAS A TIME WHEN THE CITY OF
TORONTO — THEN A SMALL, MUDDY VILLAGE OF NO MORE THAN A THOUSAND
SOULS, KNOWN AS YORK — WAS ATTACKED AND CAPTURED BY AMERICAN
FORCES. THERE WAS A TIME WHEN THE SETTLED COMMUNITIES OF ONTARIO —
THEN KNOWN AS UPPER CANADA — WERE ROBBED AND BURNED BY MEN WHO
SPOKE THE SAME LANGUAGE AND SPRANG FROM THE SAME ROOTS AS
CANADIANS.

The time was 1813. The month was April, when the first buds were
sprouting on the chokecherries that lined the concession roads, and the
first robins were warbling in the cedar forests along the Humber and Don
Rivers. On the morning of the twenty-sixth, those residents of York who
had risen early were faced with a dismaying spectacle. On Lake Ontario an
American fleet, bristling with cannon, lay just off the mouth of the Don.

The war with the United States, which we call the War of 1812, was
almost a year old. Twice the previous summer the Americans had tried to
invade Canada—once from Amherstburg directly across from Fort Detroit
and again at Queenston on the Niagara River. Twice they had been hurled
back, with Detroit and Michigan Territory seized by British, Canadian, and
Indian forces. Now they were trying again, with a new army crammed
aboard fourteen ships determined to strike at the capital of Upper Canada.

A shipbuilding contest was underway on Lake Ontario. At the eastern
end, at Sackets Harbor, the Americans were frantically trying to add to their

fleet. But the British had a big warship of their own under construction at York and another already completed. The Americans intended to seize both vessels and add them to their fleet. That would upset the balance of naval power and give them control of the lake.

On the morning of April 26 the Reverend John Strachan, thirty-five years old, a stocky figure in clergyman's black, saw the American fleet through his spyglass. In the events that followed he would play a key role. Strachan had no use for the American settlers who were pouring into the province from the border states, bringing with them—in his view—a godless and materialistic way of life. Strachan believed as strongly in the British colonial system as he did in the Church of England. He was the most energetic man in town: he taught the chosen in his own grammar school; performed weddings, funerals, and christenings; attended military parades; poked his nose regularly into government; and managed to produce a hefty number of books, articles, and pamphlets.

> *The war had made him tougher. As far as he was concerned it was a just war — one that Christians could wage with vigour and a clear conscience.*

The war had made him tougher. As far as he was concerned it was a just war—one that Christians could wage with vigour and a clear conscience.

He was not alone in thinking that way. Aboard the tall ships lurking outside the harbour, bristling with cannon, other men—Americans—equally determined, were preparing for bloody combat. And, as in all wars, their leaders were as certain as John Strachan that *their* cause was just, and that the god of battle stood firmly in their ranks.

The leader of the invasion force was Zebulon Montgomery Pike, the army's newest brigadier-general. At that very moment in his cabin on the American flagship he was scratching out a letter to his wife. Pike knew that it might be his last. "Should I fall," he wrote, "defend my memory and only believe, had I lived, I would have aspired to deeds worthy of your husband."

For most of his military life Pike had yearned to perform deeds of glory that would bring him everlasting fame. But, in spite of a flaming ambition, the laurel had eluded him. He had been a soldier for nineteen of his thirty-four years, but his only action had been an inglorious skirmish on the

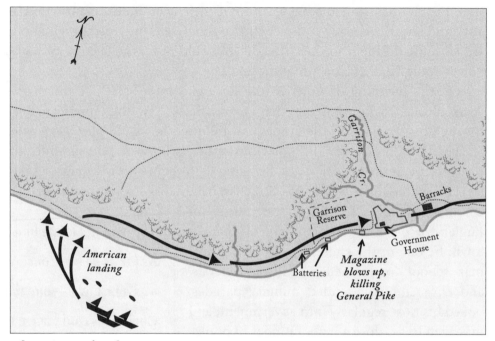

The Capture of York

Canadian border the previous November in which his troops shot at their own men.

He was better known as an explorer than an officer. Pike's Peak, a mountain in the Rockies, bears his name today, even though he didn't discover it, didn't climb it, and didn't come within fifteen miles (25 km) of it.

He was a bold, impulsive man. Serenely confident in his own ability, he felt he was headed for greatness. But promotion had been maddeningly slow. Now, at last, opportunity beckoned. "If we go into Canada," he wrote to a fellow officer, "you will hear of my fame or of my death, for I am determined to seek the Bubble even in the cannon's mouth."

Pike had been chosen to lead the attack on York because his commanding general, Henry Dearborn, was ill, or pretended to be. An indecisive, grotesque pudding of a man, Dearborn was so gross he had to be trundled about in a wheelbarrow. His troops called him "Granny."

The American sailing ships were jammed with fourteen hundred men, six hundred of whom were crowded aboard Pike's flagship *Madison*. As they

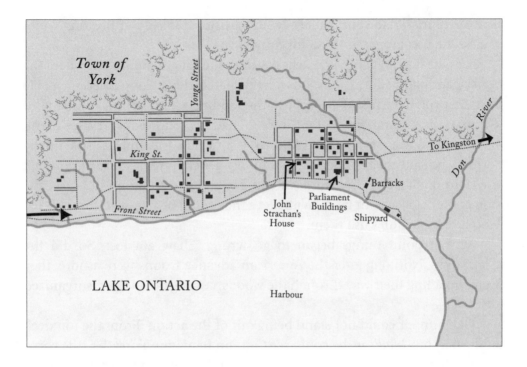

dropped anchor off what was to become Sunnyside Beach, John Strachan, through his spyglass, could see them clambering into the small boats.

The clergyman felt a sense of frustration. Why were there no British or Canadian troops rushing to repel them? The British general, Roger Sheaffe, had a tendency to delay. That maddened Strachan, who saw himself as a military expert.

It is a military axiom that a landing from the water must be halted at the edge of the beach before the enemy can dig in. Because the Americans would have to come ashore in waves, then send the boats back for more troops, Sheaffe's forces would outnumber the invaders in the early stages of the attack. Surely now, Strachan thought, was the time to rush every available man through the woods that separated the garrison from the landing point and hurl the Americans back!

But if Sheaffe faced a dilemma, he didn't show it. Even his critics—and he had many—remarked on his coolness in the events that followed. He was a bulky man, a little ponderous, who hadn't wanted to fight the Americans.

The Revolution had split his family, and a sister still lived in Boston. Nonetheless, he was prepared to do his duty.

Alas, he was no gambler. He had waited too long to figure out where the Americans planned to land. Worse, he dispatched his troops piecemeal. He first sent off the Indians to oppose the landing along with a company of Glengarrys. A company of the King's grenadiers followed, and after them, three companies of regulars. And at last, when the militia was finally formed, he sent them under their adjutant-general, Aneas Shaw, to protect the right flank along the Dundas Road. He had two six-pound (3-kg) cannon at his disposal, but he didn't believe they could be trundled through the woods and so didn't use them.

At that point things began to go wrong. Shaw got lost. So did the Glengarrys. Not long after the American advance troops were ashore, they were threading their way through the woods, cutting down the disorganized defenders.

Pike himself could not stand being out of the action. From the foredeck of the flagship *Madison*, he could see Captain Benjamin Forsyth's rifle corps pulling for the Canadian shore. A stiff wind blew them past the chosen landing place. As the soldiers struggled with the oars, the painted forms of the Indians emerged from the woods and opened fire.

"Rest on your oars," Forsyth whispered, and told his men to prime their muskets. As the Indians opened fire, the Americans returned it. That was Pike's moment.

"By God! I can't stand here any longer," he shouted, and turning to the staff, cried out, "Jump, come, come, jump into the boat."

Off he went, surrounded by his aides, heading directly toward the centre of the fray, a square, serene figure in blue—and an obvious target.

Forsyth got his men to shore, where they sought the protection of the woods—the natural habitat of American sharpshooters. Pike waded ashore with his men and formed the infantry into two platoons under a high bank. They were ordered to scale the incline and charge across the field with their bayonets. But the British grenadiers poured out of the forest and drove them down the bank back to the water's edge.

The light draught schooners, moving in at close range, sprayed the British with grapeshot and did terrible damage. The Indians, their morale shattered, vanished from the scene. Caught in a crossfire between the naval guns and the American sharpshooters, the British regulars stumbled back into the woods. They weren't used to this kind of warfare. Their training had been on the broad plains of Europe. And in their scarlet jackets they made easy targets for the American riflemen hidden between logs and trees.

"Show us our enemy, Pike," the British soldiers cried. But they disdained the natural protection of the forest and dropped like grouse at a highland shoot. Of 119 grenadiers, only thirty survived. Two are believed to have fallen through the rotting ice of a deep pond, which is today known as Grenadier Pond.

It didn't occur to them to retreat, any more than it occurred to them to seek cover. At last, unable to dislodge the Americans, their surviving officers led them back toward the Western Battery that guarded the lake road.

By now the din in the woods was deafening—the shouts of the combatants, the war whoops of the Indians, the roar of cannon and musket, and above all this, the piercing notes of Forsyth's bugler trumpeting success.

The naval guns continued to pour a hail of shot into the woods as Pike formed his men into columns and, with a fife and drum corps playing "Yankee Doodle," marched toward York through the woods along the road that hugged the lake.

Ely Playter, a farmer and militia lieutenant, back from scouting the east end of town, turned up just as the first of retreating British staggered out of the woods. Above the sound of music he could hear the cheers of the American sailors as six ships moved up toward the Western Battery. It was here that Sheaffe intended to make a stand. But that would not be easy, for the battery was jammed with men all jostling each other and harassing the gunners.

The six American ships could throw more than two hundred pounds (90 kg) of iron at the battery in a single volley. The twelve British gunners, working largely with old cannon, had scarcely one-third that fire power. And Pike's men had managed to haul two field guns through the woods— a feat that Sheaffe had believed impossible.

But before they could fling themselves at the battery, a dreadful accident occurred. In the cramped quarters, somebody jostled one of the gunners. A spark from a British gunner's slow match fell into a powder magazine. The explosion killed more than a dozen men, scorching others horribly and tearing away the gun platform.

Badly rattled, the regulars tried to remount the big gun. The militia fled. Nobody seemed to know what was to be done. General Sheaffe had left. Outnumbered, he had decided that the town could not be defended. Already he was laying plans to save his regulars and deny the public stores to the enemy.

And so Pike's forces had little opposition as they pushed on along the lakeshore toward Government House and the garrison.

The fleeing militia lost all sense of order. Ely Playter and others tried to rally them without success. Playter realized the garrison was about to be evacuated but did not know that Sheaffe had already decided to pull out and blow up the main magazine on the waterfront below Government House. Within this underground fort were two hundred barrels of gun powder and a vast quantity of cartridge, shells, and round shot. Concerned only with saving his regulars, Sheaffe gave little attention to the straggling militia. Several dozen were within a whisper of the magazine.

With the fuses burning, Playter and his men had already been ordered to march off. But the young farmer had left his coat in his quarters. He ran to retrieve it, unaware that the magazine was about to blow.

Pike was within four hundred yards (370 m) of the garrison and ordered his men to hug the ground while he brought up a six-pounder (3-kg) and a howitzer that his men had dragged through the mud and the stumps. He was on the verge of victory and he knew it.

It would be the first American victory after ten months of bitter defeat.

He sat on a stump, waiting for the final attack. One of his men had captured a Canadian militia sergeant and two of his aides. Pike was about to question them. But at that very instant the ground shook and the world turned dazzling white. An enormous roar split the ears of the attackers as a giant cloud spurted from the blazing magazine to blossom in the sky. From that vast canopy there burst in all directions an eruption of debris—great chunks of masonry, broken beams, gigantic boulders, rocks, and stones of every size. This terrifying hail poured down upon the attackers, covering the ground for a thousand feet (305 m) in every direction, killing or maiming more than a hundred men, striking off arms and legs, crushing chests, and beheading bodies.

Ely Playter, who had got his coat back and reached the barrack gate, had an appalling close-up view. Miraculously, he was untouched. He could see the huge boulders dropping all around them, some skipping across the ground, others burying themselves in the mud. He saw men smashed to a pulp.

The British casualties ran to forty, most of them militia. The Americans suffered more than five times that number and the general was among the dying. Zebulon Pike lay helpless among his mangled followers. A huge boulder had crushed his ribs. His aide was dead and so was the unfortunate Canadian sergeant.

Pike's wounds were mortal and he knew it. How humiliating, to be killed by a falling rock! Not for him the gallant death, waving his sword in the teeth of the battle, achieving the instant martyrdom of a Nelson or a Brock. Time only for a few gasping phrases for the history books: "Push on, my brave fellows, and avenge your general!"

Unfortunately for the Americans, the British regulars who ought to have surrendered slipped out of the bag before the noose could be pulled tight. The British army escaped to fight another day. And Pike would not go down in history as a military hero, but as one who accidentally gave his name to a mountain that somebody before him had discovered and somebody after him had climbed.

CHAPTER TWO

John Strachan Reigns Supreme

JOHN STRACHAN, BUSTLING ABOUT TOWN SEEKING THE ACTION, HURRIED BACK TO HIS HOUSE TO FIND HIS WIFE IN A STATE OF TERROR. HE BUNDLED HER AND THE CHILDREN OFF TO A FRIEND'S HOME OUTSIDE THE TOWN AND THEN RUSHED BACK TOWARD THE GARRISON. HE FOUND SHEAFFE AND THE REGULARS IN A RAVINE GETTING READY TO LEAVE. STRACHAN LATER DEMANDED TO KNOW WHY THE MAJOR-GENERAL DIDN'T SEIZE THAT MOMENT TO COUNTERATTACK, BUT SHEAFFE HAD NO WAY OF KNOWING OF THE HAVOC THE EXPLOSION HAD CAUSED AMONG THE ENEMY. THE MOST SENSIBLE THING HE COULD DO WAS TO BURN THE NAVAL STORES AND THE BIG VESSEL, *ISAAC BROCK,* UNDER CONSTRUCTION IN THE HARBOUR, AND GET HIS MEN OUT OF TOWN TO REINFORCE KINGSTON. HE WAS CERTAIN THAT IT WOULD BE THE NEXT TARGET OF AMERICAN ATTACK.

The Americans were furious. The whole object of the expedition had been to capture two British ships. But Sheaffe had burned one, and the other had escaped from the harbour before the attack began. Worse, the real army was out of reach—en route to Kingston and safety. Now they had to deal with amateur soldiers and a clergyman—for Strachan volunteered his services and soon became chief negotiator for the people of York.

Under the terms of the peace treaty, all arms and public stores had to be given to the Americans. The militiamen were not made prisoners but were paroled—released on the understanding they would no longer take up arms—and thus neutralized for the remainder of the war. Only officers were imprisoned. And private property was to be respected.

There was looting that night, though it was comparatively light. When Mrs. Grant Powell, a prominent society hostess, returned to her home that evening, she found Americans in her house, one of them munching on a piece of loaf sugar. A spirited argument followed with a soldier, a six-footer (1.8-m), getting much the worst of it.

Mrs. Powell told him to go home and mind his own business.

"I wish I could," the soldier replied miserably.

Mrs. Powell relented a little and asked him where he lived.

"Down to Stillwater, New York," he told her. "I've one of Major Bleeker's farms."

Mrs. Powell burst into laughter at that. She was American-born and Major Bleeker was her father. For the War of 1812, fought back and forth across the Canadian border, was very much a civil war in which families who had known each other for generations found themselves opposed.

As night deepened, silence fell over the occupied town. Only in the garrison hospital was there activity. There, scores of desperately wounded men from both sides screamed without let-up into the darkness. An American soldier's mate, Dr. William Beaumont, had seen death, but the ghastly scene before him broke his heart—the men groaning and screaming, the surgeons wading in blood, "severing limbs with knife and saw or trepanning shattered skulls." The most hardened assassin, the cruellest savage, Beaumont thought, would be shocked at the spectacle. For forty-eight hours, without food or sleep, the young doctor cut and slashed, sickened by the carnage of war.

In his eyes, these mashed and mangled men were no longer friends or enemies, only fellow creatures. Nobody, he thought, could view such a spectacle without the blood chilling in his veins; none could behold it without agonizing sympathy.

The following morning, John Strachan, angered because the Americans had not agreed to the terms of surrender, demanded to see Dearborn himself. The American general was in a bad humour, clearly nonplussed by the presumption of this cleric badgering him over minor details of a surrender the general considered a *fait accompli.*

Strachan brandished the articles of surrender, still unsigned. Dearborn glanced at the document without comment. Strachan persisted. When would Dearborn parole the officers and men of the militia? When would he allow the townspeople to care for their sick and wounded? Dearborn's irritation grew. Who were the conquered here? Who the conqueror? Who was the strange civilian with the thick Scots burr who seemed to think he could deal with generals? He told Strachan, harshly, that the Americans had been given a false return of the captured officers, and then warned him away.

But Strachan was not to be shoved aside. He wouldn't be duped, he said, or insulted. Either the document would be signed at once, or it would not be signed at all. There would be *no* capitulation! Let the Americans do their worst! With that he turned on his heel and walked back to the garrison.

These rough tactics were successful. Dearborn, in a better humour, signed the document. The militiamen were paroled and the community began to return to something resembling normality. But the Americans threatened to burn the town if the public funds, which had been concealed, were not given up. They managed to get the paper money but not the gold. A young clerk, dressed up as a market woman, complete with sunbonnet and flowing skirts, was spirited out of town with the precious metal loaded onto a one-horse wagon and covered with vegetables.

When William Playter arrived back in town after hiding in Newmarket, he found the town plundered. The garrison buildings were shattered, the council office stripped bare, every window broken. The legislative building, a low one-storey brick structure with two wings, one for each house, was ablaze. No one knew who set the fire. The Americans were blamed without any hard evidence. The best guess is that the culprits were individual American sailors who wore no uniforms.

Although the upper class in York was opposed to the American invasion, scores of ordinary citizens either welcomed it or accepted it. For every man concealing himself to escape parole, there seemed to be another eager to sign a paper that would take him out of the war. A number joined the enemy. When it became clear that the Americans intended to leave town, panic seized those who supported the invaders, some of whom urged the American officers to hold on to York and give them protection.

Suspicion and sedition went hand in hand, as neighbour broke with neighbour over idle remarks or disloyal outbursts. In Michael Dye's tavern in Markham township, Alfred Barrett offered a toast: "Success to the American fleet!" Two friends raised their glasses in agreement. They were overheard by another, who also heard two others agree that it was foolish to support the government of Upper Canada. The country, they said, really belonged to the U.S. and they hoped the Americans would win. All four eventually found themselves in the York jail, charged with sedition.

Another man, Elijah Bentley, an Anabaptist preacher, was jailed for telling friends he had seen more liberty during the four hours of the Americans in York than he had seen in the whole of the province.

The Americans also made themselves popular with some farmers by distributing a number of farm implements that had been sent out by Britain and intended for the settlers but, as the result of bureaucratic inertia, never distributed. Many were convinced that the ruling class was reserving all that treasure for its friends.

Strachan's church was looted. Lawlessness prevailed. Once again the tireless clergyman went after the hard-pressed Dearborn. Now, all the American general wanted to do was to get out of York. There was no advantage in holding the town. The brig in the harbour was destroyed. The public stores destined for the frontier had been captured. All the arms and equipment for the British squadron on Lake Erie had been seized and couldn't be replaced. That loss would badly cripple the British right division, which held Detroit and most of Michigan Territory. It could, in fact, affect the balance of naval power on Lake Erie, where the Americans were building another fleet.

If the Americans could win Lake Erie, Detroit would be regained, and the entire right wing of the British army would be in peril. For the Americans that was the plus side of the triumph at Little York.

But Dearborn was embarrassed by the continued looting which made a mockery of the terms of surrender. He realized he couldn't control his own troops and wanted nothing more than to leave as soon as the fleet was ready. He was only too happy to turn civilian control of the town back to the magistrates.

On May 1 the fleet made ready to sail. A storm kept the troops trapped and seasick on board the fleet for the best part of the week. The fourteen hundred troops that attacked York were reduced through injury, illness, and death to one thousand effective fighting men, but reinforcements were on their way. Dearborn expected six hundred men to join him at Oswego and more at Buffalo, while another thousand were waiting at Sackets Harbor.

For the people of York, the invasion marked a watershed. Nothing could ever be quite the same again. Those who fought the good fight with weapons or with words would occupy a special place in the community— especially Strachan, who became one of the leaders of the future. The lines were drawn. Those who aided the Americans, by word as much as by deed, were seen as traitors.

The militia, though it saw little action, was the darling of the community. The regulars, who bore the brunt of the fighting, were criticized as men who cared only about saving their skins. That was completely unfair. Seven eminent citizens berated Sheaffe, whose name "is odious to all ranks of people." Strachan wrote that the citizens were "indignant rather than dispirited and while they feel the disgrace of their defeat they console themselves with a conviction that it was owing entirely to their commander." His message to the Governor General, Sir George Prevost, was blunt: "Sheaffe must go."

Prevost couldn't agree with that armchair assessment, especially as neither the chaplain of York nor any of his colleagues could suggest what they might have done in the circumstances. But the Governor General was a practical politician and a diplomat. Sheaffe had outlived his usefulness. He was not sent back as an administrator. Eventually he was replaced by a Swiss-born major-general, Francis De Rottenburg. That was two months in the future. In the meantime, without any official rank, but all the power he needed, John Strachan reigned supreme.

CHAPTER THREE

The Fall of Fort George

FOLLOWING THE ATTACK ON YORK, THE AMERICANS DECIDED ON AN IMMEDI-
ATE LANDING AT THE MOUTH OF THE NIAGARA RIVER TO SEIZE FORT GEORGE,
NEAR THE PRESENT SITE OF NIAGARA-ON-THE-LAKE. THE PLAN WAS TO SEIZE
THE DEFENDING ARMY AND THEN ROLL UP THE ENTIRE NIAGARA PENINSULA.
FOR THIS THEY HAD SIXTEEN WARSHIPS AND SEVEN THOUSAND MEN. THE
BRITISH HAD EIGHTEEN HUNDRED REGULAR SOLDIERS SPREAD ALONG THE
NIAGARA FRONTIER. MOST OF THE MILITIA, HOWEVER, HAD RETURNED TO
THEIR FARMS — FOR IT WAS THAT KIND OF WAR, WHEN MEN PLOUGHED THE
FIELDS ONE DAY AND SHOULDERED A MUSKET THE NEXT.

Major-General Dearborn, ill and indecisive, dallied for a fortnight
before launching his invasion. It came on May 27, 1813.

Like John Strachan before him, Brigadier-General John Vincent, the
commander of the fort, looked out that morning at another alarming spectacle.

The curtain of fog lifted, as in a theatre, and there was now revealed to
him and his staff a spectacle he would never forget—sixteen ships standing
out from the lakeshore, sweeping toward him in a two-mile (3-km) arc.
Behind them on tow lines, 134 open boats, scows, and bateaux, crowded
with men and artillery, moved steadily toward the Canadian side.

Now the cannon began to thunder—fifty-one guns in action on the
lake, and another twenty from the American Fort Niagara across the river,
pouring a hail of iron and exploding shells across the fields and roads. The
barrage was so powerful that the people of York, forty miles (65 km) across
the lake, distinctly heard the rumble of the guns.

The enemy was manoeuvring to catch the British batteries in a crossfire
and the effect was shattering. One battery at the lighthouse managed to get
off a single shot before it was destroyed. Another at Two Mile Creek to the

west had to be abandoned. As the fleet continued its majestic movement forward, three schooners moved close to the shore to cover the landing at Cookstown, a huddle of farmhouses near the mouth of Two Mile Creek.

In a thicket overlooking this potential invasion point, Vincent had hidden a guard of fifty Mohawk under their celebrated Scottish chief, John Norton. A hail of missiles fired at point-blank range pierced the hiding place, killing two Indians and wounding several others before the main body fled.

On board his flagship, General Dearborn, still too ill to lead the attack himself, watched nervously as the assault boats moved toward the shore.

He could see a young naval officer, Oliver Hazard Perry, directing the fire from an open boat, standing tall in the stern, in full uniform, ignoring enemy musket fire. He was rowed from vessel to vessel telling each where to anchor to achieve the best field of fire. With that done, he boarded the *Madison*, determined to have nothing further to do with the invasion, which he believed to be badly planned and poorly carried out. He was eager for action, but his advice was ignored, and he had no intention of taking the blame for any disasters that might result.

Then he had a sudden change of heart. The one man he admired, Colonel Winfield Scott, Dearborn's adjutant-general, was in danger. Perry saw that he was being blown off course in the leading flatboat and was about to miss the landing point. Perry begged to be allowed to avert that disaster, leaped into his boat, picked up Scott, and with his help herded the scattered assault craft back on course. At that point a lookout on the mast of the schooner, *Hamilton*, shouted that the whole British army was advancing on the double to block the landing.

Most of the American officers didn't believe the British would make a stand. That view was reinforced by a high bank which concealed the defending troops. But Perry sensed danger. He set off to warn Scott, slipping in and out between the advancing ships. As he reached the lead assault boat, the British fired a volley. Confusion followed. The soldiers began firing wildly in every direction. Perry, fearing they would shoot each other, yelled to them to row to shore.

Scott echoed the order. He was in charge of twenty boats containing eight hundred men and a three-pound (1.4-kg) cannon. He ordered his men to advance three hundred paces across the beach and then wait for the first wave of infantry—fifteen hundred troops under Brigadier-General John Boyd.

Into the water they went, through the spray and onto the sand. As they dashed for the bank, the next wave approached the beach. The water turned to foam under the torrent of musketry.

At the same time, Scott's assault force reached the crest of the twelve-foot (4-m) clay bank. The British hurled them back down the cliff. Scott—a gigantic figure, six feet five inches (2 m) tall—was unmistakable. One of the Glengarrys attacked him with a bayonet but Scott dodged away, lost his footing, and tumbled back down the bank.

Dearborn, on board the *Madison*, saw this and uttered an agonizing cry: "He is lost! He is killed!"

But Scott picked himself up and led a second charge up the bank. The British retreated to the cover of the ravine. Then Lieutenant-Colonel Christopher Myers, Vincent's acting quartermaster-general, led a second attack and Scott was again forced back.

Now two lines of men faced each other at a distance of no more than ten yards (9 m). For the next fifteen minutes they fired away at point-blank range, and a scene of carnage followed. On the British side every field officer and most junior officers were casualties. The British were forced back, leaving a hundred corpses piled on the bank. An American surgeon counted four hundred dead and wounded men strewn over a plot no longer than two hundred yards (180 m) and no broader than fifteen (14 m).

As reinforcements arrived, the British retreated stubbornly from ravine to ravine back toward the little town of Newark. By now with more troops landing on the beach, and another American column massing farther up the river, Vincent realized that nothing could save the fort.

With tears in his eyes, he sent a note ordering that the magazine be blown up, and the garrison evacuate the fort to rejoin the retreating army on the Queenston Road.

The British retreated swiftly and silently toward the village of St. Davids as a main magazine blew up, hurling a crowd of debris into the air and causing a piece of timber to knock Scott off his horse and break his collarbone. But the Americans were in danger of winning another hollow victory and

Scott knew it—for the British were melting away. He hoisted his big frame back on his injured horse and galloped off in the wake of his own troops, who were already picking up British stragglers.

Scott did not reckon on the timidity of his commanding officer. Dearborn couldn't make a decision. He turned direct command over to Major-General Morgan Lewis, a politician, not a soldier, who loved playing commander and revelled in pomp and ceremony, but was terrified of making a mistake.

Lewis sent two messengers forward to restrain Scott, who was eager to bag the British. Scott had to abandon his plans, under a direct order to withdraw to Fort George. He could see the rearguard of the British army disappearing into the woods. The defeated columns were marching off in perfect order with much of their equipment intact, which lessened the American triumph. Once again the invaders had cracked the shell of the nut, but lost the kernel. Trapped all year in Fort George, unable to break out for long because of Vincent's raiders lurking on the outskirts, an entire American army would shortly be reduced to illness, idleness, and frustration.

> *He turned direct command over to Major-General Morgan Lewis, a politician, not a soldier, who loved playing commander and revelled in pomp and ceremony, but was terrified of making a mistake.*

Dearborn's immediate instinct was to move his troops to the head of the lake by water and cut off the British retreat. For that venture, he needed the enthusiastic cooperation of the fleet and its commodore, Isaac Chauncey, aged forty-one—a pear-shaped figure with a pear-shaped head, double-chin, and sleepy eyes. The navy had been Chauncey's life. He was determined to win naval superiority on Lake Ontario. It was this that obsessed him more than anything else. As he saw it, his task was to build as many ships as possible and then preserve them from attack, and to destroy the enemy's fleet. But the fear of losing the contest, and thus losing the lake, made him wary and overcautious.

Chauncey did not dare. Before he attacked the British flotilla, everything had to be right—wind, weather, naval superiority. But since nothing could ever be quite right for Chauncey, this war would be a series of frustrations.

He and his equally cautious opposite number, Sir James Yeo, flitted about the lake, avoiding decisive action—always waiting for the right moment, which never came.

Finally, word came that a British fleet was at the other end of the lake, attacking Sackets Harbor. That attack failed, but the Americans panicked. They briefly set fire to their own partially built warship, *General Pike*, thus delaying its launch date. That was enough for Chauncey, who left the Niagara frontier, taking all his ships and two thousand troops. It was a withdrawal that allowed Vincent's army to reach the protection of the heights above Burlington Bay (near the present city of Hamilton). If the Americans were to dislodge them, they would have to proceed by land.

The Battle of Stoney Creek

NOW THE GREATER PART OF THE NIAGARA PENINSULA WAS IN AMERICAN HANDS. THE INVADERS, HAVING SEIZED FORT GEORGE AT THE MOUTH OF THE NIAGARA AND ALSO FORT ERIE, SOME THIRTY MILES (50 KM) UPRIVER, WERE ADVANCING TOWARD THE BURLINGTON HEIGHTS. THERE, VINCENT'S SMALL FORCE OF SEVEN HUNDRED REGULARS WAS DUG IN. BUT HOW COULD HE HOLD OUT AGAINST THREE THOUSAND AMERICANS?

None of that concerned young Billy Green, a high-spirited youth of nineteen, living near Stoney Creek, not far from Burlington. For Billy, the war was a lark. When he and his older brother, Levi, heard the Americans were only a few kilometres away, they couldn't restrain their excitement. They simply had to have a good look at the advancing army.

Billy was the youngest of Adam Green's seven children. Left motherless almost at birth, he was known as a loner and a woodsman who could shinny up any tree and swing from branch to branch like a monkey. Now, at six o'clock on the humid spring morning of June 5, he and Levi clambered up the Niagara escarpment and made their way south until they reached a point above the American camp at the mouth of Forty Mile Creek.

That noon, hidden from view, they watched the Americans marching by and waited until almost all had passed. Then they began to yell like Indians—a sound that sent a chill through the stragglers.

"I tell you, those simple fellows did run," is the way Billy described it.

They scampered back along the ridge and then scrambled down to the road the soldiers had just passed over. There they ran into one lone American, one boot off, tying a rag onto his blistered foot. When he went for his musket, Levi Green hit him with a stick. The resulting yells of pain drew a rattle of musket fire from the rearguard. At that the brothers dashed back up the slope, whooping like Indians, until they reached Levi Green's cabin on a piece of benchland.

The sound of war whoops and gunfire drew several settlers from their homes. A small crowd looked down from the brow of the hill at the Americans marching through the village of Stoney Creek—a scattered huddle of log cabins and taverns. Some of the marchers halted long enough to fire at the hill. One musket ball came so close it struck a fence rail directly in front of Levi's wife, Tina, who was holding their oldest child, Hannah, in her arms.

Now the brothers went down to the village, where their sister, Kezia Corman, told them the Americans had taken her husband, Isaac, a prisoner. Billy started off at a dead run across Stoney Creek, whistling for his brother-in-law. A few moments later he heard an owl hoot and knew it was Isaac. The missing man had made his escape by pretending to be friendly to the American cause—a believable enough pretence in this province.

Isaac simply told the major who captured him that he was a Kentuckian. And the major promptly let him go. When Corman explained he couldn't get through the American lines, his captor gave him the countersign of the day. It was Wil-Hen-Har—the first syllables of the name of the American general, William Henry Harrison.

Billy Green now owned a vital piece of information. He knew what he had to do. He had to get a message to the British at Burlington. He borrowed his brother's horse, Tip, and rode him as far as he could. Then he tied him to a fence and made his way to the British lines on foot.

At that very hour the British were planning to gamble on a night raid on the American camp. Lieutenant-Colonel John Harvey had already scouted the American position and thought it vulnerable. He was by far the most experienced officer in the division. At thirty-four, he was thirteen years younger than his commander, Vincent, and had spent more than half his life in active service around the world.

The hawk-faced Harvey was a firm believer in accurate information bought at any price, and also in a series of bold and active offensive moves to throw the enemy on the defensive. Now he acted on these two convictions. He had not only scouted the enemy himself, but one of his subalterns, James FitzGibbon of the 49th, an especially bold and enterprising officer, had disguised himself as a butter peddler and actually entered the American camp to observe the location of troops and guns.

Harvey, then, was able to report that the Americans were badly scattered, their cannon was poorly placed, and their cavalry too far in the rear to be useful. He urged an immediate attack by night at bayonet point. It was their only chance, for ammunition was low; the American fleet might arrive at any moment.

Now, thanks to young Billy Green, Harvey had the countersign. He asked Billy if he knew the way to the American camp.

"Every inch of it," replied Billy proudly.

Harvey gave him a corporal's sword, which Billy kept for the rest of his long life, and told him to take the lead. It was eleven thirty. The troops, sleeping on the grass, were aroused and the column set off on a seven-mile (11-km) march through the black night. It was so dark the men could scarcely see each other. The moon was masked by heavy clouds. The tall pines added to the gloom. A soft mist blurred the trails. Only the occasional flash of heat lightning relieved the blackness.

It was so dark the men could scarcely see each other. The moon was masked by heavy clouds. The tall pines added to the gloom.

The soldiers plodded forward in silence, their footfalls muffled by the mud of the trail. Harvey had cautioned against uttering so much as a whisper. Even the flints had been removed from the firelocks to prevent the accidental firing of a musket. Billy Green, loping on ahead, found he had left the column behind and had to retrace his steps to urge more speed—otherwise it would be daylight before the quarry was flushed. "Well," someone in the ranks was heard to mutter, "that would be soon enough to be killed."

By three, on this sultry Sunday morning, Harvey's force reached the first American sentry post. Later, nobody could remember the exact order of events that followed. Someone fired a musket. One sentry at least was quietly bayonetted. Another demanded the countersign and Billy Green gave it to him, at the same time seizing his gun with one hand and killing him with his new sword held in the other.

An American advance party of fifty men, quartered in a church, were overpowered and taken prisoner. The Americans were camped on a low grassy meadow through which a branch of Stoney Creek trickled. The main road ran over the creek and climbed the ridge. Its crest was marked by a tangle of trees and roots behind which most of the American infantry and guns were located.

The British could see the glow of the American campfires directly ahead. Moving forward to bayonet the sleeping enemy, they discovered to their disappointment that the meadow was empty. The Americans had left their cooking fires earlier to take up a stronger position on the ridge.

Now the attackers fixed flints. But all hope of surprise was lost, because they were easily spotted in the campfire glow. As they dashed forward whooping like the Indians to terrify the enemy, they were met by a sheet of flame. All was confusion. The musket smoke added to the thickness of the night, and the howls of the British mingled with the sinister *click click click* of muskets being reloaded. All sense of formation was lost. As some fled, others advanced, and friend had difficulty distinguishing foe in the darkness.

The enterprising FitzGibbon, seeing the men retreating on the left, ran along the line to restore order. The left flank held. Five hundred Americans were put to flight. But on their right the British were being pushed back by more than two thousand men. The guns on the ridge were doing heavy damage. But as Harvey had guessed, the Americans' centre was weak, because the guns did not have close infantry support.

Major Charles Plenderleath of the 49th realized his men had no chance unless the guns were captured. He called for volunteers. Alexander Fraser, a huge sergeant, only nineteen years old, gathered twenty men and with his commander sprinted up the road to rush the guns. Two volleys roared over their heads, but before the gunners could reload they were bayonetted. Plenderleath and Fraser cut right through, driving all before them, stabbing horses and men with crazy abandon. The American line was cut, four of six guns captured, and one hundred prisoners seized.

The American commander, Brigadier-General John Chandler, a former blacksmith, tavern keeper, and congressman, received his appointment because of political influence rather than military experience, of which he had none. He was up at the first musket shot, galloping about on his horse, shouting orders, trying to rally his scattered troops. He spent the rest of his life defending his actions that night.

His horse stumbled, threw him to the ground, and knocked him sense-less. By the time he recovered, all was confusion. He saw a group of men by the guns, which to his dismay did not seem to be firing. He rushed forward, mistaking the men of the British 49th for his own, realized his error too late, tried to hide under a gun carriage, and was quickly hauled out by Sergeant Fraser, who made him prisoner.

His second-in-command, William Winder, a former Baltimore lawyer and another political appointee, was also lost. He was about to fire when Fraser appeared. "If you stir, you die," said the sergeant. Winder threw down his pistol and his sword and surrendered.

The American command now fell to the cavalry officer, Colonel James Burns, whose troops were too far in the rear to be effective during the attack. Burns and his horsemen roared down on the British, cut through the lines and opened fire, only to find they were shooting at their own comrades who were wandering about firing at one another. Friend and foe were now entangled, both sides taking prisoners and neither knowing how the battle was going. Vincent himself was knocked from his horse and separated from his staff, lost somewhere in the woods, stumbling about in the wrong direc-tion.

Each force left the field believing the other victorious. Harvey decided to withdraw without Vincent before the Americans could recover from their confusion. But the Americans were also preparing to flee, as William Hamilton Merritt, the leader of the volunteer dragoons, discovered when he rode back to the field shortly after dawn, seeking his missing commander. He was able to report the Americans were in a panic, destroying everything that couldn't be removed. In their haste, they didn't even stop to bury their dead.

The British returned to the Stoney Creek battlefield that afternoon to find guns, stores, and baggage still scattered about the field among the litter of the dead. Vincent turned up last, exhausted and half-famished, his sword, hat, and horse missing.

The American retreat continued. Dearborn, at Fort George, ordered Morgan Lewis to attack the British again at Stoney Creek. But Lewis moved so slowly that he was of little use. Meanwhile the British fleet, under Sir James Yeo, appeared outside the mouth of the Niagara River apparently threatening Fort George. Dearborn sent a note to Lewis to get back as fast as he could.

As the British vessels moved up to Forty Mile Creek, Lewis retired, abandoning his supplies in such haste that the occupying British seized 600 tents, 200 camp kettles, 140 barrels of flour, 150 muskets, and a baggage train of 20 boats for which the Americans had neglected to supply an escort.

Within three days of the battle of Stoney Creek, the situation along the Niagara frontier had been reversed. The Americans had been in full possession of the peninsula, outnumbering the British defenders at least three to one. The command at Montreal was prepared to evacuate most of the province, to sacrifice the militia, and pull back the regulars to Kingston. But as the result of a single unequal contest, hastily planned at the last moment and fought in absolute darkness by confused and disorganized men, the invaders had lost control.

On June 9, the Americans burned Fort Erie and evacuated all the defence posts along the Niagara River, retiring in a body behind the log palisades of Fort George. Except for a few brief raids, that would be their prison until winter forced them back across the river to American soil.

CHAPTER FIVE

Laura Secord's Journey

THE AMERICANS WERE BOTTLED UP IN FORT GEORGE AND THE BRITISH MEANT TO KEEP THEM THERE. THE AMERICANS, ON THEIR PART, WANTED TO BURST OUT AND MAKE ANOTHER ATTEMPT TO SEIZE THE NIAGARA PENINSULA. AND SO THE WAR, THAT SUMMER OF *1813*, BECAME A SECRET WAR. SOLDIERS FROM BOTH ARMIES, OFTEN DISGUISED AS CIVILIANS, SOMETIMES PRETENDING TO BE ON THE OPPOSITE SIDE, CREPT THROUGH THE FORESTS TO LAUNCH LIGHTNING ATTACKS AGAINST THEIR FORMER NEIGHBOURS. CIVILIANS, TOO, BATTLED CIVILIANS AND, SINCE EVERYBODY SPOKE THE SAME LANGUAGE, IT WAS DIFFICULT TO TELL FRIEND FROM FOE.

Lieutenant James FitzGibbon headed a troop of British mounted soldiers ("dragoons") known as "The Bloody Boys" and disguised as civilians. At the same time, an American surgeon, Dr. Cyrenius Chapin, rode at the head of a body of American mounted volunteers, plundering the homes of Canadian settlers. Chapin was a medical man who had once practiced on the Canadian side of the border and so knew most of his adversaries by sight.

FitzGibbon was determined to stop Chapin and his forays. On June 21 he left his men hidden near Lundy's Lane, not far from Niagara Falls, and moved up the road on his own, seeking information about Chapin's movements. He spotted a fluttering handkerchief waved by Mrs. James Kerby, the wife of a local militia captain, who ran to him and urged him to flee. Chapin, she told him, had just passed through at the head of two hundred men.

FitzGibbon had no intention of running away. He spotted an enemy's horse hitched to a post in front of Deffield's Inn. He rode up, dismounted, and burst in. An American rifleman covered him, but FitzGibbon, who was wearing a grey-green overall over his uniform as a disguise, clasped him by the hand, claiming they were old friends. Having thus thrown the enemy off guard, he seized his rifle barrel and ordered him to surrender.

The man refused and clung to his own weapon, trying to fire it while his comrade levelled his own piece at FitzGibbon. FitzGibbon turned about, kept the first rifle clamped in his right hand, caught the other's with his left and forced it down until it pointed at his comrade. Now he exercised his great strength to drag both men out of the tavern, all three swearing and calling on one another to surrender.

Up ran Mrs. Kerby, begging and threatening. Up scampered a small boy, who hurled rocks at the Americans. The trio continued to struggle, until one of the Americans managed to pull FitzGibbon's sword from its sheath. But just as he was about to thrust it into his opponent's chest, Mrs. Deffield, the tavern keeper's wife, kicked the weapon out of his hand.

The trio continued to struggle, until one of the Americans managed to pull FitzGibbon's sword from its sheath. But just as he was about to thrust it into his opponent's chest, Mrs. Deffield, the tavern keeper's wife, kicked the weapon out of his hand.

FitzGibbon threw one of his assailants against the steps and disarmed him. The other was attacked by the tavern keeper. FitzGibbon mounted his horse and, driving his two prisoners before him, made his escape before Chapin's main force arrived.

At this point the Niagara Peninsula was a no man's land. The populace was split between those loyal to the British cause and the others who had flocked to the American side. For most people the best policy was to lie low and try to keep out of trouble. But there were some who were prepared to risk their lives to harass the Americans. It was FitzGibbon's task to aid these partisans and help keep the enemy off balance and penned up in Fort George by ambushes and skirmishes. His fifty volunteers were disguised in the same grey-green coveralls and trained in guerrilla warfare. FitzGibbon was the perfect leader for such a force—a popular officer, unconventional, immensely strong and lithe.

The day after he escaped from Cyrenius Chapin's marauders, FitzGibbon took his men to the two-storey stone house owned by a militia captain, John De Cew, not far from Beaver Dams on Twelve Mile Creek, about seventeen miles (27 km) from Fort George.

The De Cew house formed the apex of a triangle of defence the British had thrown up to keep the Americans bottled up at Fort George. At the left base of the triangle, seven miles (11 km) away at the mouth of Twelve Mile Creek, Major Peter De Haren was stationed with three companies of regulars. At the right base, farther up the lake on the heights above Twenty Mile Creek, Lieutenant-Colonel Cecil Bisshopp was posted with a small brigade of light infantry. Merritt's provincial dragoons, FitzGibbon's Bloody Boys, Norton's Mohawks, and Captain Dominique Ducharme's band of Caughnawaga Indians patrolled the intervening countryside.

It was all very romantic—men on horseback, often disguised, riding at night, cutting and thrusting, taking prisoners, making hairbreadth escapes. But for those whose homes were plundered and whose menfolk were killed and wounded, it was also tragic.

Then, on June 23 just after sunset, a Canadian legend was born. A slight and delicate little Loyalist arrived at the De Cew house to announce that she had an important message for FitzGibbon. This was Mrs. James Secord— Laura Secord—aged thirty-eight, wife of a militia man badly wounded at the Battle of Queenston Heights, and mother of five.

Mrs. Secord told FitzGibbon that she had heard from Americans in Queenston that an attack was being planned on the De Cew headquarters the following day. To carry her warning, she had made her way on foot through the dreaded Black Swamp that lay between Queenston and De Cew's house, staying clear of the main roads in order to avoid capture. She was exhausted but game, triumphant after her long journey, which had apparently taken her, at some risk, through the camp of the Caughnawagas.

Mrs. Secord's warning caused FitzGibbon to alert Norton's Mohawks to keep his men posted all night to warn of an impending attack. None came. Was her story then a fabrication? Hardly. She was the daughter of a Loyalist family. Her husband was still crippled from wounds caused by American soldiers. She hadn't struggled nineteen miles (30 km) in the boiling sun from Queenston, through St. Davids and across a treacherous morass, on a whim.

But there was a mystery to all this. Laura Secord never made it clear exactly how she had heard the rumour of an impending attack on the afternoon or evening of June 21. She was vague and contradictory about this detail, telling FitzGibbon that her husband learned of it from an American officer, but telling her granddaughter years later that she herself overhead it.

Her exhausting journey was even more baffling because it was undertaken on the thinnest evidence—an unproven rumour, flimsy as gossamer. On June 21 the Americans had yet to make any firm plans to attack De Cew's headquarters. Even Lieutenant-Colonel Charles Boerstler, the man chosen to lead the eventual attack, didn't know of it until the afternoon of June 23.

Who were those Americans in Queenston on June 21? They must have been Chapin's followers, for the regular troops had been called back to Fort George for fear of being cut off. Yet Chapin, by his own statement, knew nothing of any attack and would not hear of it until the orders were issued on June 23.

Yet *something* was in the wind. Had someone whispered a warning in Mrs. Secord's ear? Who? It was not in her interest to give her source. News travelled on wings on the Niagara frontier. Who knew what damage might be done if Laura revealed what she knew? Her invalid husband and children could easily be the objects of revenge on this peninsula of tangled loyalties.

Like everybody else who lived along the border, the Secords had friends on both sides. Before the war the people moved freely between the two countries, buying and selling, owning land, operating businesses without regard to nationality. Chapin's men were virtually neighbours. The Secords would have known most of them.

It may be that, in later years, when the past became fuzzy, Mrs. Secord simply couldn't remember the details of her source, though she seems to have remembered everything else. It was equally possible that she refused to identify her informant to save him and his descendants from the harsh whispers and bitter scandal of treason.

For all of her long life, Laura Secord told her story many times, adding to it more than once. A cow became part of the legend although, in truth, there never was a cow.

Her story was used to underline the growing myth that the War of 1812 was won by true-blue Canadians—in this case a brave Loyalist housewife who single-handedly saved the British army from defeat. That was an exaggeration, but it fitted neatly with John Strachan's own conviction that the Canadian militiamen, and not the British regulars or the Indians, were the real heroes.

CHAPTER SIX

The Battle of Beaver Dams

COOPED UP IN FORT GEORGE, THE AILING AMERICAN GENERAL, HENRY DEARBORN, KNEW HE MUST DO SOMETHING TO RESTORE HIS SHATTERED REPUTATION. THE ENEMY HAD ESCAPED HIM AT FORT YORK AND BEATEN HIM AT STONEY CREEK. NOW FITZGIBBON'S MOUNTED MARAUDERS WERE CREATING HAVOC ALONG THE PENINSULA.

Dearborn decided to mount a massive excursion to wipe out the Bloody Boys. He had just learned that FitzGibbon had made his headquarters at the De Cew house. He figured that five hundred men and two guns, guided by Chapin and his followers, could do the job.

He turned the details over to his second-in-command, Brigadier-General John Boyd, a former soldier of fortune. Boyd was no more popular than his predecessor, Morgan Lewis, who thought him a bully and a show-off and who had warned against just the sort of attack that Boyd and Dearborn were now contemplating.

In fact, the command at Fort George was torn with petty jealousies. There was little love lost between Dr. Chapin, who would guide the expedition, and the officer chosen to lead it, Lieutenant-Colonel Charles Boerstler. Boerstler was a thirty-five-year-old regular from Maryland, who despised the self-appointed civilian leader. Yet the surgeon appeared to be the more warlike of the two. The sallow-faced Boerstler was unusually sensitive to imagined insults. Chapin was a lithe six-footer (2 m) with a great beak of a nose and piercing blue eyes, known for his boldness as well as for his ego. He couldn't stand Boerstler, whom he called "a broken down Methodist preacher." Boerstler in his turn had no use for Chapin, whom he called "a vain and boasting liar."

Nor did Boerstler like either Boyd or Winfield Scott, both of whom had been involved in what he considered insults to his abilities. Chapin tried to put off Boerstler's appointment, but the high command, knowing Boerstler to be touchy, wasn't prepared to offend him.

The expedition was hastily and imperfectly planned. No attempt was made to divert the posts at the other two corners of the defensive triangle while De Cew's house was being attacked. There was no reserve on which Boerstler could fall back in case of disaster. The problem was the lack of men—half the army being too sick to fight. Boerstler had been promised a body of riflemen, essential in the kind of bush fighting that was certain to take place, but these sharpshooters were needed for guard duty. He marched off without them.

Boerstler sent patrols to prevent any citizen from escaping with news of the troops' advance. (Laura Secord had been at FitzGibbon's headquarters for more than twenty-four hours.) At daybreak the detachment moved on to St. Davids, where it surprised two Caughnawagas. One was shot, but the other escaped to warn Major De Haren of the Americans' advance.

The Americans moved in a column up the side of the Niagara escarpment, halted at the top, moved on again for about a kilometre past an open

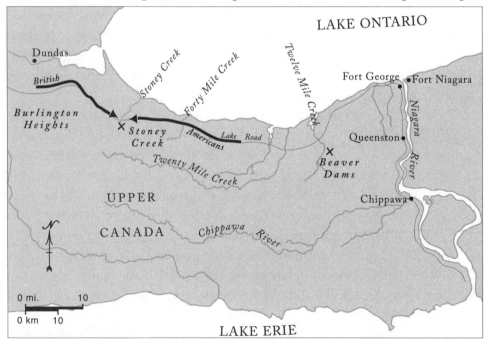

Niagara Peninsula 1813

field and into a narrow ravine bordered on both sides by thick woods. It was here that the Battle of Beaver Dams began.

Francis Dominique Ducharme, a forty-eight-year-old veteran of twenty-five years' service in the western fur country, was the leader of the Caughnawaga Indians. He persuaded De Haren to allow him to move out of his original position, in order to ambush the Americans in the woods. The Indians killed every one of Chapin's advance guard at the outset of the battle.

Boerstler ordered his wagons and horses to the rear, out of the enemy fire, formed up Chapin's men, and led a charge against the Indians—a charge made futile by his lack of experienced sharpshooters.

To Chapin he was a blunderer. It was Chapin who, according to his later account, foresaw the Indian ambush and warned his commander. He was in the act of driving the Natives through the woods when he was called back against his will by the timid and hesitant Boerstler.

There were several versions of the Battle of Beaver Dams, but one thing was clear: by noon the attacking troops were exhausted. Boerstler, feeling

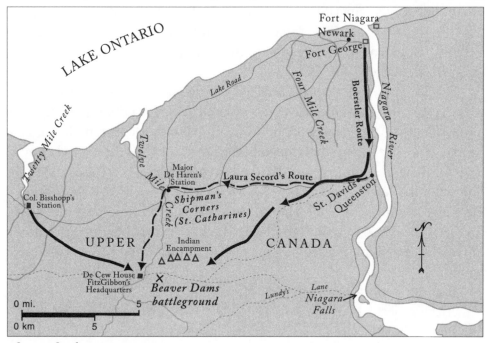

The Battle of Beaver Dams

hemmed in by the woods and the hidden Indians, had made the mistake of leading his men forward and keeping them for too long under heavy fire. In fact, his detachment was too small and his plans imperfect and hurried. The troops had been up since dawn, had marched eleven miles (18 km) without refreshment, had fought for three hours under the blazing sun, and had exhausted their ammunition.

At that moment, James FitzGibbon appeared on the scene, carrying a white flag and demanding an American surrender. He had actually been in the area for some time. He had been alerted in the morning, by Ducharme's Caughnawaga scouts, to the presence of an enemy column advancing on his post. He had scouted the battlefields and sent for his men. But he could not depend on the Indians, who were coming and going on whim. No one was capable of forcing a surrender, and Ducharme couldn't speak English. So FitzGibbon decided upon a bluff and strode forward, white flag in hand.

Boerstler sent his artillery captain, McDowell, to meet him. The two parleyed. FitzGibbon resorted to a tried-and-true threat. He said he had been dispatched by Major De Haren to inform the Americans that they were surrounded by a superior force of British, that they couldn't escape, and that the Indians were infuriated to the point of massacre. But Boerstler refused to surrender. He wasn't accustomed, he said, to surrender to an army he hadn't seen.

FitzGibbon's bluff had been called. There was no unseen army—only Ducharme and his Caughnawagas. Nonetheless, FitzGibbon boldly proposed that the Americans send an officer to examine De Haren's force. That would convince them that the odds against them were overwhelming, he said. Boerstler agreed, but declared he would not surrender unless he found himself badly outnumbered. FitzGibbon then retired to pretend that he was consulting with De Haren, who wasn't anywhere near the scene. Instead he ran into Captain John Hall, who had just ridden up with a dozen provincial dragoons. FitzGibbon persuaded him to impersonate the absent major.

Back he went to report that De Haren had agreed to receive one of the American officers. Boerstler sent a subaltern, who encountered Hall, thinking him to be De Haren. Hall, thinking quickly, declared that it would be humiliating to display his force, but insisted it was quite large enough to compel surrender. Boerstler, weak from loss of blood from wounds sustained in the battle, asked for time to decide. FitzGibbon gave him five minutes, explaining he couldn't control his Indians much longer.

"For God's sake," cried Boerstler, "keep the Indians from us!" And with the spectacle of massacre never far from his mind, he agreed to surrender.

FitzGibbon now faced a problem. How could his tiny force disarm five hundred of the enemy without his deception being discovered—especially when the real Major De Haren was nowhere to be found? Fortunately a more senior officer, Lieutenant-Colonel John Clark, arrived, followed shortly after by De Haren himself with a body of troops.

But FitzGibbon had one other problem. He must explain his deception to De Haren before the major unwittingly revealed it to the enemy. In addition, he wanted credit for the surrender and feared that De Haren would rob him of it. To his discomfiture, De Haren brushed him aside. He was clearly about to offer surrender conditions on his own to Boerstler.

At this, FitzGibbon stepped up quickly, laid his hand on the neck of the major's horse, and spoke in a low, firm voice: "Not another word, sir; these are my prisoners."

Then he stepped back and cried loudly, "Shall I disarm the American troops?"

To that De Haren had to agree.

FitzGibbon still feared the major, by some remark, might ruin everything. The Americans could easily overwhelm them if the deception was revealed. He quickly ordered the troops into file and, as soon as some were formed, rapped out an order to the men to march, thus driving Boerstler and De Haren forward to prevent conversation between them.

The marching Americans, still armed, were rapidly approaching FitzGibbon's small force of Bloody Boys. He suggested to De Haren that the captives ground arms at once.

"No," said De Haren harshly, "let them march through between our men and ground their arms on the other side."

"What folly," thought FitzGibbon. "When they see our handful, will they really ground their weapons?"

He turned to De Haren: "Do you think it prudent to march them through with arms in their hands in the presence of the Indians?"

At the mention of the dreaded word *Indians*, Boerstler threw up a hand. "For God's sake, sir, do what this officer bids you!"

De Haren agreed, the prisoners dropped their weapons, and the Indians appeared from behind trees and bushes and rushed toward them. FitzGibbon, springing up on a stump, shouted that no one would be hurt and allowed the Indians to plunder the muskets, knives, swords, and other equipments.

The Battle of Beaver Dams had confirmed the inability of the invaders to break out of their prison at Fort George. Boerstler had lost more than five hundred men, including Chapin and twenty-one of his mounted corps. The big doctor wasn't a prisoner for long. Later on he succeeded in overpowering his captors and escaping.

Dearborn was stunned by the disaster, describing the Battle of Beaver Dams as "an unfortunate and unaccountable event." But generals must be accountable. When the news reached Washington, there was an immediate demand for the sick old soldier's removal. His officers urged him to move the army back to American soil, but a council of war agreed to hold fast. Dearborn, however, was himself removed, as much to his own relief as to that of his officers.

CHAPTER SEVEN

The Second Attack on York

Panic again struck York at the end of July 1813. Square sails were seen on the lake — white jibs, red stripes and blue stars flying from the stern. With a new American warship finally launched at Sackets Harbor, the naval balance on Lake Ontario had changed again. The Americans were back in force on this humid summer morning of July 31 — at least a dozen vessels nearing the harbour.

By the time the leading vessels anchored off the garrison, the town was all but empty of men. It was true that they had given their parole but they did not trust the Americans. Along the Niagara frontier other paroled military officers had been bundled up and taken across the border to captivity on foreign soil, and so the men of York were taking no chances.

William Allen, a merchant and militia major, reached the Playter farmhouse on north Yonge Street. There, with the help of Ely Playter and his brother, he concealed a boatload of five thousand cartridges and another crammed with baggage in a marsh near the Don River. Then he moved north and hid out in the woods.

Through the silent streets of the empty town, two men made their way to the garrison. Grant Powell, the son of the chief justice, had elected to stay. And so, of course, had the Reverend Dr. Strachan. (Who would dare imprison *him*?) They reached the garrison about two o'clock and waited for developments.

They watched the largest vessels come to anchor at three o'clock. The wind was so light that the schooners, trailing behind, had to use their sweeps. At four, they saw the boats put off. Two hundred and fifty men landed without opposition. All the available British troops had long since retired to defend Burlington Heights.

Carrying a white flag, Strachan tackled the first officer to reach the shore and demanded to be taken to the commodore, Isaac Chauncey. With Winfield Scott at his elbow, Chauncey was cordial enough. Indeed, he expressed regret at the theft of the books from the library the previous April, said he had made a search of the fleet for these books, had found several, and would return them. Strachan demanded to know what his intentions were. He pointed out that the present inhabitants of York were all women and children. Did he mean to destroy the community? If so, would he allow the removal of these non-combatants?

Chauncey reassured him. He planned no looting, only the seizure of public stores and the burning of all fortifications. The major purpose of the expedition was retaliation for British attacks on the far side of the lake. He did not say it, but the real reason for the expedition, surely, was the need to do *something*. Cooped up in Sackets Harbor and Fort George, the Americans were denied a naval confrontation by the elusive British commodore, Sir James Yeo. Stalemated in their attempts to seize the Niagara Peninsula, they needed action, any action.

Chauncey asked where the public stores were. Strachan and Powell would not tell him. It didn't matter because Chauncey already knew, or soon found out. He knew the state of York's defences. He knew the position of the army on Burlington Heights and knew every single transaction that had taken place in the town.

He also knew that some public stores had been hidden in William Allen's store and that Allen, himself a militia officer under parole, had been collecting and sending information to the British army and aiding in the forwarding of troops. Winfield Scott offered a five-hundred-dollar reward for Allen's capture and sent his men to break into the store. They seized everything, broke open several officers' trunks, gave away the contents, and burned a large quantity of hemp. Others opened the jail and released all the prisoners. When Strachan attempted to protest to Scott, the American colonel brushed him off and declared he would seize all the provisions he could find.

In this he had the aid of a group of disloyal Canadians. One of them, John Lyon, brought his wagon down Yonge Street to help the Americans move the captured flour to the boat. His crony, Calvin Wood, jailed for sedition, was one of those released from the York jail. Wood and several others went aboard the American ships to give the enemy information; in gratitude, his new-found friends gave him seven barrels of flour.

From these informants Chauncey learned that boatloads of arms, baggage, and ammunition had been hauled up the Don River. It was late in the evening. A half-hearted attempt to storm Burlington Heights had been called off. The fleet was about to leave. Now, however, the commodore postponed his departure. The following morning the troops disembarked, and three armed boats moved up the Don seeking the hidden supplies. But Ely Playter and his brother had already squirreled most of them away, and the searchers returned disappointed.

Charges of sedition and taunts of treason would be thrown at any who, by deed, word, or even gesture, appeared to support the American cause. It would no longer be wise to praise the American way of life.

The troops evacuated the town, burned the barracks and blockhouses, and returned to the ships. The fleet weighed anchor the following dawn and set sail for Sackets Harbor. Again, unaccountably, the Americans had decided not to occupy the capital and cut the line between Kingston and the British forces on the Niagara. The town breathed more freely. The inhabitants could not know that this was the last time a hostile flotilla would anchor in Toronto Bay. The new centre of action would be on Lake Erie two hundred miles (320 km) to the southwest.

War passed York by, but its effects lingered on long after hostilities ended. John Lyon, Calvin Wood, and a clutch of other dissidents would soon find themselves in jail. Charges of sedition and taunts of treason would be thrown at any who, by deed, word, or even gesture, appeared to support the American cause. It would no longer be wise to praise the American way of life.

A "committee of information" was about to come into being to take evidence from all loyal subjects who wished to inform on their neighbours. Its members were men of absolute loyalty and substance, the core of the Family Compact. For York—the future city of Toronto—the war was over. But in Upper Canada individual liberties were not a matter of pressing concern. Individualism, after all, was an American concept. "Liberty" was a Yankee word.

And so the campaign on the Niagara Peninsula ended where it had begun some three months before—in stalemate. The American invaders were still hived in Fort George. The rest of Upper Canada was scarred but defiant. The war was by no means over, but for the settlers, desperately trying to preserve their fields of barley and wheat, hostilities had passed them by.

INDEX

"Attack of Fort Oswego on Lake Ontario,
North America. May 6th 1814" by Captain William Steele.
Not since the War of 1812 have Canada and the United States
seen battles on the Great Lakes that straddle their borders.

THE BATTLE OF LAKE ERIE

CONTENTS

A Bloody Little War

WAR HAS ALWAYS BEEN A PAINFUL BUSINESS. WHETHER YOU ARE STRUCK BY A
SWORD, AN ARROW, A LANCE, A CANNONBALL, A PIECE OF SHRAPNEL, OR A BUL-
LET, IT HURTS DREADFULLY. YOU BLEED — SOMETIMES TO DEATH. YOU LOSE
YOUR ARM OR YOUR LEG. YOU ARE CRIPPLED, OFTEN FOR LIFE. IT HAS ALWAYS
BEEN, AND IT ALWAYS WILL BE.

The War of 1812 was a minor conflict in which the United States
attempted to invade Canada in order to punish Britain. It was also a bloody
affair, and the lake battle described in this book was as gory a skirmish as
any that took place in the larger arena of Europe. The decks of the ships that
fought each other on Lake Erie on that bright September day in 1813 were
slippery with the blood of seamen torn to pieces by cannon fire.

The Americans were furious because the British, locked in a life-and-
death battle with Napoleon Bonaparte's France, were boarding American
ships at sea and seizing every seaman born in Britain. The Americans could
not attack Britain three thousand miles (4,800 km) across the water, and so
they invaded the nearest British possession, Canada.

By the fall of 1813, the war had been raging for fifteen months. Three
American armies had tried to invade Canada and had been hurled back.
The British had seized Fort Detroit; the Americans had briefly occupied
Little York (Toronto) but were now hived behind the walls of Fort George
on the Niagara River, the only piece of Canadian territory they occupied.
The British, who had captured most of Michigan Territory, controlled Lake
Erie, where the bloodiest contest of the war would soon take place.

The Americans outnumbered the British regulars by seventeen thousand to seven thousand, but those figures don't tell us much. Many of
the American "regulars" were untrained recruits, and the British had an

additional two thousand Indians under the brilliant Shawnee war chief Tecumseh.

Both sides also had reserves of civilian soldiers: the militia. The American draftees, however, were called up only for short terms—as little as sixty days, as much as a year. With the exception of the Kentuckians, who loved to fight, most refused to serve beyond their term. Moreover, under the Constitution, they did not have to fight on foreign soil.

In Canada, all fit males between eighteen and sixty were obliged to serve in the Sedentary Militia. They were largely untrained and incompetent, but available in times of crisis.

The Incorporated Militia of Upper Canada was more efficient, its members having volunteered to fight for the duration of the war. Many, indeed, had joined up for patriotic reasons. In addition to the British regulars, there were also several Canadian regular units who fought as bravely and as efficiently as the British.

But these were not the neat-looking soldiers of the war paintings. On both sides, their uniforms were patched, tattered, and sometimes hanging in shreds. Shoes, tunics, and pantaloons were in short supply. There were times when the fighting men were described in official dispatches as "literally naked." Sanitation was primitive, and sickness widespread. Men sometimes went a year without being paid and hundreds deserted for that reason alone.

In battle after battle, the combatants on both sides were at least half-drunk. The doctors believed that a daily issue of spirits was essential to good health. In spite of that, the troops suffered and often died from measles, malaria, typhus, typhoid, influenza, and a variety of diseases that went under the vague names of "ague" or "lake fever."

The British were given a daily glass of strong Jamaica rum; the Americans were fed a quarter pint (200 mL) of raw whisky. Many a farm boy got his first taste of spirits in the army, and many were corrupted by it.

The lack of hospital supplies and proper food helped to lengthen the sick list. In Canada, almost every item the army and navy needed, from

> *In Canada, all fit males between eighteen and sixty were obliged to serve in the Sedentary Militia. They were largely untrained and incompetent, but available in times of crisis.*

rum to new uniforms, came by ship from overseas. Every scrap of canvas, every yard of rope, every anchor, cannonball, bolt, cable, and rivet came across the ocean to Montreal and was then taken by sleigh in winter or flat-boat in summer to places like Fort Amherstburg. There, the British were engaged in a mad race to finish their fleet before the Americans could complete theirs and fight the battle for control of Lake Erie. When our story opens in the summer of 1813, that race was at its height.

CHAPTER ONE

The Race to Build Fighting Ships

ON A SOFT DAY IN MAY 1798, A TWELVE-YEAR-OLD ENGLISH BOY, ROBERT BARCLAY, TAKES HIS LEAVE OF HIS FAMILY TO GO TO SEA. HE IS A SMALL, PLUMP CHILD WITH ROSY CHEEKS AND DARK EYES WHICH ARE ALREADY FILLED WITH TEARS. BUT, TEARS OR NOT, HE MUST SET OFF BY COACH TO JOIN A BRITISH FRIGATE AT GREENOCK. HE WEEPS BITTERLY AS HE TELLS AN INNKEEPER'S WIFE, "I AM ON MY WAY TO SEA AND WILL NEVER SEE FATHER, MOTHER, BROTHERS OR SISTERS AGAIN."

Sixteen years later, Captain Robert Heriot Barclay is a British naval commander in charge of the flotilla being built at Amherstburg, near the present site of Windsor, Ontario. He has spent half his life in the service of the British navy, rising from the rank of midshipman at twelve, to commander at the age of twenty-eight. Now he faces his greatest trial: Canada and Britain are at war with the United States. The ships of two opposing fleets are being hammered together out of green wood on the shores of Lake Erie. It is a race against time. Soon, Barclay knows they must face each other on these shallow, wind-blown waters. And no one can tell the outcome …

This is the story of the bloody battle that Barclay fought against his American opposite number, twenty-seven-year-old Commodore Oliver Hazard Perry. It was the only battle ever fought on any Canadian lake. We will never see another like it, because warfare has changed, ships have changed, and weapons have changed. But it makes an exciting tale, for the two fleets were evenly matched, and either side might have won.

This was the day of the sailing ship—a vessel driven solely by the uncertain wind. Thus, as Barclay and Perry both realized, they were the playthings of the weather. The wind could drive one flotilla directly into the midst of the other. If the wind was against you, however, you could only wait for the other side to attack, unless you attempted the awkward and often dangerous technique of zigzagging across the unruly waters.

A commander was, of course, trained to manoeuvre his ship, but he was faced with a second hazard: gunfire. Cannonballs wreaked terrible havoc in those days, tearing into the rigging, causing masts to topple, sails to rip, and lines to end up in a tangled confusion.

Without sails a ship would come to a dead stop; if its rudder was smashed by enemy fire, it couldn't be steered. As more cannonballs pounded the vessel and more men were mangled, the decks would become so slippery with blood that it was difficult for the seamen to go about their duties. Ships' commanders could be killed as they walked the deck, and often enough, when the next in line took over, he was killed too, until the entire vessel was under the command of an inexperienced junior, unable to manoeuvre in the heat of battle.

The ungainly ships with their tall masts and complicated rigging might then blunder into one another and become tangled with the rigging of a sister vessel. Driven by wind and inexpertly handled, they often collided. All these things happened during the Battle of Lake Erie.

Think of it—fifteen wooden sailing ships, prisoners of the wind, most of them built on those very shores that same summer, locked in a combat that see-sawed back and forth as the cannon roared and men died, half-hidden by the smoke of battle.

It was the second year of the War of 1812, and the United States was still trying to seize Canada. In those days, travel by land was difficult and sometimes impossible. The roads weren't much more than muddy trails—where there *were* roads. The only efficient way to move about was by ship on the Great Lakes.

And so the side that controlled the lakes in this bloody, senseless war controlled the war itself.

Therefore, in the late summer of 1813, the Americans were determined to seize all of Lake Erie so they could land another invading force on Canadian soil. That touched off a frantic race to build fighting ships on those empty, forested shores, each side racing to be the first to launch an attack on the other.

The carpenters had been at work all winter building an American fleet on the shores at Presqu'Isle Bay in the best natural harbour on the lake.

Now, in June, the half-constructed fleet was to be increased by five small vessels that Commodore Perry had seized from the British earlier that summer.

Let us meet Perry as he tosses in his bunk aboard the captured brig *Caledonia*, in June of 1813, en route from Buffalo, New York, to Presqu'Isle. He is tall and well built, his plump cheeks framed by dark curly sideburns; but at the moment he is not well.

He comes from Quaker stock and the sea is bred in him, for his father was a naval captain. There are eight in the family. One older brother, Matthew, will soon go down in history as the first man to open up the mysterious island of Japan to western commerce.

Though Perry has a quick temper, he has learned to control it, so his colleagues find him quiet, courteous, unemotional, and rather humourless. Dr. Usher Parsons, his surgeon, thinks he is the most remarkable officer he's ever known, because the seamen under him are not only fond of him, they're in awe of him. This is no narrow-minded commander. Perry is well-read, plays the flute, and is a capable fencer. A student of history and drama, he is also a fearless and elegant horseman.

He has only two chinks in his armour. His main flaw is his tendency to get sick after a period of stress. The other is simpler and not much of a drawback to a man who spends his working life on the water. Perry, for reasons that have never been explained, is terrified of cows!

Perry, in his sickbed, was frustrated—as all naval commanders must have been on that squall-ridden lake—by the unpredictable weather. As he headed for Presqu'Isle, the wind dropped. The squadron could go no farther and so was forced to zigzag back to its anchorage at Buffalo.

The next morning Perry tried again. His ships crawled along the shoreline, their sails drooping in a waning breeze. In the first twenty-four hours, he had moved no more than twenty-five miles (40 km).

Captain Barclay, meanwhile, was trying to guess the strength of his enemy. How many ships did the Americans have? How close were they to completing the two big brigs that would control the course of the battle? Barclay decided to send a small flotilla up the lake to try to find out.

He knew that if the Americans completed their work they would out-gun him. He knew he should attack them now, but he wasn't ready. The British high command was denying him both supplies and men. Once again Barclay found himself "ill used," a phrase he had first scribbled into an old family register in his midshipman days.

His life since that time had been neither easy nor distinguished. As a run-of-the-mill officer he was no better and certainly no worse than hundreds of others. "Ill used" fits his career. He had been wounded at Trafalgar, fighting the French under Nelson. He had narrowly escaped drowning when a boat capsized. He had lost an arm in another battle, and as a result carried a combination knife and fork with which to cut up his meat, one-handed.

Officially, Barclay was only a commander, though he was called "captain." And his was a miserable command. His crude vessel, *Detroit*, hammered together from green lumber cut on the spot and still unfinished, seemed pitiful after the great three-decked ships of the British navy.

Barclay was also painfully aware that he was second choice for the job. Another officer had turned it down because he did not want to command a badly equipped fleet in what the high command clearly viewed as a Canadian backwater. Barclay was stuck with it.

And so he did his best to figure out the odds. He sent a small flotilla to stand off the shores of Presqu'Isle Bay to spy on the American shipbuilders and try to discover how soon they'd be ready to fight.

Meanwhile, after a frustrating twenty-four hours spent creeping along the shoreline of Lake Erie, Perry had anchored close to the shore to escape detection. He was eager to be back at Presqu'Isle to oversee construction of his fleet, but he feared the enemy might be lurking about. The tension increased his illness.

A man signalled from the shore, and Perry sent a boat to bring him aboard. The news was ominous. Barclay's fleet of five vessels, led by the flagship *Queen Charlotte*, had appeared off Presqu'Isle. Perry would have to battle them before he could get into the harbour.

Sick or not, he leaped from his bunk prepared to fight. But when, on June 19, he reached his destination, Barclay's fleet had unaccountably left. They had, apparently, seen what they wanted to see and sailed off.

This was one of the strokes of good fortune that marked Perry's career.

If Barclay was "ill used," Perry was blessed with good luck. The British clearly outgunned him, even without their big ship *Detroit*, still under construction at Amherstburg. The fleets would not be equal until Perry's men completed his two big brigs, *Lawrence* and *Niagara*.

Barclay might easily have destroyed Perry's little flotilla as it tried to enter Presqu'Isle harbour, but he had no way of knowing where Perry was and left before encountering him.

The harbour, a placid sheet of water three miles (4.8 km) long and more than a mile (1.6 km) wide, was protected from the vicious storms on the lake by a six-mile (9.6-km) finger of land that curled around the outer edge. A sandbar, just six feet (1.8 m) below the surface of the lake, joined the peninsula to the far shore. That made it impossible for enemy ships to sail into the bay itself. Once Perry manoeuvred his craft over that bar the British could not get at him.

But there was one obvious disadvantage. The two big warships being built on the bay might draw too much water to clear the sandbar, especially if a British fleet was waiting outside to blast them with cannon fire as they attempted that difficult manoeuvre.

As the pilots brought their light vessels through the narrow channel, Perry's men could see the village of Erie crowding along the shoreline—some fifty frame houses, a blacksmith's shop, a tannery, and a courthouse, the last serving as a sail loft. The shipbuilders were all young, energetic men—their average age was thirty-five—and for good reason. They had to be husky, for the problems of building state-of-the-art fighting vessels hundreds of miles from a centre of civilization seemed almost insurmountable.

The only resource Presqu'Isle had was timber. Everything else had to be hauled in by boat and then by ox cart over roads that were no more than tracks wriggling through the forests, pocked by mud holes, blocked by stumps and deadfalls.

Perry and his troubleshooter, Daniel Dobbins, had to travel to Meadville, Pennsylvania, to scrape up steel to make axes. Iron came all the way from Bellefonte, spike rods from Buffalo, cable and hawsers from Pittsburgh, canvas from Philadelphia. There was no oakum to caulk the seams in the ships' sides; old rope had to do instead. And Dobbins had to plunder an ancient schooner for scrap iron, rigging, and shot.

Noah Brown, Perry's building superintendent, had organized an army of axemen, choppers, and sawyers, who were now stripping the surrounding forest. They worked from dawn to dusk, hacking down cucumber, oak, poplar, and ash for ribs, white pine for decks, black oak for planking and frames, red cedar and walnut for supports. This was all handwork; there were no sawmills. The race to finish the fleet before the battle began was so swift that a tree on the outskirts of the settlement could be growing one day and be part of a ship the next.

Perry's designer, a Scottish-born genius named Henry Eckford, had outfitted all the vessels brought from Black Rock and had also designed four of the six being built at Presqu'Isle, including the two great brigs. Because no conventional craft of their size could get across the harbour's mouth, Eckford had to design fighting vessels that had extremely shallow draughts.

It was difficult work. Food shortages caused more than one strike. Delays were maddening. Anchors ordered for the first of May had not yet arrived. In spite of that, all the ships were in the water, nearing completion.

Perry confidently expected his fleet to be ready by mid-July. But he had two problems. He didn't have enough seamen to man the ships, and he still faced the difficult task of getting his big ships across that sandbar. And now, as he looked out onto the lake, he could see that the British were again lurking, ready to tear the brigs to pieces before they could even make sail.

CHAPTER TWO

Desperate for Sailors

ON JULY 4, INDEPENDENCE DAY IN THE UNITED STATES, THE SMALL FORCE OF BRITISH SOLDIERS STATIONED AT SANDWICH (NEAR PRESENT-DAY WINDSOR) COULD SEE THE AMERICANS' ROCKETS EXPLODING IN THE SKY AND HEAR THE SOUND OF CHURCH BELLS. THE COMMANDER OF THE BRITISH RIGHT DIVISION STATIONED HERE, MAJOR-GENERAL HENRY PROCTER, HAD NEVER FELT SO FRUSTRATED.

Barclay had returned from his inspection of Presqu'Isle full of gloom. He had seen the new American brigs already in the water, but his own ship, the huge *Detroit*, was still on land. Procter knew what he should do. He should attack at once and destroy Perry's fleet before it could be finished. Alas, he had neither men nor supplies for the job.

Nor could he expect any. The commander of the forces in Upper Canada had promised to send troops. But the troops hadn't come. Procter was convinced they never would. The British were short of gunners, clerks, servants, as well as fighting men. They were also short of food and money to pay the men. Things were so bad, Procter wrote in a letter to his commanding officer, that "we have scarcely the Means of constructing even a Blockhouse."

Captain Barclay was equally desperate for seamen. He had arrived with only a handful, and most of these were incompetent. He desperately needed three hundred trained sailors and marines to man his fleet. But his superiors wouldn't even send him a shipwright.

The problem was that the war was also being fought on Lake Ontario, where an American and a British fleet were chasing each other about without ever coming to blows. The British command wanted to hold every man and every scrap of material to meet the American threat there.

Obviously, the high command had given up on Lake Erie and was prepared to lose it to the Americans. This was part of the British strategy since the start of the war. Montreal and Quebec were to be defended at all costs, even if it meant abandoning Upper Canada (present-day Ontario) to the enemy.

The British didn't have the resources to fight everywhere. An American force was already threatening the Niagara Peninsula. A thin British force held the heights at Burlington (above what is today the city of Hamilton). Another force was garrisoned at Kingston, on the St. Lawrence River. If the British weakened these strongholds by sending some of the defenders to Lake Erie, they might easily fall to the Americans.

And so the orders to Procter and Barclay were simple, if maddening: they must seize control of Lake Erie. Once they did that the British would have no trouble protecting Lake Ontario.

Procter felt abandoned. He was certain that if he had received the promised men and supplies he could have destroyed all of Perry's vessels at Presqu'Isle. That would have given him command of the lake and acted as a diversion to protect the British.

The American fleet was rapidly approaching fighting trim. When Barclay's new ship, *Detroit*, and two gunboats being built at Amherstburg were finished, the odds would again be even. But Barclay knew the *Detroit* would not be in the water until July 20. After that she would have to be rigged with masts and sails.

The British faced even more difficulties than Perry when it came to building warships. Canada had no steel or iron mills, no Pittsburghs or Philadelphias, and no manufacturing worthy of the name. Everything except timber—nails, bolts, pulleys, lead, copper, glass, paint, resin, cordage, sails— had to come from Montreal and Quebec and, ultimately, from England.

The cannon Barclay had ordered for the big ship were taken over by the British at Kingston for other purposes. Now he had to order new guns, which would have to be shipped across the Atlantic, up the St. Lawrence, and across Lake Ontario, where the American fleet was waiting. The Niagara Peninsula was in flames, which meant that the guns would have to be transported by a long land route through the forests of Upper Canada to Amherstburg.

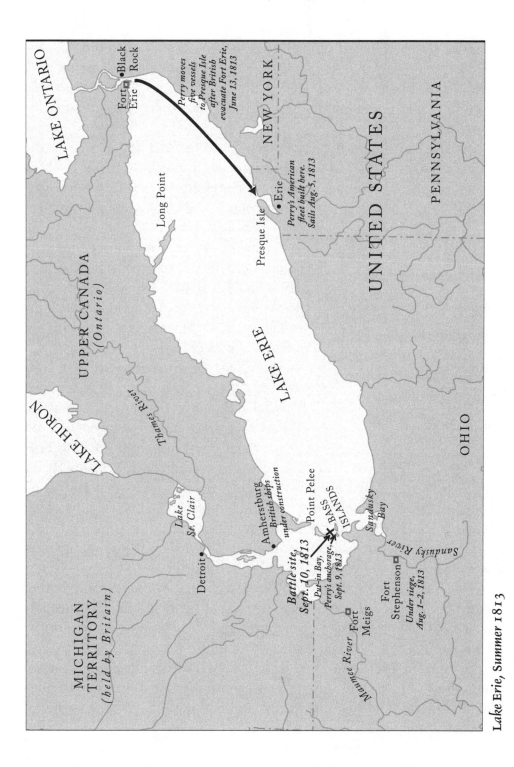

Lake Erie, Summer 1813

Within the map:

LAKE ONTARIO

Black Rock

Fort Erie

NEW YORK

Perry moves five vessels to Presque Isle after British evacuate Fort Erie, June 13, 1813

Long Point

Presque Isle

Erie

Perry's American fleet built here. Sails Aug. 5, 1813

UNITED STATES

PENNSYLVANIA

UPPER CANADA (Ontario)

LAKE HURON

Thames River

LAKE ERIE

Lake St. Clair

Amherstburg British ships under construction

Point Pelee

BASS ISLANDS

Sandusky Bay

OHIO

Detroit

Battle site, Sept. 10, 1813

Put-in Bay, Perry's anchorage, Sept. 9, 1813

Sandusky River

Fort Stephenson Under siege, Aug. 1–2, 1813

MICHIGAN TERRITORY (held by Britain)

Maumee River

Fort Meigs

That spring, when the Americans had attacked York (Toronto), the British had lost fifty thousand dollars' worth of stores—guns, ammunition, cables, cordage, canvas, tools—all destined for Barclay's fleet. When he'd asked his superiors for more, he had been told to get it by fighting the Americans.

But Barclay knew his force wasn't strong enough to attack the Americans. Presqu'Isle was too well guarded. Meanwhile, General Procter's Indian allies were becoming restless. Supplies were so short they were existing on bread. And the traditional presents, which the military always distributed, hadn't arrived.

He and his people were still full of fight, and the Shawnee was convinced that Fort Stephenson, a more lightly held bastion, could easily be taken. Again, Procter had no choice but to follow Tecumseh's lead.

Procter knew he must do something. The Indians needed the excitement of a battle. If they didn't get it they would drift away to their villages, and the army would be terribly weakened. For, in this strange war, the Indians were a key force.

Tecumseh, the great Shawnee war chief who hated the Americans, was Procter's chief Native ally. He was eager to mount an attack on Fort Meigs, the American stronghold on the Maumee River, just south of Lake Erie. This was the headquarters of the American commander, William Henry Harrison, a future U.S. president. Procter was convinced that Harrison's stronghold was too tough a nut to crack, but he had no choice: if he didn't go on the attack he would lose his Indian allies.

He set off with an army of five thousand, placed his troops on the right bank of the river, and planned an ambush. It failed.

The Americans drove the British back, but that didn't really bother Tecumseh. He and his people were still full of fight, and the Shawnee was convinced that Fort Stephenson, a more lightly held bastion, could easily be taken. Again, Procter had no choice but to follow Tecumseh's lead.

Fort Stephenson lay a mile or so upriver from Sandusky Bay on the south shore of Lake Erie. With its weak garrison of 150 soldiers and its huddle of wooden buildings, it certainly couldn't be held against an army of 5,000. Harrison realized that.

But now an incredible incident took place. Harrison sent an order to the fort's young commander, Major George Croghan, to set the fort on fire and get out. But Croghan pretended he hadn't understood! When the British gunboats swept up Sandusky Bay, propelled by a spanking breeze, Croghan held his ground.

Procter had Croghan outgunned. He had six-pounders (3-kg) to destroy the palisades and howitzers to lob more cannonballs over the walls to maim the defenders inside. All Croghan had was one ancient six-pounder (3-kg), left over from the Revolution, known as "Old Betsey."

Procter's force outnumbered Croghan's by at least seven to one. But in battle it is not always the largest force that wins but the character of the fighting men.

Neither side expected victory in this strange contest. Harrison looked at the odds and was prepared to give up. Croghan, however, had no intention of withdrawing. Procter, on the other hand, didn't believe the fort could be taken; but with Tecumseh pushing him he had no course but to attack.

Procter felt his command slipping away. Droves of his Native allies had already deserted because of the failure to grab Fort Meigs. So Procter now planned a two-pronged attack, with the British regulars storming the fort from one side, the Indians from the other.

Croghan had only one thing on his side: the will to win. Procter was within 250 yards (230 m) of the fort by dawn, August 1. That day he hurled five hundred cannonballs and shells at the Americans. He planned a fake attack at the south end to deceive the defenders, but Croghan was prepared for that. He was convinced, rightly, that the real attack would come from the northwest.

The British began the assault at four that afternoon. But Procter was a flawed commander. He tended to panic when steadfastness was required. His men were ill prepared. They had no scaling ladders to launch against the sixteen-foot (5-m) palisade, and their axes were dulled from weeks of misuse.

A deep ditch encircled the fort. The British reached a point twenty paces from this obstacle and formed themselves in line for a frontal assault—the most difficult and dangerous of all military manoeuvres.

At that point Croghan's Kentucky sharpshooters opened up. The palisade was higher and the ditch deeper than the attackers had expected. Soon the ditch was clogged with dead and dying men, struck down as they attempted vainly to breach the double obstacle.

When darkness fell, a rising moon cast a pale light on the carnage. In the ditch and the ravine beyond, men were groaning, dying, and cursing Procter for deserting them.

The assault had been a failure. The general had been bested by a youth who had just passed his twenty-first year. It did not bode well for the battle that was looming on the grey waters of the lake.

CHAPTER THREE

Perry's Luck

ON AUGUST 1, WHEN THE BRITISH MOUNTED THEIR FLAWED ATTACK ON FORT STEPHENSON, OLIVER HAZARD PERRY ROSE AT LAST FROM HIS SICKBED. HE HAD HAD ANOTHER STROKE OF GOOD FORTUNE — "PERRY'S LUCK," IT WOULD COME TO BE CALLED. HE LEARNED THAT THE BRITISH FLEET, WHICH HAD BEEN HOVERING JUST OUTSIDE THE BAY FOR ALMOST TWO WEEKS, HAD VANISHED.

The blockade was ended. His own ships were now ready to sail. The moment had come to get them across the sandbar that blocked the entrance. So Perry shook off the "bilious" fever that seemed to strike him after long periods of stress and fatigue.

These had not been easy weeks. He still didn't have enough experienced seamen or officers to man his ships. He was mortified that he couldn't give naval help to Harrison during the siege of Fort Meigs. The high command had only sent him a handful of men, the dregs of the fleet: "a motley set, blacks, soldiers and boys," in Perry's description. But he was eager to attack Barclay, even with ships that were partially manned. "I long to have at him," he declared.

A second detachment of sixty men arrived, but these weren't much use to Perry. Most were worn down by disease; one-fifth were suffering from fever and dysentery.

Two hundred soldiers had accompanied him from Black Rock, but these had long since been ordered back to Lake Ontario. His only defence force was a comic opera regiment of Pennsylvania militia, too afraid of the dark to stand watch at night. Perry demanded to know why they weren't at their posts and received a jarring comment from their commander.

"I told the boys to go, Captain," he said, "but the boys won't go."

Perry wasn't worried about Procter, who was wary now of attacking *any* defensive position. Perry didn't contemplate defence—he was determined to attack. His force, at that moment, was clearly superior to Barclay's, because the British brig *Detroit* remained unfinished.

"What a golden opportunity if we had men," Perry wrote. Yet, because he didn't have enough, he was "obliged to bite [his] fingers in vexation." Fortunately, the enemy was out of the way for the moment. He could at last get his ships into the open lake without fear of attack. Or were the British faking? Perhaps, but he intended to try anyway.

Now he suffered a new frustration. The water had dropped to a depth of only four feet (1.2 m) at the sandbar. The two brigs, *Lawrence* and *Niagara*, drew nine feet (2.7 m). That meant they were trapped.

Luckily, Noah Brown had foreseen just such a calamity. His solution was ingenious. He built four huge box-like scows, known as "camels." These could be floated or sunk at will. By placing a camel on either side of a ship and sinking both camels below the surface, the vessel could be raised up by means of ropes and windlasses. Then it was set on a series of wooden beams resting on the camels. The scows were then plugged, pumped out, and brought to the surface. With the big ship resting on the supports, the entire ungainly contraption could be floated easily across the bar.

But that wasn't easy. Before the big brigs could be raised up on the camels, the smaller vessels in the fleet had to be lightened and hauled across the sandbar to act as a protective screen in case the British squadron should reappear. More guns were needed to meet that threat. And so the brig *Niagara* was brought up close to the bar to act as a floating battery. If the British returned, she would fire broadside at the advancing ships.

Now *Niagara*'s twin, *Lawrence*, a fully rigged brig, pierced for twenty guns, was hauled forward. For three hours the sweating seamen stripped her of her armaments. The camels were brought alongside and the brig was hoisted two feet (60 cm). It wasn't enough; she still drew too much water. The process had to be repeated. It wasn't until mid-morning on August 4 that she was finally floated free.

The officers and men had spent two sleepless nights, but the work still wasn't over. Now *Lawrence* had to be refitted—a task that took them until midnight. And then *Niagara* had to be floated over the bar, protected by *Lawrence*'s guns. Could they get the ships out of the harbour before the

British returned? Alas, before *Niagara* could be freed of the bar, two sails were seen through the haze on the horizon. Barclay was back.

Again Perry's luck held. Barclay simply could not believe that Perry could get those two big ships over the bar. The British commander was elated at the prospect of treating them as sitting ducks. Barclay had gone off to attend a dinner in his honour at Port Dover. There, in reply to a toast, he announced he expected to return "to find the Yankee brigs hard and fast aground on the bar at Erie … in which predicament it would be but a small job to destroy them."

Now, nature helped to deceive the British. The wind cast such a haze across the mouth of the bay that Barclay thought that Perry had somehow got his whole fleet over the bar and into the open lake. Perry sent two of his smaller vessels out to the lake to fire a few shots, and Barclay, believing himself outgunned, retired. He did not yet have his big ship *Detroit* in fighting trim. But it wasn't until midnight on August 5 that Perry's fleet of ten ships, all fully armed, headed out into the lake for a two-day trial run, vainly seeking the elusive British.

Perry's worries still weren't over. The trouble was that many of the men serving under him were volunteers, and, under the terms of their enlistment, ready to go home. He had to pay them off and was left only with those men who had signed up for four months' service. Thus, he had less than half the men he needed to man his fleet. Of these, less than a quarter were regular naval personnel. As for his officers, they had little experience. Perry realized that delay was dangerous, but he knew that he wasn't yet prepared to face the enemy.

He was still suffering from fatigue and fever. The struggle to get the *Lawrence* over the bar had worn him down. For two days he had gone without food or sleep. He had also received a taunting letter from his superior officer on Lake Ontario, Admiral Chauncey. The sensitive Perry decided to quit. He told the secretary of the navy that he could not "serve longer under an officer who has been so totally regardless of my feelings." But the dispute was patched up, and to Perry's delight he got his reinforcements—several officers and eighty-nine seamen under Jesse Elliott.

As events would prove, Elliott was a bit of a problem. Though junior in rank to Perry, he was far better known to the American public—a national hero because he had led a daring raid against the British the previous summer, the only victory in a string of scandalous defeats. He was four years older than Perry, and at one time had been picked to command the U.S. naval force on Lake Erie—until Perry overtook him. He was vain, boastful, and not always generous with subordinates, for he liked to get credit for any victory. He was also a bit of a troublemaker, having already fought one duel. Perry, however, was glad to see him when he arrived on August 10.

The men Elliott brought were better than the previous seamen. Perry, whose flagship would be *Lawrence*, gave Elliott command of *Niagara* and allowed him to choose his own crew. The ambitious Elliott grabbed the pick of the crop. *Lawrence*'s sailing master complained that the vessels now were unequally manned, the best men having been taken for *Niagara*. But Perry was so happy to see them that he overlooked Elliott's rudeness.

He was far more concerned about the big British ship *Detroit*, now nearing completion at Amherstburg. It was larger than any of his own vessels, and so he took care to cruise the lake ready for battle.

Since he only had forty men who knew anything about guns, he started to drill his force. His plan was to force Barclay out of his harbour at Amherstburg and, if that failed, to transport General Harrison's army across the lake to attack Procter. Meanwhile, he took his fleet into Put-in Bay, a safe anchorage not far from Sandusky Bay, at the western end of the lake.

There, sickness struck once more. Perry fell dangerously ill again with fever. His thirteen-year-old brother, Alexander, was also sick. The chief surgeon was too ill to work. His assistant, also ill and flat on his back on a cot, had to be carried from ship to ship to minister to the sick.

On August 31, more reinforcements arrived: one hundred Kentucky riflemen. Their job was to act as marines and sharpshooters in the battle to come. Most had never seen a ship before and couldn't hide their astonishment or curiosity. They climbed the masts, plunged into the holds, trotted about each vessel from sick bay to captain's cabin, exclaiming over the smallest details.

The next day Perry was well enough to put his squadron in motion toward Amherstburg, hovering outside the harbour just as Barclay had once blockaded him. He could see *Detroit* was now fully rigged. But Barclay declined to come out.

A few days later, three escaped prisoners from Amherstburg warned him that Barclay was preparing for battle. Perry now had a pretty good idea of his adversary's strength, but he overestimated Barclay's manpower, which was in fact no greater than his own. Actually, in firepower Perry now outgunned Barclay two to one.

Again sickness struck him. In spite of this, he called a council in his cabin. Of his 490 men, he learned, almost a quarter were ill, and all three surgeons were now sick. Some of the invalids, however, would still be able to fight.

Here, each commander was given his instructions. Perry, in *Lawrence*, would attack Barclay's flagship, *Detroit*. Elliott, in *Niagara*, would attack the next largest vessel, *Queen Charlotte*. And so on down the line.

British and American tactics in the battle to come would depend on the kind of guns with which each ship was equipped. The Americans preferred short, stubby, powerful guns called "carronades." The British favoured long guns that could pound the American ships from a distance.

With his carronades Perry would be forced to fight at very close quarters. Unless he could get close to the British and hammer them hard, the British, with their longer range, could batter him to pieces while he could not reply.

He left nothing to chance. He had already worked out a series of signals for the day of action. Now he handed every officer written instructions, telling them to make sure they engaged their opposite number in close action at half cable's length (91 m).

He left nothing to chance. He had already worked out a series of signals for the day of action. Now he handed every officer written instructions, telling them to make sure they engaged their opposite number in close action at half cable's length (91 m). Those long guns bothered him. If he had his way, his powerful short-range carronades would batter Barclay's at point-blank range.

As the officers rose to leave, Perry called them back and went over the plan again. He wanted to make absolutely sure they would bring the British fleet into close action. When he dismissed them he echoed a phrase of Horatio Nelson's: "If you lay the enemy close alongside you cannot be out of your place."

But that still wasn't enough for Perry. He stood on the deck and repeated Nelson's phrase. He couldn't get those British long guns out of his mind. Barclay, he knew, could easily stand out of range, especially if the wind was right, and reduce his fleet to matchwood before a single American shot could strike him.

It was ten o'clock on a lovely September evening. The moon was full, the lake like black glass tinselled with silver. From the shore came the hum of voices around campfires and the *peep-peep* of frogs in nearby Squaw Harbour. From the quarterdecks of the anchored vessels, the low murmur of officers could be heard, discussing the coming battle, and also the crackle of laughter—sailors telling jokes.

Perry went to his cabin. He had letters to write. If the battle should come and he was victorious, they wouldn't have to be sent. But if he should fall and die, these would be his final messages.

CHAPTER FOUR

The Eve of Battle

IN AMHERSTBURG THAT FATEFUL SEPTEMBER 9, ROBERT HERIOT BARCLAY KNEW THAT HE MUST LEAD HIS SQUADRON INTO LAKE ERIE AND FIGHT THE AMERICANS — HE HAD NO OTHER CHOICE. HE REALIZED THE ODDS WERE AGAINST HIM AND THAT ONLY A MIRACLE COULD BRING HIM VICTORY. BUT AMHERSTBURG WAS ON THE VERGE OF STARVATION. HIS OWN CREWS WERE ON HALF RATIONS. THEY DIDN'T EVEN HAVE A BARREL OF FLOUR LEFT.

Procter's fourteen thousand followers, mostly Indians with wives and children, had been reduced to a few barrels of pork, some cattle, and a little unground wheat. Barclay held off until the last moment, hoping for the promised reinforcements, guns, and equipment for his new ship, *Detroit*. Now he could hold out no longer. He must attempt to run down the lake to bring provisions from Long Point, on the northern shore of Lake Erie. He also knew that Perry's fleet was waiting to intercept him at Put-in Bay, thirty miles (48 km) to the southeast. Perhaps he could get past Perry unseen, though that seemed unlikely. But he did not intend to shirk the encounter.

Like Perry, he was badly undermanned. Indeed, he was in far worse condition than his adversary. His officers didn't know their own men. The men didn't know their ships. Barclay had been pleading for weeks for reinforcements, but the merest handful had arrived, most of them untrained.

The troops had not been paid for months. The civilian workers had refused to work on the ships without wages. Procter had warned the high command that "there are not in the Fleet more than four and twenty *seamen*." Barclay had echoed these remarks to his own command.

"If you saw my Canadians, you would condemn every one … as a poor devil not worth his Salt."

All the Canadian Governor General, George Prevost, could do was write foolish letters likely to infuriate both commanders. The Governor General had reached the Niagara frontier on August 22 and ignored all his subordinates' worries. He said that the situation "may be one of some difficulty," but "you cannot fail in honourably surmounting it"—as if mere words could win a battle!

"Captain Barclay … has only to dare, and the enemy is discomfited," he said. The Governor General was a prisoner of his own optimism.

Prevost wrote glibly of seamen "valorous and well disciplined." Procter replied, "Except, I believe, the 25 Captain Barclay brought with him, there are none of that description on this lake."

Barclay was also short of guns and equipment because of the American attack on York that spring. To outfit his new ship he had to borrow a weird collection of cannon from the ramparts of Fort Amherstburg. The big guns came in half a dozen sizes. Each needed separate ammunition. That meant that confusion would reign among the untrained gunners in the heat of battle.

The guns could not be fired efficiently. The matches and tubes were spoiled or corroded. To fire a gun, an officer had to snap his flintlock pistol over the touch-hole—an awkward procedure that slowed the rate of fire. Indeed, everything on *Detroit* was makeshift. Some of the sails, cables, and blocks had been borrowed from *Queen Charlotte* and other vessels, there being no others available in Amherstburg.

The Governor General kept promising that more guns and men were on their way. On September 1, the British landed a dozen twenty-four-pound (11-kg) carronades at Burlington, on Lake Ontario. But the guns got no farther. A few more reinforcements did arrive—two lieutenants, two gunners, and forty-five seamen who turned out to be, in Barclay's opinion, "totally inadequate." Sixteen were mere boys.

Prevost assured him that more were on the way, but Barclay couldn't wait. At ten o'clock on that calm, moonlit night, as Perry paced his own deck a few leagues away, Barclay's fleet of six warships slipped their moorings and moved out into the Detroit River onto the shining waters of the shallow lake.

In Europe, the noose was tightening around Napoleon. Austria had joined the Allied cause. The Prussians had already dealt the French a stunning setback at Katzbach. In St. Petersburg, Russia, three distinguished American diplomats were attempting peace talks with Britain, with the Tsar acting as mediator. But none of this could have the slightest effect on the contest being waged here on a silent lake in the heart of a continental wilderness.

And so, here is Barclay, walking the quarterdeck of his untried ship. What is he thinking? Certainly he has looked at the odds, which are against him. Perry has ten vessels—three brigs, six schooners, and a sloop. Barclay has six—two ships, a brig, two schooners, and a sloop. Ships and brigs are square rigged, the former with three masts, the latter with two. It is largely on these big vessels that the contest will depend.

Barclay's flagship, *Detroit*, was the largest vessel on the lake. It was 126 feet (38 m) long, at least fifteen feet (4.6 m) longer than either of Perry's two brigs. But firepower counts more than size, and here Perry had the advantage, especially at close quarters. Long guns were most effective at eight hundred yards (732 m). At three hundred (274 m), the stubby carronade could do greater damage. Perry's could shatter the British fleet with a combined broadside weighing a total of 664 pounds (299 kg). The British, who preferred the longer range, could hurl only 264 pounds (119 kg) of metal at the enemy.

Barclay was also short of trained gunners and seamen. Of his total crew of 440, at least 300 were soldiers, not sailors. But three of every five men in Perry's crews were seamen.

Barclay had one advantage only. Perry's two largest vessels, *Lawrence* and *Niagara*, were inferior to him in long-range firepower. At long range the American flagship faced nine times its own firepower. No wonder Perry was desperate to fight at close quarters.

Barclay had a pretty good idea of the two fleets' comparative strength. He had looked over the opposing squadron off Amherstburg, climbing to the highest house in the village to examine the vessels through his glass. His strategy was the opposite of Perry's. He intended to use his long guns to batter the Americans before they could get within range with their stubby carronades.

But here both men were faced with the limitations of wooden sailing ships. A great deal depended on forces over which neither man had any control. If Barclay had the "weather gauge"—that is, if the wind was behind him so that he could manoeuvre his ships easily—then Perry would be in trouble. But if Perry had the gauge, the wind would drive him directly into the heart of the British fleet and allow him to use his short-range weapons.

For both men, the next day would tell the tale. For all Barclay knew, it might be his last day on earth—as it might be Perry's. He might emerge a hero, honoured, promoted, decorated. More likely, he thought, he would have to shoulder the blame for defeat.

How would fate, fortune, wind, and circumstance use him in the approaching battle? The next day would tell.

CHAPTER FIVE

Launching the Attack

I<small>T WAS SUNRISE</small>, S<small>EPTEMBER</small> 10, <small>AT</small> P<small>UT-IN</small> B<small>AY</small>. P<small>ERRY'S LOOKOUT, HIGH UP</small>
<small>ON THE MAST OF</small> *L<small>AWRENCE</small>,* <small>SPOTTED A DISTANT SILHOUETTE BEYOND THE</small>
<small>CLUSTER OF ISLANDS.</small>

"Sail, ho!" he cried.

In an instant Perry leaped from his bunk. The cry seemed to act as a
tonic to his fever. Up the masthead went his signal: *Get underway.* Within
fifteen minutes his men had hauled in sixty fathoms (110 m) of cable, hoisted anchors, raised the sails, and steered the nine vessels for a gap between
the islands that shielded the harbour.

The wind was against Perry. He could gain the weather gauge only by
beating around to the windward of some of the islands. That would require
much time, and Perry was impatient to fight.

"Run to the lee side," he told his sailing master, William Taylor.

"Then you will have to engage the enemy to leeward, sir," Taylor
reminded him. That would give the British the advantage of the wind.

"I don't care," said Perry. "To windward or leeward, they will fight
today." So off they went.

The fleet was abustle. Decks had to be cleared for action so that nothing
would get in the way of the recoil of the guns. Seamen were hammering in
flints, lighting rope matches, placing shot in racks or in coils of rope next to
the guns. Besides round shot, to pierce the enemy ships, the gunners would
also fire canister—a menacing cluster of iron balls encased in a tin covering—or grapeshot, a similar collection arranged around a central core in a
canvas or quilted bag.

Perry's favourite black spaniel ran about the deck in excitement until his
master ordered him confined in a china closet where he would no longer be

underfoot. Then he collected the ship's papers and signals in a weighted bag, which could be thrown overboard in the case of surrender, denying that information to the enemy. At the same time his men were getting out stacks of pikes and cutlasses to push back the British if they attempted to board the ship. In addition, they sprinkled sand on the decks to prevent slipping when the blood began to flow.

The assistant surgeon, Usher Parsons, was setting up a makeshift hospital in *Lawrence*'s wardroom. The brig was so shallow that there wasn't any secure place for the wounded. They would have to be kept in a ten-foot (3-m) square patch of floor, level with the waterline—as much at the mercy of the British cannonballs as were the men on deck above.

Suddenly, just before ten, the wind shifted to the southeast—Perry's Luck! The commodore now had his weather gauge. Slipping past Rattlesnake Island, he bore down on the British fleet, five miles (8 km) away.

Barclay had turned his ships into the southwest. The sun bathed his line of vessels in a soft morning glow, shining on the spanking new paint, the red ensigns, and the white sails against the cloudless sky. Perry picked up a glass and stared at the British fleet. He realized that Barclay's line of battle wasn't what he had expected. The small schooner *Chippawa*, armed with a single long gun at the bow, was at the head of the line. Behind it was a big three-master, which must certainly be *Detroit*. Perry had thought the British lead vessel would be the seventeen-gun *Queen Charlotte*, designated as Elliott's target.

As a result of this new information, Perry had to change his battle order to bring his heaviest vessels against those of the enemy. The ambitious Elliott, up ahead in *Niagara*, had originally asked to be in the forefront, but now he was moved farther back, much to his chagrin. Perry himself intended to take on Barclay. Two American gunboats would operate off his bow to act as dispatch vessels. *Caledonia* would engage the British brig *Hunter*, and Elliott in *Niagara* would follow to take on the larger *Queen Charlotte*. Four smaller vessels would bring up the rear—nine ships in all. (The sloop did not take part.)

All hands were piped to quarters. Tubs of rations, bread bags, and the standard issue of grog were on hand for the battle. Perry produced a flag he had prepared for the moment with the words "Don't give up the ship!" embroidered on it.

"Shall I hoist it?" he asked. A cheer went up. Even the sick—those who could walk—came out as Perry, moving from battery to battery, examined each gun, murmured words of encouragement, exchanged a joke or two with the Kentuckians he knew best, and saved his special greeting for men from his home state of Rhode Island.

"Ah, here are the Newport boys! *They* will do their duty, I warrant!"

To a group of old hands, who had experience of earlier contests and had removed their cumbersome headgear and tied handkerchiefs around their foreheads, he said, "I need not say anything to you: *you* know how to beat those fellows."

Now a silence descended on the lake. The British line, closed up tight, waited motionless in the light breeze. The American squadron, with the breeze behind it, approached at an angle of fifteen degrees. The hush was deadly. To David Bunnell, a seaman aboard *Lawrence*, it resembled "the awful silence that precedes an earthquake." Bunnell had been at sea a long time and had served in both navies, but now he found his heart beating wildly as all nature seemed "wrapped in awful suspense."

In the wardroom below, its single hatch closed tight, the only surgeon available, Usher Parsons, sat in the half-light, unable to shake from his mind the horrors he knew would follow.

At the guns, the men murmured to each other, giving instructions to comrades in case they should fall, relaying messages to wives and sweethearts. Perry, in his cabin, reread his wife's letters, then tore them to shreds so the enemy wouldn't get them. "This is the most important day of my life," he said quietly.

Slowly the distance between the two fleets narrowed. Minutes dragged by. Both sides held their breath. Perry had little control over the speed of his vessels. At their rear, the slower gunboats were already lagging badly behind.

Soon only a mile (1.6 km) separated the two big flagships. Suddenly a British bugle broke the silence, followed by cheers from Barclay's fleet. A cannon exploded. The sound seemed electrifying. A twenty-four-pound (11-kg) ball splashed into the water ahead. The British were still out of range. But the battle had begun.

CHAPTER SIX

The Strange Behaviour of Jesse Elliott

SLOWLY THE AMERICAN FLEET SLIPPED FORWARD UNDER THE LIGHT BREEZE. FIVE MINUTES WENT BY, AND THEN ANOTHER EXPLOSION. A CANNONBALL TORE ITS WAY THROUGH LAWRENCE'S BULWARKS. A SEAMAN FELL DEAD, KILLED BY A FLYING SPLINTER. THE BRITISH HAD FOUND THEIR RANGE. "STEADY, BOYS, STEADY," SAID PERRY.

Up from below came an odd whimpering and howling—Perry's spaniel. The cannonball had torn its way through the planking of the china closet, knocking down all the dishes and terrifying the animal, who would continue to bark throughout the course of the battle.

Perry called out to his first lieutenant, John Yarnell, to hail the little *Scorpion*, off his windward bow, by trumpet. He wanted her to open up on the British with the only long gun she had. He ordered his own gunners to fire *Lawrence*'s long twelves, but with no effect, for the British were still out of range.

Now Barclay's strategy became apparent. He had decided to ignore all the other vessels in Perry's fleet and have his ships concentrate their combined fire, a total of thirty-four guns, on *Lawrence*. He intended to batter Perry's flagship to pieces before she could get into range, then attack the others.

The British vessels formed a tight line, no more than a hundred yards (91 m) apart. At this point Perry's superior numbers didn't count for much. As he pulled abreast of the British, his gunboats were too far in the rear to do any damage. He signalled all his vessels to close up and for each to engage her chosen opponent. Finally, at twelve fifteen, he brought *Lawrence* into carronade range of *Detroit*—so close that the British believed he was about to board their ship.

As the thirty-two-pound (14.5-kg) canisters sprayed the decks of his flagship, Robert Barclay suffered a serious stroke of bad luck. His seasoned second-in-command, Captain Finnis, in charge of *Queen Charlotte*, had been unable to reach his designated opponent, partly because the wind had dropped and partly because Elliott, in *Niagara*, had remained out of range. So Finnis, under heavy fire from the American *Caledonia*, determined to move up the British line ahead of *Hunter* and punish *Lawrence* at close quarters with a broadside from his carronades.

But just as his ship shifted position, Finnis was felled by a cannonball and died instantly. His first officer died with him, and a few minutes later the ship's second officer was knocked senseless by a shell splinter.

And so, at twelve thirty, *Queen Charlotte*, the second most powerful ship in the British squadron, fell under the command of a young, inexperienced lieutenant in the Provincial Marine, Robert Irvine. He was no replacement for the expert Finnis, and all he had to support him was a master's mate of the Royal Navy, two boy midshipmen from his own service, a gunner, and bo'sun. Barclay had lost his main support.

Despite that, *Lawrence* was reeling under the British hammer blows. The tumult aboard the American flagship was appalling. Above the shrieks of the wounded and the dying and the rumblings of the gun carriages came the explosion of cannon and the crash of round shot splintering masts, tearing through bulwarks, ripping guns from their carriages.

The decks were soon a rubble of broken spars, tangled rigging, shredded sails, and dying men. And over the whole scene hung a thick pall of smoke, blotting out the sun and turning the bright September noon to gloomy twilight.

Here now was the true horror of naval warfare. Lieutenant John Brooks, the head of Perry's marines, the handsomest officer at sea this day, turned, smiling, to pass a remark to Perry, when a cannonball tore into his hip, ripped off a leg, and hurled him to the deck. In terrible agony, Brooks screamed for a pistol to end his life. Perry ordered the marines to take him below.

As they bent over him, Brooks's young black servant, just twelve years old, bringing cartridges to a nearby gun, saw his fallen master and flung himself, sobbing, to the deck. Usher Parsons could do nothing for Brooks. He had only a few hours to live.

Perry's first lieutenant, John Yarnell, presented a grotesque appearance. His nose, perforated by a splinter, had swollen to twice its normal size. Blood from a scalp wound threatened to blind him, but Parsons bound it up with a bandanna and Yarnell went back to the deck.

At that point he walked into a cloud of cattail down, torn from a pile of hammocks by a cannonball. Wounded a third time, he came below once more for medical help, his bloody face covered with down, looking like a gigantic owl. At this bizarre spectacle, the wounded men couldn't help laughing. "The devil has come for us!" they cried.

Perry himself seemed to bear a charmed life. Men were dropping all around him, but he didn't suffer a scratch. As Perry stopped to give aid to one of his veteran gun captains, the man, drawing himself up, was torn in two by a twenty-four-pound (11-kg) cannonball.

Perry himself seemed to bear a charmed life. Men were dropping all around him, but he didn't suffer a scratch. As Perry stopped to give aid to one of his veteran gun captains, the man, drawing himself up, was torn in two by a twenty-four-pound (11-kg) cannonball.

Perry's second lieutenant, Dulaney Forrest, was standing close to him when a shower of grapeshot struck Forrest in the chest, knocking him to the deck. But the shot was spent. Perry asked him if he was badly hurt, whereupon the stunned officer, regaining consciousness, cried out, "I'm not hurt, sir, but this is my shot!" and he pulled out a handful from his waistcoat and pocketed it as a souvenir.

Perry's little brother, Alexander, acting as a messenger during the din of battle, was also knocked senseless by a splinter, though otherwise unhurt—and still the commodore remained untouched. For the next century, American naval men would speak in awe of Perry's Luck. Luck … mingled with good sense. Unlike Nelson, who stood on the decks at Trafalgar in a glittering full-dress uniform, an easy target for the enemy, Perry had donned the plain blue jacket of a common sailor.

By one thirty, *Lawrence*'s sails were so badly shredded that the brig could no longer be controlled. In spite of the sand, the decks were slippery with blood, which seeped through the seams and dripped on the faces of the wounded in the wardroom below.

The wounded were taken down the hatch so quickly that the surgeon could do little more than tie up the bleeding arteries and attach a few splints to shattered limbs. There was no time for amputations—that would have to follow. Only when a leg or an arm hung by a shred did the ailing surgeon stop to sever it.

Nor was there any protection from the battle raging above. At least five cannonballs ripped through the walls of Parson's makeshift hospital. The doctor had just finished applying a tourniquet to the mangled arm of a young midshipman when a ball passed through the room and tore the boy out of the surgeon's arms, throwing him against the wall, his body half-severed. One seaman, brought down with both arms fractured, was scarcely in splints before another ball tore off his legs.

On the deck above, the carnage was dreadful as the gun crews were felled by the British grapeshot. Perry called down through the skylight asking the surgeon to send up one of his assistants to man a gun. Every few minutes he called again, until there was no help left for the doctor.

Those who survived that battle would remember, years later, small, bizarre incidents. At one point two cannonballs passed through the powder magazine—and didn't ignite it. Another entered the "light room" next to the magazine and knocked the snuff from a candle, but a gunner put it out with his fingers before the magazine could explode.

One shot punctured a pot of peas boiling on deck and scattered them. David Bunnell, working his gun, noticed a pig had got loose and was greedily eating the peas even though both its hind legs had been shot away.

Another shot struck a nearby gun, showering its crew with tiny pieces of gunmetal. One man was riddled from knees to chin with bits of cast iron, some as small as a pinhead, none larger than a buckshot. He recovered.

All the marines had been ordered down from the masts to replace the gunners. When the marines were put out of action, Perry called down the hatch, "Can any of the wounded pull a rope?"

Two or three managed to crawl on deck and lend a feeble hand. One of the sick men insisted on helping at the pumps so that the others could help with the guns. He was very ill and had to sit down to do the job. And at the end of the battle he was still sitting there, dead, a bullet through his heart.

The main battle took place between *Lawrence* on one side and the two largest British vessels—*Detroit* and *Queen Charlotte*—on the other. Elsewhere, things were going badly for the British. A cannonball carried away the rudder of *Lady Prevost,* one of the smaller British craft, and she drifted helplessly out of action. Her commander had been driven temporarily insane by a wound to his head. Another small British ship, *Little Belt,* lost her commander, ran to the head of the line, and was out of the fight.

But where was Jesse Elliott in the new brig *Niagara*? Perry's officers and men were in a fury to see that she was standing well off, using her long guns to little effect and too far out of range to bring her carronades into action. Elliott's orders were to attack *Queen Charlotte,* which was hammering away at Perry's flagship. He had not done that. *Niagara* lurked behind the slower *Caledonia,* every spar in place, her crew scarcely scratched, her bulwarks unscarred.

Elliott and others had many explanations for this curious and dangerous lack of action, but none made any sense. In fact, it seemed that Elliott, angry at having been overtaken by a younger man and being removed from the lead at the last moment, was stubbornly following Perry's instructions (but only part of them) to stay at cable's length (182 m) from the vessel ahead. More than that, Elliott undoubtedly saw himself as the saviour of the day. When Perry was driven to surrender his flag, he, Elliott, would move on.

On *Lawrence,* even the wounded were cursing Elliott.

"Why don't they come and help us?" one seaman asked the bleeding Yarnell.

"We can expect nothing from that ship," came the bitter reply.

By two thirty, Perry's flagship was in a shambles. Most of her guns were useless, smashed by the enemy's shot. A handful of gunners stuck to their posts, firing as quickly as they could. David Bunnell, in his haste, stuck a crowbar down the muzzle of his cannon and fired that, too. The gun grew so hot from constant use that it jumped from its carriage. By now five of Bunnell's crew of eight were casualties.

He moved to the next gun and, finding only one man left, brought up his surviving crew members and tried to get that weapon into action. As he did, he looked down the deck and was shocked by what he saw: a tangle of bodies—some dead, some dying—the deck a welter of clotted blood, brains, human hair, and fragments of bones sticking to the rigging and planking.

Of 137 officers and men aboard the flagship, only 54 had escaped injury or death.

One by one, *Lawrence*'s guns fell silent until she lay like a log in the water. Now another extraordinary event took place. Suddenly *Niagara* got underway. Apparently Elliott thought that Perry was dead. Now he took over, shouting an order to *Caledonia* directly ahead to move out of the line and let him pass—apparently to go to the aid of the disabled flagship. But he didn't do that. Instead he passed *Lawrence* on the windward side, leaving that vessel to the mercies of the British.

Aboard *Detroit*, Barclay, though badly wounded in the thigh, was secure in the belief that he had won the day. His ship, too, had taken a fearful pummelling. Its first officer was dead. Its spars and yards were shattered. Many of its guns were out of action. The deck was clear of corpses, however, for the British did not share the American reverence for the dead and threw all the bodies, except those of the officers, immediately overboard. Here, too, was one of the bizarre spectacles that highlighted this bizarre action—a pet bear, roaming the deck unhurt, licking up the blood.

But with Perry's flagship dead in the water, the wounded Barclay felt safe in his belief that the British had won a victory.

As it turned out, that was premature.

CHAPTER SEVEN

"We Have Met the Enemy ... "

OLIVER HAZARD PERRY HAD NO INTENTION OF GIVING UP. WHATEVER MOTIVE ELLIOTT HAD HAD FOR STAYING OUT OF THE BATTLE, HE HAD LEFT PERRY A SEA-WORTHY BRIG TO CONTINUE THE CONTEST. AND SO PERRY MADE A DECISION THAT WOULD TURN HIM INTO A NATIONAL HERO. HE CALLED FOR A BOAT, TOOK FOUR MEN, AND THEN TURNED TO YARNELL.

"I leave you to surrender the vessel to the enemy," he said, and with that he ordered his men to pull for *Niagara*.

At the last moment he remembered his special flag and called for it. "If victory is to be gained, I'll gain it," he said.

He couldn't control his excitement. He refused to sit down until his men threatened to ship their oars because they feared for his life. The British, aboard *Detroit*, caught a glimpse of the little boat half-hidden by the gunsmoke. Musket balls whistled past Perry's head. Oars were shattered. Round shot sent columns of spray into the boat. But Perry's Luck held. When a twenty-four-pound (11-kg) ball hit the side of the rowboat, he took off his jacket and plugged the hole.

On *Lawrence*, some of the wounded wanted to fight on instead of surrendering.

"Sink the ship!" they cried, and "Let us sink with her!"

But Yarnell did not intend to indulge in further sacrifice. As he reached *Niagara*, Perry turned and saw *Lawrence*'s flag come down. The British, however, couldn't board the prize—all of their lifeboats had been shattered.

Now the astonished Elliott saw the American commodore come over the side, a scarecrow figure, hatless, his clothes in tatters, blackened from head to foot by gunsmoke, spattered with blood.

"How goes the day?" asked Elliott needlessly.

"Bad enough," said Perry. "We have been cut all to pieces." Then: "Why are the gunboats so far behind?"

"I'll bring them up," said Elliott.

"Do so, sir," Perry replied shortly.

Elliott took a rowboat and started off through the heavy fire, using a speaking-trumpet to call the smaller craft forward into battle. He took command of the little *Somers*, and there he indulged in a strange display of temperament. When a cannonball whizzed across the deck he ducked and a gun captain laughed. In a fury Elliott struck him across the face with his trumpet and arrested the sailing master, whom he believed to be drunk. But he got his gunboats quickly into action and poured a heavy fire on the British ships.

Perry was also in action. He hoisted his personal flag on *Niagara* and was intent on cutting directly through the British line, dividing it in two. Barclay, who was back on deck with his wounds dressed, saw what Perry intended to do. A fresh breeze had sprung up. *Niagara* was bearing down at right angles to his ship. In a few minutes she'd be able to rake the full length of the British vessel with her broadside of ten guns. That was a manoeuvre that every commander feared.

Barclay knew what to do. He would have to bring his ship around before the wind so that his own broadside of undamaged guns could face Niagara.

Barclay knew what to do. He would have to bring his ship around before the wind so that his own broadside of undamaged guns could face *Niagara*. But before he could do that he was struck down again by a charge of grapeshot that tore his shoulder blade to pieces, leaving a gaping wound and rendering his one good arm useless. At the same instant his second-in-command fell mortally wounded, and the ship was in charge of the young Lieutenant George Inglis.

Now the American gunboats in the stern began to rake the British vessels. Inglis tried to bring his badly mauled flagship around. But *Queen Charlotte*, which had been supporting Barclay in his battle with *Lawrence*, had moved in too close. She was lying directly astern in the lee of *Detroit*, which had literally taken the wind out of her sails.

Queen Charlotte's senior officers were dead. Robert Irvine had little experience in working a big ship under these conditions. As *Detroit* attempted to come around, the masts and the bowsprits of the two ships became hopelessly entangled and they were trapped. *Queen Charlotte* couldn't even fire at the enemy without hitting fellow Britons.

Only seven minutes had passed since Perry boarded *Niagara*. Now he was passing directly through the ragged British line, a half pistol-shot from the flagship.

"Take good aim, boys, don't waste your shot!" he shouted. His cannon were all double-shotted—two balls hurling through the air instead of one. That increased the carnage.

Niagara came directly abeam of the entangled British ships, and as it did so Perry fired his broadside, raking both vessels and also *Hunter*, which was a little bit astern. On the left, Perry fired his other broadside at two smaller British craft, *Chippawa* and the rudderless *Lady Prevost*.

The damage was frightful. Perry could hear the shrieks of newly wounded men above the roar of the cannon. At this point every British commander and his second was a casualty and unable to remain on deck.

Looking across at the shattered *Lady Prevost*, Perry's gaze rested on an odd spectacle. Her commander, shot in the face by a musket ball, was the only man on deck, leaning on the companionway, his gaze fixed blankly on *Niagara*. His wounds had driven him out of his mind and his crew, unable to face the fire, had fled below.

Detroit's masts crumbled under Perry's repeated broadsides. *Queen Charlotte's* mizzenmast was shot away. The ships were hopelessly entangled and taking a terrible beating. An officer appeared with a white handkerchief tied to a pike. He couldn't haul down the flag because Barclay had nailed his colours to the mast.

Queen Charlotte, *Hunter*, and *Lady Prevost* all surrendered. Two British gunboats, *Chippawa* and *Little Belt*, attempted to make a run for it but were quickly caught. To Perry's joy, his old ship, *Lawrence*, drifting far astern, had once again raised her colours because the British had been unable to board her.

At three o'clock Perry's victory was absolute and unprecedented—the first time in history that an entire British fleet had been defeated and captured intact by its adversary. The ships built on the banks of the wilderness lake had served their purpose. They would not fight again.

When Elliott boarded *Detroit* there was so much blood on the deck that he slipped, drenching his clothing in gore. The ship's sides were studded with iron—round shot, canister, and grapeshot—so much metal that no man could place a hand on its starboard side without touching some.

Down came Barclay's colours. And Barclay said to Elliott, ruefully, "I would not have given sixpence for your squadron when I left the deck." He was in bad shape: weak, perhaps near death from loss of blood and the shock of his mangled shoulder.

Perry, sitting on a dismounted cannon aboard *Niagara*, took off his round hat and, using it for a desk, scrawled out a brief message to Harrison on the back of an envelope. It was a sentence destined to be the most famous of the war: "*We have met the enemy and they are ours. Two Ships, two Brigs, one Schooner, and one Sloop.*"

Around the lake the sounds of battle had been heard, but none could be sure who had won. At Amherstburg, Procter's deputy believed the British to be the victors. At Cleveland, seventy miles (112 km) away, a carpenter working on a new courthouse could hear the sound of the cannons. The villagers assembled to wait until the firing ceased. And because the last five reports came from heavy guns—American carronades—they concluded that Perry had won and gave three cheers.

Aboard *Lawrence*, as Perry returned to receive the official surrender, a handful of survivors greeted him silently. Twenty corpses lay on the deck, including close friends with whom he had dined the night before. He looked around for his little brother, Alexander, and found him sound asleep in a hammock, exhausted by the battle.

Perry put on his full-dress uniform and received those members of the enemy still able to walk. They picked their way among the bodies and offered him their swords, which he refused to accept. Instead he inquired after Barclay. His concern for his vanquished enemy was real and sincere.

That night, as the September shadows lengthened, Perry lay down among the corpses, his fever having subsided under the adrenalin of battle. He folded his hands over his breast and, with his sword beside him, slept the sleep of the dead.

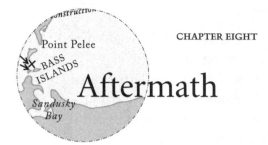

CHAPTER EIGHT

Aftermath

THE AMERICAN FLEET, WITH ITS PRIZES AND ITS PRISONERS, WAS BACK AT PUT-IN BAY BY MID-MORNING ON SEPTEMBER 11. IN THE WARDROOM, DR. USHER PARSONS HAD BEEN TOILING SINCE DAWN AMPUTATING LIMBS. HE HAD WORKED ON NINETY-SIX MEN AND SAVED NINETY-THREE.

A special service was held for the officers of both fleets. Barclay, in spite of his wounds, insisted on attending. Perry supported him, one arm around his shoulder. The effort was too much for the British commander, who had to be carried back to his berth on *Detroit*. Perry sat with him until the soft hours of the morning, when the British commander finally dropped off to sleep.

The prisoners were struck by the American's courtesy. Now that the heat of battle had passed, he looked on his foes without rancour, making sure his officers treated them well. To Barclay he was "a valiant and generous enemy."

The British commander would never again be able to raise his arm above his shoulder, and so he wrote to his fiancée offering to release her from their engagement. For once in his life, he was not "ill used." The spirited young woman replied that if there was enough of him left to contain his soul, she would marry him.

Elliott's behaviour had enraged Perry's officers. But Perry, intoxicated by victory, was in an expansive mood. He knew that Elliott had acted disgracefully, but he was too happy to take action against him. It was in his power to ruin Elliott's career, but that was not in his nature.

However, the contest between Perry and Elliott was not over. As the news of the great victory spread across the United States, as bonfires flared and public dinners, toasts, orations, songs, and poems trumpeted the country's triumph, the seeds of a bitter controversy began to sprout.

For the next thirty years, the Battle of Lake Erie would be fought again and again with affidavits, courts of inquiry, books, pamphlets, newspaper articles, even pistols. By 1818 Perry's own good nature had evaporated. He called Elliott "mean and despicable."

When Elliott challenged him to a duel, Perry responded by demanding his court martial. It never took place. Even after Perry's death from yellow fever in 1819, the verbal war did not end: a literary battle went on. Nor did it die until the last of the participants had gone to their final rest to join those others who, in the bloom of youth, had bloodied the raw new decks of two fleets that tore at each other on a cloudless September afternoon in 1813.

INDEX

"Meeting of Brock and Tecumseh, 1812"
by Charles William Jefferys. The meeting of Brock and
Tecumseh, two of the most charismatic leaders in the
War of 1812, was a seminal moment.

(ARCHIVES OF ONTARIO, AC621231)

THE DEATH OF TECUMSEH

CONTENTS

CHAPTER ONE

The Shawnee's Dream

TECUMSEH! THAT NAME ECHOES DOWN THE CORRIDORS OF HISTORY—AS WELL IT MIGHT. OF ALL THE GREAT NATIVE LEADERS ON BOTH SIDES OF THE CANADA–U.S. BORDER, HE IS WITHOUT DOUBT THE GREATEST.

A master strategist, his handling of his Native followers helped General Isaac Brock capture Detroit in the summer of 1812.

A brilliant orator, he could bring tears to the eyes of white men who did not understand a word he said.

A compassionate leader, he was opposed to the ritual killing or torture of prisoners.

A champion of his people, his dream was to unite the various tribes who occupied American territory and to form an independent Native state.

This is the story of Tecumseh's last brave days in the second year of the War of 1812. But the beginnings of the story go back to the Battle of Tippecanoe in 1811.

Tecumseh—a muscular Shawnee with golden skin and hazel eyes—had every reason to hate the Americans. They were driving his people farther and farther west, stealing Native land. When Tecumseh and his mystic brother, the Prophet, tried to set up an independent community called Prophet's Town on the Wabash (in what is now Indiana), his old nemesis, William Henry Harrison, governor of Indiana Territory, attacked and destroyed it.

It was this attack—the Battle of Tippecanoe—that caused Tecumseh to gather his followers and cross the border into Canada. For years he had dreamed an ancient dream of a confederacy which would unite the tribes and set up a Native state in the heart of North America. We can see his passion and his commitment in a rare published report of a speech he made in 1806:

It is true I am Shawnee. My forefathers were warriors. Their son is a warrior. From them I take only my existence. From my tribe I take nothing. I am the maker of my own fortune. And oh!, that I might make that of my red people, and of my country, as great as the conceptions of my mind, when I think of the Spirit that rules the universe ...

The way, and the only way, to check and stop this evil, is for all the red men to unite in claiming a common and equal right in the land; as it was at first; and should be yet; for it never was divided, but belongs to us all, for the use of each. That no part has a right to sell, even to each other, much less to strangers who want it all and will not do with less ...

Sell a country! Why not sell the air, the clouds, and the great sea, as well as the earth? Did not the Great Spirit make them all for the use of his children?

At Tippecanoe, Harrison, hungry for Indian land, determined to stop any attempt by the Shawnee chief to form such a confederacy, and while he destroyed the community, he could not shatter Tecumseh's dream.

Harrison's senseless destruction of Prophet's Town drove the Shawnee and his followers—representing a dozen tribes—into the arms of the British and Canadians. When war broke out the following June, Tecumseh was determined to fight against the Americans. And so, in trying to stop the formation of an Indian confederacy, Harrison had succeeded in strengthening Tecumseh's plans.

In the summer of 1812, the British, Canadians, and Indians hurled back every American attempt to invade Canada. But now, as our story begins, in September 1813, the tide was turning.

Tecumseh's old enemy, Harrison, was on the march following the American victory in the Battle of Lake Erie earlier that summer. All the British ships were sunk or lost in that lake battle, and Erie was now in American hands. Their vessels could cruise those waters at will, landing soldiers anywhere.

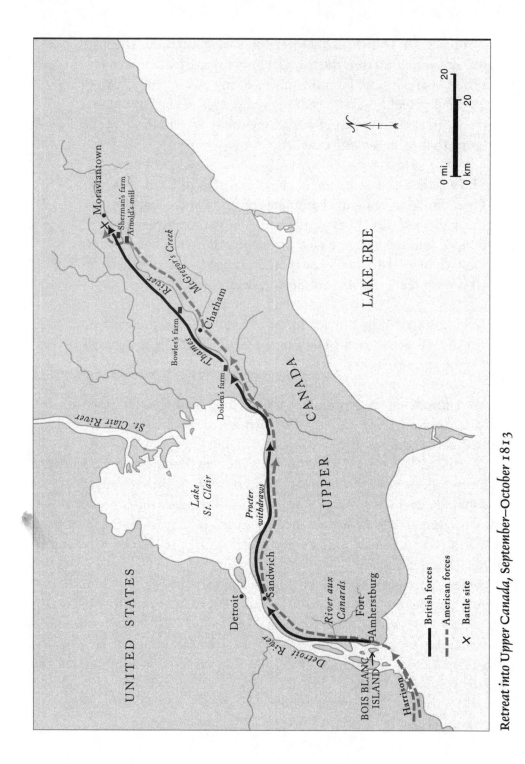

Retreat into Upper Canada, September–October 1813

The British could not hope to hold the American territory that Brock and Tecumseh had captured the previous summer. Detroit would have to be evacuated. Amherstburg, on the Canadian side, was threatened.

The British had two choices: either to stand and fight at the water's edge or to retreat up the valley of the Thames, dig in, and try to stop the American advance. The British command wanted to retreat, but to Tecumseh retreat was out of the question. He and his followers wanted to stand and fight.

Tecumseh must have wished that the British commander at Amherstburg, Major General Henry Procter, had some of the brilliance of Isaac Brock, at whose side he had fought the previous summer. But Brock had been killed at Queenston Heights. And Procter lacked Brock's drive, his sense of leadership, and his easy way with his men. He was in his fiftieth year, a good enough soldier, but not very imaginative. There was a heaviness about him, his face was fleshy, and his body tended toward fat. He was "one of the meanest looking men I ever saw," in the words of an American colonel.

Procter had three failings: he couldn't make up his mind quickly, as good leaders must; he kept his plans to himself without telling others; and, in moments of stress, he tended to panic.

Tecumseh was in a violent passion. He had just come over the lake from Detroit, which the British, to his fury, had decided to abandon. Now it looked as if Procter was also trying to retreat from Amherstburg.

Procter, as usual, was being secretive. He insisted, against all evidence, that the British had won the lake battle! That further angered Tecumseh. The Shawnee was no fool and didn't like to be treated as one. He had been quarrelling with Procter since Brock's death. In Tecumseh's view, Brock was a *man*, whereas Procter was only fit to wear women's clothes. And now here he was, a British general, afraid to face his Shawnee ally with the truth.

We cannot blame Tecumseh for being disillusioned. He had, since 1809, been an optimist, convinced that he could somehow gather the various tribes into a mighty union. By helping the British, he thought, they would be able to hold onto their hunting grounds and their traditional way of life.

But the war had gone sour. Tecumseh had just come back to Canada from the south, where he had tried to convince the other tribes to join him.

He had failed. He was still obsessed with a single goal, but that goal now seemed to be in doubt, and Tecumseh was close to despair.

He told his followers that the King over the water had broken his promise to them. The British had pledged that there would be plenty of white men to fight along with the Indians. But where were they?

"The number," said Tecumseh, "is not now greater than at the commencement of the war; we are treated by them like the dogs of snipe hunters; we are always sent ahead to *start the game*; it is better that we should return to our country and let the Americans come and fight the British."

Many of Tecumseh's people agreed. But the Sioux, and their one-time enemies, the Chippewa, who had come over to the British side, persuaded him to remain.

Now, with Fort Detroit being dismantled, Tecumseh had further evidence of Procter's distrust. Off he went in a fury to the home of Matthew Elliott of the Indian Department at Amherstburg, who cringed under Tecumseh's fury. Tecumseh warned Elliott that if Procter retreated, his followers would make a public spectacle. He threatened to bring out the great wampum belt that was a symbol of British-Indian friendship and cut it in two to indicate eternal separation. Worse, Tecumseh warned, the Indians would fall on the British army, which they outnumbered three to one, and cut the British to pieces.

Retreat was not in Tecumseh's makeup. He believed only in attack. His one goal was to kill as many of the enemy as possible. Now in his mid-forties, he had been fighting white Americans all his life to prevent them moving into land that had always been Native territory.

There was no love lost between the Kentucky frontiersmen and the Indians. The whites were moving westward, seizing the land as their own; the Shawnee were engaged in a vain attempt to stop them. At the age of fifteen, Tecumseh was fighting Kentuckians. At sixteen, he was ambushing their boats. At twenty-two, he was serving as a raider and scout against the United States, which sided with the white frontiersmen.

When his elder brother was killed, Tecumseh became band leader in his stead, going north again to take part in the disastrous Battle of Fallen Timbers. There, in August 1794, not far from the present site of Toledo,

Ohio, General "Mad Anthony" Wayne attacked and destroyed the Northwest Indian Confederacy, ending the Natives' attempt to retain their land. Three thousand Americans destroyed a force of fourteen hundred Natives. Most of the present state of Ohio and parts of Indiana, Illinois, and Michigan were lost to the tribes, which included the Shawnee.

On that black day, Tecumseh, his musket jammed, tried vainly to rally his followers, waving a useless weapon as they scattered before the American bayonets. Tecumseh was a man who didn't believe in holding back, but now his British allies wanted him to do just that.

CHAPTER TWO

"I Feel I Shall Never Return"

ONCE AGAIN TECUMSEH WAS FACING HIS OLD ENEMY, WILLIAM HENRY HARRISON. ON MORE THAN ONE OCCASION HE HAD USED HIS GOLDEN VOICE TO FRUSTRATE HARRISON'S HUNGER FOR INDIAN LANDS. NOW HARRISON HAD LAKE ERIE TO HIMSELF AND COULD LAND ANYWHERE.

Harrison had a score to settle with Tecumseh, who had frustrated his land grab. But Tecumseh had a score to settle with Harrison, who had destroyed the capital of his confederacy in the Battle of Tippecanoe. He could not wait to get at the general, and he used the weapon of his oratory to rally his people and to blackmail the British into standing fast.

On the morning of September 14—just four days after the Americans won the Battle of Lake Erie—he summoned his followers at Amherstburg. They squatted in their hundreds on the fort's parade ground as he strode over to a large stone on the riverbank. It was here that announcements of importance were made and here that Tecumseh made the last speech of his life. It was addressed to Procter, who was standing nearby with a group of officers.

First Tecumseh spoke of his suspicions, born of long experience going back to the peace that followed the American Revolution:

Father, listen. Our fleet has gone out, we know they have fought. We have heard the great guns, but know nothing of what has happened to our father with one arm. [A reference to Captain Robert Barclay, commander of the British fleet.] Our ships have gone one way and we are much astonished to see our father tying up everything and preparing to run the other, without letting his children know what his intentions are.

You always told us to remain here and take care of our land ...
You always told us you would never draw your foot off British
ground. But now, Father, we see that you are drawing back,
and we are sorry to see our father doing so without seeing the
enemy. We must compare our father's conduct to a fat animal
that carries its tail upon its back. But when affrighted, it drops
it between its legs and runs off.

He urged Procter to stay and fight any attempted invasion. If
Procter was defeated, Tecumseh promised he would remain on the
British side and retreat with the troops. If Procter wouldn't fight,
the Indians would:

Father, you have got the arms and ammunition ... If you have
any idea of going away, give them to us ... Our lives are in the
lands of the Great Spirit; we are determined to defend our
land; and if it is his will, we wish to leave our bones upon it.

With these words, some of his people leapt up prepared to attack the
British immediately if their leader gave the word. But they did not act,
because Procter promised to hold a council with the tribesmen two days
later.

Procter was faced with a serious problem. His fort was defenceless. He
had stripped it of its cannon to arm one of the big ships now captured by
the Americans. A third of the troops had also been lost to him in that battle. He was out of provisions. The new supplies would have to be sent over-
land because they could no longer move by water, which the Americans
controlled.

What's more, Harrison had a strong attack force and also the means to
get across the lake unmolested and into Canada. Procter's own men were
battle weary, starving, and in despair over the loss of the fleet.

Procter was not daring. He had often opposed the bold Isaac Brock, who
had captured Detroit in a single thrust. Procter had been against that. He
was a man who went by the book, and, in doing so, often wasted precious
time.

The British felt they had reason to withdraw from Fort Amherstburg. With the lake battle lost, they knew that Harrison could land troops anywhere along the north shore of Lake Erie and get around the British to take them from the rear. But if Procter moved up the Thames Valley, Harrison's supply lines would be stretched to the limit.

Harrison's army was composed mainly of volunteers who had signed on for only six months. After that term was up, experience showed that most of them would hightail it back to their farms in the United States.

But if Procter was to move, he would have to move at once, for Harrison would be at his heels, giving him no chance to prepare a defence. There, Procter showed his hesitancy. A week went by and nothing happened. Then at last he held his promised meeting with the tribesmen.

Here was his problem: ten thousand Native women and children would have to be brought across the lake and moved up the Thames Valley ahead of the army, together with those white settlers who didn't wish to remain under foreign rule. The sick would also have to be removed, and that would be awkward. Furthermore, they would have to take all the military stores with them—a cumbersome business.

This was an enormous undertaking. It required drive, organizational ability, decision, and a sense of urgency—qualities that Procter didn't have.

Indeed, this evacuation posed as many problems for Procter as did the advancing American forces. Harrison was not encumbered by thousands of Natives and civilians clogging the narrow trails along the Thames.

Procter met the Indians on September 18. Again Tecumseh urged that Harrison be allowed to land and march on Amherstburg. He and his Indians were prepared to attack on the American flank, with the British facing the front. If the attack failed, Tecumseh said, he would make a stand at River aux Canards, three miles (4.8 km) north of Amherstburg. He had defended it successfully the previous year, when an American force had earlier tried to invade Canada.

Procter rejected the plan. Tecumseh, in a fury, called him "a miserable old squaw." At that the chiefs leapt up, brandishing tomahawks, their yells echoing down from the vaulted roof of the lofty council chamber.

Finally Procter abandoned the secrecy that had caused so much trouble up to this point. He unrolled a map and explained his position. He pointed out that if gunboats came up the Detroit River they could cut off the Indians camped on the American side. That would make it impossible for them to help the British. It would allow Harrison to move to the mouth of the Thames River and attack the British from the rear, cutting off all retreat.

Tecumseh considered this carefully. He asked some questions and made some shrewd remarks. He had never seen a map like this before. This part of the country was new to him, but he quickly saw the significance of the problems the British faced.

Procter promised to make a stand near the community of Chatham, at the forks of the Thames River. He said he would fortify the position and would "mix our bones with [your] bones." Tecumseh asked for time to confer with his fellow chiefs. He managed to convince them to reverse their own stand and follow him up a river unknown to them and into a foreign country. But Tecumseh still had doubts.

On September 23 the British destroyed Fort Amherstburg, wrecking the dockyards and burning all the public buildings. The army set off for Sandwich (near the present city of Windsor), directly across from Detroit. "We are going to follow the British," Tecumseh remarked sadly, "and I feel that I shall never return."

CHAPTER THREE

"We Must Not Retreat"

THE BRITISH WITHDRAWAL MOVED AT A SNAIL'S PACE. IT TOOK TEN DAYS JUST
TO GET ALL THE STORES AND BAGGAGE A FEW MILES UP THE DETROIT RIVER BY
WAGON AND SCOW. THE TOWNSPEOPLE INSISTED ON BRINGING THEIR PERSON-
AL BELONGINGS — AN UNNECESSARY BURDEN THAT TIED UP THE BOATS AND
CAUSED A DELAY IN MOVING THE WOMEN, CHILDREN, AND THE SICK.

The military stores were in a snarl. Entrenching tools, for instance,
which should have been carried with the troops, were placed at the bottom
of the boats and so were difficult to reach when the soldiers needed them.

Finally, on September 27, the British destroyed the barracks and public
buildings at Detroit. The rearguard moved across the river. The rest of the
troops marched out of Sandwich.

That same evening, Jacques Bâby, a prominent merchant and a lieutenant-colonel in the militia, gave a dinner for the senior officers of the 41st
Regiment in his stone mansion at Sandwich. Tecumseh attended wearing
deerskin trousers, a calico shirt, and a red cloak. He was in a black mood,
eating with pistols on each side of his plate, his hunting knife in front of
him.

A knock came at the door. A British scout announced that the enemy
fleet had entered the river and was sailing north near Amherstburg.
Tecumseh rose, his hands on his pistols, and turned to General Procter.

Father, we must go to meet the enemy ... We must not retreat ...
If you take us from this post you will lead us far, far away ... tell
us Goodbye forever and leave us to the mercy of the Long
Knives. I tell you I am sorry I have listened to you thus far, for
if we remained at the town ... we could have kept the enemy

from landing and have held our hunting grounds for our children.

Now they tell me you want to withdraw to the river Thames ... I am tired of it all. Every word you say evaporates like the smoke from our pipes. Father, you are like the crawfish that does not know how to walk straight ahead.

Procter did not reply, and the dinner broke up. Tecumseh had no choice but to follow the British with those warriors who were still loyal to his cause. But many were not. His force now numbered no more than one thousand. The Ottawa and Chippewa bands had already sent three warriors to make peace with Harrison. The Wyandot, Miami, and some Delaware were about to do the same. In 1812 these tribesmen had been necessary for a victory. Without them Upper Canada would have become an American state. Now Procter saw them only as a nuisance.

In the days that followed, the British general seemed unable to make any decision. Procter literally failed to burn his bridges behind him to delay Harrison. He believed that if he did so the Indians would think themselves cut off and abandon his cause. He purposely held back the army to wait for the Indians. Aware of his pledge to Tecumseh to make a stand at the forks of the Thames, he dashed ahead to look over the ground. He left his second-in-command, Lieutenant-Colonel Augustus Warburton, in charge—but with no instructions of any kind.

He couldn't get the Indians out of his mind. Their presence haunted him. The promises wrung from him at the council obsessed him. Tecumseh's taunts stung.

There was something more. His own superiors had stressed again and again the necessity of keeping on good terms with the tribes. They knew that without the Indians the war would have already been lost.

Procter had been ordered to keep the Indians happy "by any means in your power" and to promise them mountains of presents if they would only follow the army.

There was another fear. What if the Indians did defect? Would they fall upon the British, destroy the army, and swell the ranks of the invaders?

And so Procter was caught in a trap. If he lost his Native allies he would be blamed; but if Tecumseh remained his ally, Procter wasn't really in charge. He sent his engineering officer upstream to the forks of the Thames, at the community of Chatham. The officer reported that this was not the best place to make the promised stand. But something had to be done.

Finally Procter selected Moraviantown (near the present community of Thamesville), twenty-six miles (41.6 km) farther upstream—a slightly better position.

Procter's intentions were clear. The army would stand and fight at Moraviantown and not at the forks of the Thames. So, Henry Procter would always be able to say he had kept his promise to Tecumseh. But somehow, in his haste, he didn't get around to informing Lieutenant-Colonel Warburton, who was leading the army up the valley.

> *Johnson made no bones about his belief that the English should be driven from the New World. "I shall never die contented until I see ... her territories incorporated with the United States," he said.*

The British had abandoned Detroit, and with it control of all American territory captured the previous year. Now with the army back on Canadian soil, fleeing up the Thames Valley with Harrison close behind, another American force was also heading for Canada. Twelve hundred mounted Kentucky riflemen galloped along the Detroit road to help reinforce Harrison's invasion army. Their leader was a fiery young congressman, Colonel Richard Mentor Johnson.

Johnson, a handsome, stocky figure with a shock of auburn hair, had made a name for himself as an eloquent politician. He was the first native-born Kentuckian to be elected to both the state legislature and the federal congress. He was also a leading member of the group of War Hawks who had goaded the United States into declaring war on Canada in 1812.

Like so many of his colleagues, Johnson was reared on tales of Indian attacks. His family were all Indian-fighters. Unlike the New Englanders and the Pennsylvanians, the Kentuckians regarded the invasion of Canada as a holy war, "a second revolution as important as the first," in Johnson's words. It was also seen as a war of conquest.

Johnson made no bones about his belief that the English should be driven from the New World. "I shall never die contented until I see ... her territories incorporated with the United States," he said.

That, of course, had not been the original intention of the Americans when they invaded Canada. They were simply infuriated because, although the United States had not taken sides during the Napoleonic Wars, the English had insisted on mounting a blockade to prevent American ships bringing supplies into French ports.

Angered by the British, but unable to attack them across three thousand miles (4,800 km) of Atlantic water, they decided instead to give Britain's main colony—Canada—a bloody nose. But the war had been going on for a year and that hadn't happened.

Recruits flocked to Johnson's banner—veterans of the American Revolution, former Indian-fighters, and young men raised on tales of adventure. They had all made their wills and had resolved never to return to Kentucky unless they came back as conquerors. The captain of the first battalion, Robert McAfee, was one who foresaw the shores of Lake Erie becoming the richest and most important section of the United States. "It is necessary that Canada should be ours," he wrote in his journal.

Johnson and his brother, James, had fifteen hundred six-month volunteers under their command. Each man was decked out in a blue hunting shirt with a red belt and blue pantaloons, also fringed with red. They were armed with pistols, swords, hunting knives, tomahawks, muskets, and Kentucky squirrel rifles.

Ever since mid-May, these men had been herded through the wilderness for more than twelve hundred miles (about 2,000 km) without once firing a shot at the enemy. They longed for action, and now at last it seemed they could smell it.

Johnson could hardly wait to get at Procter, whom he called a "monster," because Procter's Indians had massacred the Kentucky forces at the Battle of Frenchtown on the southwestern shore of Lake Erie the previous autumn. His men were just as eager. Off they rode toward Detroit, swimming their horses across the little streams, on the lookout for hostile Indians. The news of the British withdrawal excited them.

On the afternoon of September 30, they reached their objective. The entire population of Detroit turned out to greet them. The governor of

Kentucky himself, old Isaac Shelby, had, at Harrison's request, brought some two thousand eager volunteers to swell the ranks of the invading army.

Johnson now learned to his surprise that Procter had abandoned Amherstburg without fighting and that Harrison had already seized that fort. Harrison now had a force of about five thousand men. Two thousand were regular soldiers. The rest were amateurs.

Harrison didn't expect to catch Procter, because the British had grabbed every horse in the country. It was all he could do to find a broken-down pony to carry the aging Shelby along with the troops. But he expected and hoped that Procter would make a stand somewhere on the Thames. Harrison's greatest fear was that Procter *wouldn't* stop. The American general wanted to fight and thought he could win.

Shelby hadn't been able to resist Harrison's request that he come along. He was sixty-three years old, paunchy and double-chinned, with close-cropped white hair. But he commanded the respect of the Kentucky soldiers, who called him Old King's Mountain after his memorable victory at that place during the Revolutionary War in 1780.

Harrison wanted Shelby's opinion: should the army pursue Procter by land up the Thames Valley, or should the troops be carried by boat to Long Point, along the lake, and then march in by the Long Point road? Shelby believed Procter could be overtaken by land. Harrison's council of war agreed.

Harrison decided to take thirty-five hundred men up the Thames, leaving seven hundred behind to hold Detroit. Johnson's mounted volunteers would be in the lead. The rest, who had left their knapsacks and blankets on an island in the river, would follow.

But Harrison had real trouble persuading any Kentuckian to stay on the American side of the river. They considered it an insult to be left behind. In the end he had to conscript them to hold Detroit.

On the other hand, the Pennsylvania militia stood on its constitutional right not to fight outside the territory of the United States.

"I believe the boys are not willing to go, General," one of their captains told him.

"The boys, eh?" Harrison remarked sarcastically. "I believe some of the officers *too* are not willing to go. Thank God I have Kentuckians enough to go with you."

He knew that speed was all important. Shelby kept pointing out that "if we desire to overtake the enemy, we must do more than he does, by early and enforced marches."

And so at dawn on October 2, as Procter continued to dawdle, the Americans pushed forward, sometimes at a half-run to keep up with the mounted men. Johnson asked Harrison if he could ride ahead in search of the British rearguard, and Harrison agreed. But he added a word of caution: he was afraid of the Indians.

"Go, Colonel, but remember discipline. Be cautious, sir, as well as brave and active, as I know you all are."

Off went Johnson at the head of a group of volunteers. Not far from the Thames, they captured six British soldiers who told them that Procter's army was only fifteen miles (24 km) above the mouth of the river. It was nearly sunset, but when the regiment heard that, it was determined to move at once. In one day Harrison's army had marched twenty-five miles (40 km).

The troops set off again at dawn. Only three gunboats could get up the shallow and winding Thames. Harrison figured Procter didn't know the speed he was moving at, because Procter hadn't bothered to destroy any of the bridges to hold up the American advance.

That afternoon the army captured a British lieutenant and eleven dragoons. Now Harrison learned that the British had no knowledge of his advance.

By evening, his army was camped ten miles (16 km) up the river and just four miles (6.4 km) below Matthew Dolsen's farm at Dover, from which the British had only just departed. It had taken Procter five days to make the journey from Sandwich. Harrison managed to cover the same ground in less than half the time.

CHAPTER FOUR

Tecumseh Prepares for Battle

AUGUSTUS WARBURTON, PROCTER'S SECOND-IN-COMMAND, WAS CONFUSED AND PERPLEXED. HE HAD NO IDEA WHAT HE WAS TO DO, BECAUSE HIS COMMANDER HADN'T TOLD HIM. HE HAD LEARNED THAT THE AMERICANS WERE ON THE MARCH A FEW MILES DOWNSTREAM. HIS OWN MEN HAD REACHED THE PLACE WHERE PROCTER HAD DECIDED TO MAKE A STAND, BUT NOW PROCTER HAD CHANGED HIS MIND AND RUSHED UP THE RIVER TO MORAVIANTOWN, HAVING APPARENTLY DECIDED TO MEET THE ENEMY THERE.

Captain William Crowther had a problem, too. Procter had ordered him to fortify Dover, and Crowther wanted to throw up a temporary gun battery, cut loopholes in the log buildings, and dig trenches. But all the tools had been sent on to Bowles's farm seven miles (11 km) upriver. There were no wagons or boats to bring them back, and Crowther was unable to follow his orders.

It was too late anyway. Tecumseh was across the river on the *south* bank, and he insisted on moving three miles (4.8 km) upstream to Chatham, at the forks. It was there that Procter had originally promised to make a stand and, if necessary, lay his bones with those of the Indians. But again, he had neglected to tell Tecumseh of his change of plan.

Warburton wanted to keep the Indians on the British side and so followed Tecumseh. The army, which had lingered at Dolsen's farm for two days waiting for Procter, moved three miles (4.8 km) to Chatham and stopped again. It was Tecumseh—not Procter, not Warburton—who was calling the tune.

The Shawnee war chief was in a fury; there were no fortifications at Chatham. Procter had betrayed him—or so he believed. Half his force had left, headed by Chief Walk-in-the-Water of the senior tribe of Wyandot.

Now Matthew Elliott, his life threatened by the angry Natives, crossed the river and urged Warburton to stand and fight at Chatham.

"I will not, by God, sacrifice myself," he declared in tears.

Warburton asked Elliott to tell Tecumseh that he would try to keep Procter's promise and make a stand on any ground of the Indians' choosing. He had already sent two messages to Procter, warning him that the enemy was closing in and explaining that he had moved forward to Chatham. But Procter went on to Moraviantown regardless, after sending his wife off to safety at Burlington Heights.

The Indians were angered at Procter's absence. Tecumseh's brother, the Prophet, said he would personally like to tear off the general's epaulettes, because he wasn't fit to wear them. The army, too, was disturbed. Mutiny was in the air.

There was talk of Warburton taking over from Procter. But Warburton would have none of that. Major Adam Muir of the rearguard declared that Procter ought to be hanged for being away and Warburton hanged for shirking his responsibility.

With the American army at his heels, Warburton got two messages on the morning of October 4. The first came from Procter, announcing he would return to join the troops. The second, from Tecumseh, told him that the Indians had decided to retire to Moraviantown.

Warburton waited until ten in the morning—but still no Procter. He could hear shots across the river: the Indians skirmishing with the enemy. Just as he set his troops in motion he got another message from Procter, ordering him to move a few miles upriver to Bowles's farm. The column moved slowly, held up often by Indian women who forced it to halt time after time to let them pass by.

Bowles's was as far as the boats could go; the river above was too shallow. There, Warburton finally met up with his general, who was already giving orders to destroy all the stores—guns, shells, cord, cable, naval equipment. In short, the long shuttle by boat from Amherstburg, which had held up the withdrawal, had been for nothing. Procter even ordered two gunboats sunk in the river to slow down the Americans' progress.

By eight that evening, the forward troops had reached Lemuel Sherman's farm, about four miles (6.4 km) from Moraviantown. There they halted for the night. Ovens were built, and orders were given for bread to be baked. But there was no bread: the bakers said they had to look after their families first. And so, footsore, exhausted, and half-starved, with their morale at its lowest ebb, the men subsisted on whatever bread they had saved from the last issue at Dolsen's.

Tecumseh, meanwhile, fought a rearguard action at the forks of the Thames, near Chatham. His followers tore the planks off the bridge at McGregor's Creek, and when Harrison's forward scouts, under a veteran frontiersman, William Whitley, tried to cross on what was left of the bridge, the Natives opened fire from their hiding places in the woods.

Whitley, a sixty-three-year-old Indian-fighter and Kentucky pioneer, had insisted on marching as a private soldier under Harrison, accompanied by two black servants. As the Indians fired, he toppled off the muddy timbers and fell twelve feet (3.6 m) into the water, but he managed to swim ashore, gripping his silver-mounted rifle. The Indians were driven off with shots from two six-pounder (3-kg) cannons. The bridge was repaired, and the Americans pushed on.

Tecumseh reached Christopher Arnold's mill, twelve miles (19 km) upriver from the forks, that evening. Arnold, a militia captain, was already a friend of Tecumseh from an earlier encounter, and he offered him dinner and a bed. But he was worried about his mill: the Indians had already burned McGregor's. Tecumseh promised it would be spared, for he saw no point in useless destruction. With the other mill gone, the white settlers would have to depend on this one.

Fact mingles with myth in the reports of those last hours as Tecumseh prepared for battle. Those whose paths crossed his would always remember what was done and what was said, and they would hand it down years later to their sons and grandsons.

Young Johnny Toll, playing along the riverbank near McGregor's Creek, would never forget the hazel-eyed Shawnee who warned him, "Boy, run away home at once. The soldiers are coming. There is war and you might get hurt."

Sixteen-year-old Abraham Holmes would always remember the sight of the Shawnee war chief standing near the Arnold mill on the morning of October 5, his hand at the head of his white pony. What a scene that was:

the tall figure dressed in buckskin from neck to knees, a sash at his waist, his headdress adorned with ostrich plumes, waiting until the last of his men had passed the mill and was safe. Holmes was so impressed he would name his first-born son Tecumseh.

Years later, Christopher Arnold would describe the same scene to his grandson, Thaddeus. Arnold remembered standing by the mill dam, waiting to spot the American vanguard. It was agreed he would signal its arrival by throwing up a shovelful of earth. But Tecumseh's eyes were sharper. He was on his horse, dashing off at full speed after the first glimpse of Harrison's scouts. At the farm of Arnold's brother-in-law, he stopped to perform a small act of charity, tossing a sack of Arnold's flour at the front door to sustain the family, who had run out of bread.

Lemuel Sherman's sixteen-year-old son, David, and a friend were driving cows through a swamp when they came upon Tecumseh, seated on a log, two pistols in his belt. The Shawnee chief asked young Sherman whose boy he was, and, on hearing that his father was a militiaman in Procter's army, told him, "Don't let the Americans know your father is in the army or they'll burn your house. Go back and stay home, for there will be a fight here soon."

Years later, when David Sherman had become a wealthy landowner, he laid out part of his property as a village and named it Tecumseh.

Billy Caldwell, the half-caste son of the Indian Department's Colonel William Caldwell, would always remember Tecumseh's fatalistic remark to some of his chiefs:

"Brother warriors, we are about to enter an engagement from which I shall not return. My body will remain on the field of battle."

Long before, when he was fifteen, facing his first musket fire against the Kentuckians, when his life stretched before him like a river without end, Tecumseh had feared death and run from the field. Now he seemed to welcome it because he had no further reason to live.

Word had also reached him that the one real love of his life, Rebecca Galloway, had married. It was she who had introduced him to English literature. There had been other women and other wives (he had treated them all with disdain), but this sixteen-year-old daughter of an Ohio frontiersman was different. She spoke his language, taught him English, introduced him to the Bible, Alexander the Great, and Shakespeare's plays. He fell in love with her and brought her gifts—a silver comb, a birchbark canoe, furs, and deer meat.

He asked for her hand in marriage, offering her thirty silver brooches, and, so it was said, she was ready to accept. However, she insisted he give up Indian life and adopt white customs and dress. But Tecumseh could not bring himself to adopt a course that would cost him the respect of his people. And so, reluctantly, they parted, never to meet again.

Now he was single. His last wife, White Wing, a Shawnee whom he had married in 1802, parted from him in 1807. There would be no more women in his life. He was wedded to an ideal.

Rebecca was part of a dead past, a dream that would not come true, like his own shattered dream of a united Indian nation.

In some ways, Tecumseh seems more Christian than the Christians, with his hatred of senseless violence and torture. He was considerate of others, chivalrous, moral, and, in his struggle for his people's existence, totally selfless. But he intended to go into battle as a pagan, daubed with his customary black paint, swinging his hatchet, screaming his war cry, remembering always the example of his elder brother, Cheeseekau, the father figure who brought him up and who in the end met death gloriously, attacking a Kentucky fort, expressing the joy he felt at dying—not like an old woman at home, but on a field of conflict, where the fowls of the air would pick his bones.

CHAPTER FIVE

Procter Makes a Stand

SINCE LEAVING DOLSEN'S, PROCTER'S TROOPS HAD HAD NO RATIONS. WHEN THEY REACHED LEMUEL SHERMAN'S FARM ON THE UPPER THAMES, THEY WERE ABOUT TO ENJOY THEIR FIRST MEAL IN TWENTY-FOUR HOURS WHEN THE ORDER CAME TO PACK UP AND MARCH. THE AMERICANS WERE ONLY A SHORT DISTANCE BEHIND THEM.

Some cattle had already been butchered, but there was no time to cook the beef and not a pan in which to roast it. And there was no bread. Some of the men stuffed raw meat into their mouths or munched away on whatever crust they could still find from the last issue. The rest went hungry.

There was worse news. The Americans had seized all the British boats, capturing the extra ammunition, tools, and stores. The only cartridges the troops now had were in their own pouches. The officers tried to keep that information from their men.

The army marched two and a half miles (4 km). Procter appeared and brought it to a halt. Here, with the river on his left and a heavy marsh on his right, in a light wood of beech, maple, and oak, he had determined to make his stand.

It wasn't a bad position. His left flank was resting on the high bank of the river. That meant the enemy could not turn it. His right was protected by the marsh. He expected the Americans to advance down the road that cut through the left of his position. He planted his only gun—a six-pounder (3-kg)—at this point to rake the pathway.

He put the regulars on the left to hold the flank. The militia would form a line on the right. Beyond the militia, separated by a small swamp, would be Tecumseh's warriors.

Procter might have chosen to make his stand farther upstream, in the heights above Moraviantown. There, his position would have been protected by a deep ravine and the hundred log huts of the Christian Delaware Indians, who had lived here with their Moravian missionary since fleeing Ohio in 1792. It was to that village that Procter brought his main guns and supplies.

Why had he changed his plans so suddenly? It was the Indians who dictated the battle again. It was not their style to fight in the open plain, so Procter had no choice but to listen to them.

The tactics were simple. The British would hold the left, while the Indians, moving like a door on a hinge, would creep forward through the thicker forest on the right to attack Harrison's flank.

But there were problems. The worst was morale. The troops were slouching about, sitting on logs and stumps. They had already been turned around once, marched forward and then back again for some sixty paces, grumbling about "doing neither one thing or another." An hour passed before they were brought to their feet and told to form a line.

There was another problem. Procter had only six hundred men—not enough to stand shoulder to shoulder in the accepted fashion. In those days of musket warfare, men did not spread out, nor did they aim their weapons at any particular object. They were drilled to stand as close together as possible and fire all their muskets at the opposing force. This withering fire—a cloud of musket balls aimed in the general direction of the enemy—had worked well on the European plains.

But now the line developed into a series of clusters as the troops tried to hide behind the trees. Apparently nobody thought of building any sort of bulwark—trenches, mounds of earth, barricades of logs and branches— that might stop the enemy's cavalry. And nobody noticed that on the British side of the line there wasn't any underbrush. But what could they do? All the shovels, axes, and entrenching tools had already been lost to the enemy.

The troops stood in position for two and a half hours, patiently waiting for the Americans to appear. They were weak from hunger and exhausted from the events of the past week. They hadn't been paid for six months and were so poor they couldn't even afford soap. Their clothes were in rags. They were short of greatcoats and blankets. They were overworked and gloomy. Some had been on garrison duty far away from their homes in

England for a decade. They could not see through the curtain of trees, but they heard rumours that Harrison had ten thousand men advancing to the attack.

And then there was Procter. Many of his men believed he was more interested in saving his wife and family than in saving them. Many believed they were about to be cut to pieces and sacrificed for nothing. And so they waited—and that wait seemed an eternity.

Tecumseh rode down the ragged line, clasping the hands of the officers and murmuring encouragement in his own language. He had a special greeting for young John Richardson, whom he had known since childhood. Richardson noted the fringed deerskin ornamented with stained porcupine quills, the ostrich feathers, and, most of all, the dark, lively features and the flashing hazel eyes.

Whenever, in the future, John Richardson thought of Tecumseh—and he thought of him often—that picture would remain: the tall, sturdy chief on the white pony, who seemed now to be in such high spirits, who genially told Procter to urge his men to be stout-hearted and to take care the Long Knives did not seize the big cannon.

CHAPTER SIX

The Battle of the Thames

HARRISON, HAVING DESTROYED ALL THE BRITISH GUNBOATS AND SUPPLIES, CROSSED THE THAMES IN ORDER TO REACH THE RIGHT BANK, ALONG WHICH THE BRITISH HAD BEEN RETREATING. THE WATER WAS SO DEEP THAT THE MEN HESITATED UNTIL HARRISON'S AIDE, THE NAVAL COMMANDER OLIVER HAZARD PERRY, RODE THROUGH THE CROWD, SHOUTED TO A FOOT SOLDIER TO CLIMB ON BEHIND, AND DASHED INTO THE STREAM, CALLING ON COLONEL JOHNSON'S MOUNTED VOLUNTEERS TO FOLLOW.

In that way, with the aid of several abandoned canoes and keelboats, the three thousand foot soldiers were moved across the river in forty-five minutes.

William Whitley, the veteran scout, saw an Indian on the opposite bank and shot him. He swam his horse back across and scalped the corpse. "This is the thirteenth scalp I have taken," he told a friend, "and I'll have another by night or lose my own."

The Americans formed up on the right bank. A spy reported the British not far ahead, aiming for Moraviantown. Harrison rode up to Johnson and told him that the foot soldiers wouldn't be fast enough to overtake Procter until late in the day. He wanted Johnson to push his mounted regiment forward to stop the British retreat. "If you cannot compel them to stop with an engagement, why *fight* them, but do not venture too much," Harrison ordered.

Johnson moved his men forward at a trot. A captured French-Canadian soldier told him that eight hundred men, supported by fourteen hundred Indians, lay ahead. Johnson, though apparently outnumbered, had no intention of retreating. But Procter did not attack. The two armies remained within view of one another—no more than a few hundred yards apart—motionless, waiting.

A quarter of an hour went by. Harrison arrived with his troops—eleven regiments supported by artillery, stretching back for three miles (4.8 km)—and held a council of war on horseback. At once he saw that Procter had a good position and realized that the British would use the Indians on the edge of the swamp to get around his flanks. That he had to prevent at all costs.

His strategy was to hold the Indians back with a strong force on his left and attack the British line with a bayonet charge through the woods. At the same time, Johnson's mounted men would splash through the swamp that separated the British from the Indians and attack Tecumseh's tribesmen.

It took him an hour and a half to form up his troops. The British, peering through the oaks and beeches and the brilliant sugar maples, could catch only glimpses of the enemy three hundred yards (270 m) away. The Americans had a better view of the British in their scarlet jackets.

Now Johnson sent a man forward to look at the swamp and realized that it was impassable. Harrison's tactics wouldn't work.

Harrison wanted him to retire to the rear and form a reserve, but Johnson had another idea. "General Harrison, permit me to charge the enemy and the battle will be won in thirty minutes," he said. He meant the British on his right, and not the Indians, separated by the swamp on his left.

Harrison looked over the field. He could see that the British redcoats were spread out in open formation, not shoulder to shoulder. There were gaps between the clusters of men. The woods were thick with trees, but there wasn't much underbrush. And he knew that Johnson had trained his men to ride through the forests of Ohio, firing cartridges to get the horses used to the sound of guns. Most of them were expert marksmen, having ridden horseback since childhood.

"Damn them! Charge them!" cried Harrison, and he changed the order of battle on the spot. He was convinced that these unusual tactics would catch the British unprepared.

Now one of Johnson's scouts came back with welcome news. He had found a way through the swamp. It wouldn't be easy, for the ground was bad. Johnson turned to his brother, James: "Brother, take my place at the head of the first battalion. I will cross the swamp and fight the Indians at the head of the second battalion." He explained his reason: "You have a family, I have none." And so the younger brother would attack the British on the right, while the other Johnson would take his chances in the swamp.

A brief lull followed. One of Harrison's colonels rode out in front of his regiment and shouted, "Boys, we must either whip the British and Indians or they will kill and scalp every one of us. We cannot escape if we lose. Let us all die on the field or conquer."

Once again, Procter had bungled. He had repeatedly threatened that he couldn't control the Indians and that if the Americans attacked him they would be massacred by the tribesmen. Now the Americans believed him and were prepared, if necessary, for a suicidal attack.

"Clear the road!" Hall cried. But the road was clogged with fleeing British. He suggested to the general they take to the woods. Procter, stunned by the suddenness of defeat, didn't appear to hear him.

The bugle sounded a charge. Seated on his horse halfway between the British lines, Procter heard the sound and asked what it meant. His brigade major told him it was the advance.

An Indian scout fired his musket, and without orders the entire British front line discharged their ragged volley at the advancing horsemen. The horses recoiled in confusion.

Procter was desperate to put his six-pound (3-kg) cannon into effect. "Damn that gun. Why doesn't it fire?" he said.

But the British horses had been so startled by the gunfire that they reared back. They became entangled in the trees and dragged the cannon away with them.

James Johnson rallied his men and charged forward as a second line of British defenders opened fire. "Charge them, my brave Kentuckians!" Harrison cried, as the volunteers dashed forward, yelling and shouting. They hit the left of the British line, which crumbled.

"Stop, 41st, stop!" Procter shouted. "What are you about? For shame. For shame on you!"

The force of the cavalry charge had taken Johnson's horsemen right through both British lines. Now they wheeled around to their left to roll up the British right, which was still holding.

"For God's sake, men, stand and fight!" cried a sergeant of the 41st.

Not far away stood John Richardson, age sixteen, but already the survivor of three bloody skirmishes. A fellow officer pointed at one of the mounted riflemen taking aim at a British foot soldier. Richardson raised his musket, leaned against a tree for support, and dropped the mounted man from his horse.

Richardson now saw one of the Delaware chiefs throw a tomahawk at a wounded Kentuckian with such force that it opened his skull and killed him instantly. The Delaware pulled out the hatchet and scalped the man. That grisly scene was no sooner over than the firing in the woods on Richardson's left ended suddenly. The order came to retreat.

Procter was preparing to make off. His gun crew had fled. The Americans had seized the six-pounder (3-kg). John Hall, his brigade major, warned him that unless they moved swiftly they would both be shot.

"Clear the road!" Hall cried. But the road was clogged with fleeing British. He suggested to the general they take to the woods. Procter, stunned by the suddenness of defeat, didn't appear to hear him. No more than five minutes had passed since Harrison's bugle sounded.

"This way, general, this way," said Hall patiently, like a parent leading a child. The general followed obediently.

"Do you not think we can join the Indians?" he asked. Tecumseh's force on the right of the shattered British line was still fighting furiously. But James Johnson's charge had cut Procter's army in two, and there was no way of reaching the Indians because there were mounted Americans between the Indian and British forces.

Off Procter went, riding as fast as he could, with the Americans in hot pursuit. He knew the Kentucky volunteers' reputation. For all he knew they might skin him alive if they caught him. So he galloped away from the battle as fast as he could, with the sounds of Tecumseh's Indians, still holding, echoing in his ears.

As James Johnson's men drove the British before them, his brother's battalion plunged through the decaying trees and willows of the small swamp that separated the Indians from their white allies. Richard Johnson's plan was brutal. He called for volunteers for what was in effect a suicide squad—known in both armies as the Forlorn Hope. This screen of twenty bold men was instructed to ride ahead of the main body to attract the Indians' fire. Then, while the tribesmen were reloading, the main body would sweep down on them.

There was no problem with volunteers. The grizzled Whitley, a fresh scalp still dangling from his belt, would lead the Forlorn Hope, and Johnson would ride with them. Off they plunged through the water and mud into a hail of musket balls. Now, above the noise of battle, another sound was heard—clear, authoritative, almost melodic—the golden voice of Tecumseh urging his followers on to victory.

Johnson's tactic was working. The Indians had concentrated all their fire on the Forlorn Hope, killing fifteen of the twenty, including William Whitley. But Johnson faced a problem. The mud of the swamp had risen to the horses' bellies. His men could not charge.

Bleeding from four wounds, Johnson ordered his followers to dismount and attack. An Indian behind a tree fired, and the ball struck a knuckle of Johnson's left hand, coming out just above the wrist. The Indian advanced, his tomahawk raised, but Johnson, who had loaded his pistol with one ball and three buckshot, drew his weapon and fired, killing the man instantly. Not far away lay Whitley's corpse, riddled with musket balls.

Beyond the protecting curtain of gun smoke, the battle with the Indians raged on. Word spread that Richard Johnson was dead. An old friend, Major W. T. Barry, rode up from the rear to examine the corpse, but met a group of soldiers carrying the colonel back in a blanket.

"I will not die, Barry," Johnson assured him. "I am mightily cut to pieces, but I think my vitals have escaped." One day he would become vice-president of the United States.

The noise of the battle behind him continued to sound in his ears as the Americans pressed forward through the trees. The volume rose. The Kentuckians were shouting their battle cry. The Indians were shrieking and whooping. Wounded men were groaning and screaming. Horses were neighing and whinnying. The sound of musket and rifle fire shattered eardrums, as bugles sounded and cannon fired.

The smoke of battle lay thickly over forest and swamp, making ghosts of the dim, painted figures of Tecumseh's men, who would appear for an instant from the cover of trees to fire a weapon or hurl a tomahawk and then vanish into the gloom. They did not seem to be real to the Americans, for their faces could only be seen in death.

Who were the leaders, and who were the followers? One man, the Kentuckians knew, was in charge. They could hear Tecumseh's terrible battle cry piercing the ragged wall of sound. For five years they had heard its echo, ever since he had first made his presence felt in the Northwest.

Yet that presence had always been ghostly; no Kentuckian on the field that day had ever seen the Shawnee chief or heard his voice until this moment. He was a figure of legend, his origins clouded in myth, his image a reflection of other men's ideas. Johnson's riders were tantalized by his invisibility.

And then, suddenly, came a subtle change in the sound. Private Charles Wickliffe, who had been timing the battle, noticed it. Something was missing. Wickliffe groped for an answer and then came to realize that he could no longer hear that one clear cry. The voice of Tecumseh urging on his followers had been stilled. The Shawnee had fallen.

The absence of that sound was as clear as a bugle call. Suddenly the battle was over. The Indians withdrew through the underbrush, leaving the field to the Americans. As the firing trailed off, Wickliffe took out his watch. Exactly fifty-five minutes had elapsed since Harrison ordered the first charge. As the late afternoon shadows gathered, a pall rose over the bodies of the slain.

But one corpse was missing. Elusive in life, Tecumseh remained invisible in death. No white man had ever been allowed to draw his likeness. No white man would ever display or mutilate his body. No headstone, marker, or monument would identify his resting place. His people had spirited him away to a spot where no stranger would ever find him—his earthly clay, like his own forlorn hope, buried forever in a secret grave.

CHAPTER SEVEN

The Legend Begins

Fleeing from James Johnson's riders, even as the battle still raged, young John Richardson charged through the woods with his comrades and lost his way. He found himself unexpectedly on the road, now clogged with wagons, discarded stores and clothing, women and children.

Five hundred yards (450 m) to his right he saw the main body of the regiment, disarmed and surrounded by the enemy. Acting on instinct, he and the others turned left, only to run into a body of American cavalry, the men walking their horses.

Their leader, a stout, elderly officer dressed like his men in a Kentucky hunting jacket, saw them, galloped forward, waved his sword, and shouted in a commanding voice: "Surrender, surrender! It's no use. It's no use resisting. All your people are taken and you'd better surrender."

That was Shelby. Richardson, whose attitude toward all Americans was snobbishly British-Canadian, thought him a vulgar man, who looked more like one of the army's wagon drivers than the governor of a state. Certainly, he didn't look a bit like a chief magistrate in one of His Majesty's provinces.

Richardson quickly buried his musket in the deep mud—to keep it from the enemy—and gave up. As the troops passed by, one tall Kentuckian glanced over at the little teenager and said, "Well, I guess now, you tarnation little Britisher, who'd calculate to see such a bit of chap as you here?" Richardson would never forget that remark, which showed the difference in the languages of the two English-speaking peoples who shared the continent.

Meanwhile, Major Eleazer Wood was in full pursuit of Procter. But the general escaped, stopping only briefly at Moraviantown and then moving on to Ancaster, so tired he couldn't even write a coherent account of the day's action that evening. Wood had to be content with capturing his carriage, containing his sword, hat, trunk, and all his personal papers, including a packet of letters from his wife.

Moraviantown's single street was clogged with wagons, horses, and half-starved Kentuckians. The missionary's wife, Mrs. Schall, worked all night baking bread for the troops, some of whom pounced on the dough and ate it before it went into the oven. Others upset all the beehives, scrambling for the honey, and ravaged the garden for vegetables, which they devoured raw.

Richardson and the other prisoners fared better. Squatting around a campfire in the forest, they were fed pieces of meat toasted on skewers by Harrison's aides, who told the British that they were sorry to hear of the death of the much-admired Tecumseh.

Now began the long argument over the Shawnee's death. Who had killed Tecumseh? Some said Whitley, whose body was found near that of an Indian chief. Others, including Shelby, thought that a private from Lincoln County had shot him. Another group insisted that the Indian killed by Richard Johnson was Tecumseh. That would form the most colourful feature of Johnson's campaign for the vice-presidency.

But nobody knew or would ever know how Tecumseh fell. Only two men on the American side knew what he looked like—Harrison, his old enemy, and Anthony Shane, the mixed-blood interpreter who had known him as a boy. Neither was able to say with certainty that any of the bodies in the field looked like the Indian leader.

The morning after the battle, David Sherman, the boy who had encountered Tecumseh in the swamp, found one of his rifled flintlock pistols on the field. That same day, Chris Arnold came upon a group of Kentuckians skinning the body of an Indian to make souvenir razor strops.

"That's not Tecumseh," Arnold told them.

"I guess when we get back to Kentucky they will not know his skin from Tecumseh's," they replied.

In death as in life, the Shawnee war chief inspired myth. There were some who believed he had not been killed at all but merely wounded, and that he would return to lead his people to victory. That was a wistful hope. But "skeletons" of Tecumseh would turn up in the future. "Authentic" graves would be identified and then rejected. Yet the facts of his death and his burial remain as elusive as those of his birth almost half a century before.

John Richardson was moved back to the Detroit River with six hundred other prisoners. Luckily for him, his grandfather, John Askin, of Amherstburg, had a son-in-law, Elijah Brush, who was an American military colonel at Detroit. Askin wrote to his daughter's husband, telling him to look after his grandson. As a result, Richardson, instead of being sent up the Maumee River with the others, was taken to Put-in Bay by gunboat. There, he ran into his own father, Dr. Robert Richardson, an army surgeon captured by Perry.

Harrison's supply lines were stretched too far. The Thames Valley had been stripped of fodder, grain, and meat. His six-month volunteers were all clamouring to go home.

The double victories, first on Lake Erie and now on the Thames, tipped the scales of war. For all practical purposes, the conflict on the Detroit frontier was ended. The British expected Harrison to follow up his victory and so fell into a panic, destroying stocks of arms and supplies as they retreated to the protection of Burlington Heights, above the present site of Hamilton, Ontario. The army was in dreadful shape. Of eleven hundred men, eight hundred were sick, too ill to haul wagons up the hills or through the rivers of mud that passed for roads.

Now the British were prepared to let all of Upper Canada west of Kingston fall to the Americans. The Americans, however, could not maintain their momentum. Harrison's supply lines were stretched too far. The Thames Valley had been stripped of fodder, grain, and meat. His six-month volunteers were all clamouring to go home.

In the end, Harrison was a captive of his country's hand-to-mouth recruiting methods. He could not pursue the remnants of Procter's army as common sense dictated. Instead, he had to move back down the Thames River, try to hold on to Fort Amherstburg, and leave one of his brigadiers in charge of Detroit.

The war was by no means over; and neither side had yet won. The British still held a key outpost in the far west—the captured island of Michilimackinac, guarding the route to the fur country at the northern end of Lake Huron. It was essential that the Americans grab it. They should have been able to do so with their superior fleet, but the Canadian winter frustrated that plan.

In the United States victory bonfires lit up the sky. Songs were written for the occasion. Harrison was toasted at every table, and Congress struck a gold medal. It was this that rocketed Harrison to the presidency. An extraordinary number of those who fought with him also rose to high office.

For Henry Procter there was no praise. A court martial the following year found him guilty of negligence, of bungling the retreat, of errors in tactics and judgment. He was publicly reprimanded and suspended from rank and pay for six months.

If he had retreated promptly and without baggage, he might have saved his army. And yet it was the army he blamed for all his misfortunes—not himself. In his report of the battle and his testimony at the court martial, he threw all the responsibility of defeat on the shoulders of the men and officers serving under him. But in the end it was Procter's reputation that was tarnished and not that of his men.

To the Americans he would remain a monster, to the Canadians a coward. He was neither—merely a victim of circumstance, a brave but weak officer, capable enough except in moments of stress, unable to make the huge leap that distinguishes the outstanding leader from the run-of-the-mill: the quality of being able in moments of difficulty to rise above his own limitations. The prisoner of events beyond his control, he dallied until he was crushed. His career was ended.

He left the valley of the Thames in a shambles. Moraviantown was a smoking ruin, destroyed on Harrison's orders to prevent its being used as a British base. Bridges were broken, grist mills burned, grain destroyed, sawmills shattered. Indians and soldiers of both armies had plundered homes, slaughtered cattle, stolen private property.

And Tecumseh's dreamed-of confederacy—a union of all the tribes— was finally dead. In Detroit thirty-seven chiefs representing six tribes signed an armistice with Harrison, leaving their wives and children as hostages for their good intentions. The Americans didn't have enough to feed them, and so the women and children were seen grubbing in the streets for bones and rinds of pork thrown away by the soldiers. Rotting meat discarded in the river was retrieved and devoured. On the Canadian side, two thousand Indian women and children swarmed into Burlington Heights pleading for food.

Kentucky had been battling the Indians for half a century. Now the long struggle for possession of the Northwest was over. And that was the real significance of Harrison's victory. The proud tribes had been humbled. The Indian lands were ripe for the taking.

The personal struggle between Harrison and Tecumseh had all the elements of classic tragedy, and, as in classic tragedy, it is the fallen hero and not the victor whom history will remember.

Harrison died after a single month in office. It was his fate to be remembered as a one-month president, forever to be confused with his grandson Benjamin, a longer-lived President Harrison. But in death, as in life, there was only one Tecumseh. His last resting place, like so much of his career, is a mystery. But his memory will be forever green.

INDEX

"James Wilkinson" (1757–1825) by Charles Wilson Peale.
Wilkinson's tired leadership of the American attack on
Montreal ended in disaster for the American cause.

ATTACK ON MONTREAL

CONTENTS

The Foolish War

OF ALL THE FOOLISH WARS FOUGHT IN THE NINETEENTH CENTURY, SURELY THE SILLIEST AND MOST FOOLISH WAS THE AMERICAN ATTEMPT TO INVADE CANADA BETWEEN 1812 AND 1814. THE WAR WAS LAUNCHED IN ORDER TO GIVE A BLACK EYE TO THE BRITISH, WHO WERE INTERFERING WITH AMERICAN SHIPS TRYING TO TRADE WITH FRENCH PORTS. THE WAR OF 1812, THEN, WAS SIMPLY A FOOT-NOTE TO THE NAPOLEONIC WARS BEING FOUGHT ON THE EUROPEAN CONTI-NENT BETWEEN ENGLAND AND FRANCE.

It was not only a foolish war, it was also a very strange one. Imagine a war in which everybody stopped fighting in the fall because the soldiers on both sides had to go home to get in the harvest!

In the winter it was just too cold to fight and in the spring many of the citizen soldiers had to work in the fields. So this war took place in the hot, lazy days of summer along the U.S.–Canadian border.

It was also a war fought by children, some of whom were as young as thirteen or fourteen. Many had not had a drink of hard liquor before join-ing up and so went into battle half-sozzled from their quarter pint (200 mL) of whisky or tot of strong rum.

And it wasn't only the soldiers who were blind to what was happening. Half the time the generals didn't know what was going on. Where was the enemy? They didn't know because communication was difficult and some-times impossible. Neither the telephone nor the radio had been invented.

Both sides used spies to find out how many fighting men were on the opposite side. Generally they got it wrong. The spies were mainly local farmers who couldn't always be trusted because this was also a civil war in which the people on both sides knew each other well.

For many, the border didn't exist. For years both Americans and Canadians had been smuggling goods across it.

The real enemy in this odd conflict was disease. On both sides, measles, typhus, typhoid, influenza, and dysentery probably put more men out of action than a bullet or a cannonball. For this, the universal remedy was liquor. There were no wonder drugs, no real medicines.

The war along the St. Lawrence River was largely a war of musketry. The so-called Brown Bess musket was the basic infantry weapon, even though it was very inaccurate. The British troops and Canadian regulars were better with the musket because they were drilled to use it. They advanced in line, shoulder to shoulder, making no attempt to fire at individual targets. Instead they were taught to spray the enemy with a hail of bullets that wobbled down the unrifled barrels and might have flown anywhere.

That didn't matter. No enemy could withstand that wave of devastating lead. The forward line had been drilled to advance, to open fire on command, to drop to the ground and reload while the soldiers standing behind let go with a second volley. These tactics worked well in the open fields, such as Crysler's farm on the St. Lawrence. They were less effective in the forests, where the advance was held up by trees, stumps, and rough ground.

Under those conditions, the individualistic Americans preferred the long Tennessee rifle. It was far more accurate than the musket. Sharpshooters, hidden behind trees or folds in the ground, could take careful aim at enemy soldiers. That was how Isaac Brock, the general who led the British and Canadian forces at the Battle of Queenston Heights in 1812, was killed. A rifle bullet got him in the heart.

Brock was one of the few capable leaders in this crazy war. The American leadership was especially incompetent. They were not helped by the American volunteers, who had signed up for only a few months, and not for the duration of the war. They could refuse to cross the border into a foreign country, a right protected by the U.S. Constitution.

In many cases the Americans' hearts weren't in it. Why should they be? They weren't doing battle to save their nation as the Canadian regulars and volunteers were. Many of the people who lived along the border were newcomers to Canada. They had arrived after the American Revolution because they were loyal to the British cause. For them this war would be one of the defining moments in the history of their raw, new nation. They knew that if they lost the war they could find themselves once again citizens of a land from which they had so recently fled. These people were Loyalists. They didn't want to be Americans, and they were prepared to fight to prevent it.

Canada is an independent nation today partly because of them.

CHAPTER ONE

The Ailing General

OF ALL THE SILLY AND FOOLISH CAMPAIGNS FOUGHT IN THIS WAR, SURELY THE SILLIEST WAS THE AMERICAN ATTEMPT IN THE AUTUMN OF 1813 TO SWEEP DOWN THE ST. LAWRENCE RIVER FROM LAKE ONTARIO AND SEIZE MONTREAL.

The generals of the invading army were aging incompetents, hated by their troops and despised by their fellow officers. They did not have the will to win—an essential in warfare. The malady of defeatism infected their followers, fourteen hundred of whom refused to cross the border to do battle. The men were sickly, badly fed and clothed, often untrained and ill equipped, and no match for their opponents.

The Americans outnumbered the defenders of Canada more than two to one but didn't know it; they were led to believe that they faced overwhelming odds and so, in effect, gave up in their minds before the battle was joined.

Major-General James Wilkinson, the officer in charge of the American invasion attempt, was a poor excuse for a soldier. He was a sick man, shivering with fever, so ill he had to be helped ashore when his troops reached the St. Lawrence.

Even if he'd been in the best of health, Wilkinson would have been an odd choice for commander-in-chief of the invading forces. He was getting on in years and almost universally despised. His entire career had been a catalogue of blunders, intrigues, investigations, plots, schemes, and deceptions.

Although he seemed pleasant enough on first encounter, he was unreliable, greedy for money, boastful, and dishonest. Three times he had been forced to resign from the army because of scandal.

He had once plotted against George Washington, then president of his country. He had even come close to treason when he had secret dealings with the Spanish. In spite of that, he had managed to rejoin the army and had risen to brigadier-general. Again he faced a court martial for conspiracy, treason, neglect of duty, and misuse of public money. But the court cleared him of the charges and he bounced back.

This was the man that the American high command had chosen to lead its newest attack. And so we find him in early October 1813, at Sackets Harbor, not far from the point where the St. Lawrence River pours out of Lake Ontario.

The Americans had tried without success to capture the Niagara Peninsula and had been forced back to Fort George at the mouth of the Niagara River. Now they decided to change their plans. Their newest scheme was to cut the lifeline between Upper and Lower Canada. That would mean an all-out assault, either on Kingston or Montreal. If successful, Canada would effectively be cut in two. But neither the American secretary of war, John Armstrong, nor his ailing major-general, Wilkinson, could make up their minds which city to attack.

What a strange pair they made when they met at Sackets Harbor on October 13, 1813. The secretary was about to turn fifty-six, and he was handsome, aristocratic, and warlike. He and Wilkinson were once friends, but now he wanted Wilkinson's job.

The major-general was aware of Armstrong's ambitions but was too sick to care. He actually *wanted* to quit, but Armstrong wouldn't let him. "I would feed the old man with pap sooner than leave him behind," was the way he put it. In fact, the "old man" was scarcely a year older than Armstrong.

Armstrong himself was on shaky ground politically. U.S. President James Madison had no confidence in him. The secretary of state, James Monroe, was an enemy. Armstrong kept his job only through the support of powerful friends in New York.

Winter was approaching, but these two rivals couldn't agree on tactics. The secretary of war wanted to attack Kingston directly. Wilkinson dallied.

The two men kept contradicting one another. When Wilkinson insisted that Montreal was the target, Armstrong took the other side. Then both men changed positions until it became clear that neither expected that any attack on either stronghold could succeed. They had lost the battle in their minds before it began.

In war, one of the essentials for victory is confidence. All through history great military leaders have won out over heavy odds because they knew they could prevail. The will to win is as valuable as an extra cannon or a division of men.

In this case the Americans had three armies—one at Fort George on the Niagara would join with a second army at Sackets Harbor, while a third to the south on Lake Champlain would act in support.

By October 4, the two leading armies should have reached Grenadier Island at the mouth of the St. Lawrence, the jumping-off point for the final assault.

But Wilkinson's troops were moving at a snail's pace. The contractor had figured it would take five days to load the boats. It actually took nineteen, throwing the schedule off-kilter. Worse, the ammunition and guns needed for the attack were loaded without any plan and scattered about the flotilla.

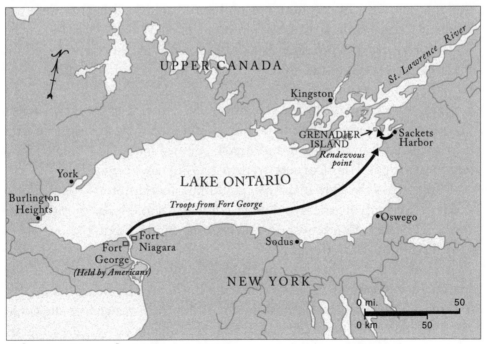

Lake Ontario, October 1813

Hospital stores took priority over guns and powder. Hundreds of men lay ill because of the bad food and the wretched sanitation. The meat was rotten, the whisky polluted, the flour so bad that the medical officer said, "It would kill the best horse in Sackets Harbor." That September seven hundred officers and men lay ill. Within two months that number had doubled. The flotilla, when it did move, was a floating hospital, in the words of the camp surgeon.

The bread was the worst. It contained bits of soap, lime, and human excrement. And no wonder! The bakers took their water from a stagnant corner of the lake, no more than three feet (90 cm) from the shore. The latrines were clustered only a few yards away. Naked men kneaded the dough. Nearby, in a cemetery, two hundred corpses lay buried in no more than a foot of sandy soil. The troops were weak from dysentery, but nothing was done for them. Wilkinson, who was supposed to be in charge, was as sick as anybody else.

Meanwhile, the supporting army from Lake Champlain under Major-General Wade Hampton was also delaying. Hampton had four thousand regular troops and fifteen hundred militiamen and he'd been ordered to support Wilkinson's attack. But Hampton hated Wilkinson so much he wouldn't take orders from him. As a result, when Wilkinson sent directions to Hampton two hundred miles (320 km) away, Hampton didn't even answer.

Hampton's army did make one attack on September 21, which failed because the weather was so hot. His horses and men were so desperate with thirst that they had to retreat and march seventy miles (112 km) back to their present spot, Four Corners on the Châteauguay River.

Armstrong—the only man who could talk to Hampton—told him to hold fast. "Keep up the enemy's doubts, with regard to the real point of your attack." The fact was, however, that Armstrong himself didn't know where the real point of attack would be.

At last, on October 16, he told Hampton to move down the Châteauguay River and cross the Canadian border. There he would be able to support a thrust against Kingston. Or, if Montreal was chosen, he could wait until the main body headed down the St. Lawrence.

By mid-October only half of the combined forces had reached the rendezvous point on Grenadier Island. A winter storm had been raging for a week, lashing the waters of the lake with rain, snow, and hail. The few boats that did set off were destroyed or forced back to the harbour. By October 19, when the storm subsided, the main body set off for Grenadier Island. The ground was now thick with snow, but no one had yet decided whether Kingston or Montreal would be the main point of the attack. Did these American generals really believe they could seize Canada before winter?

CHAPTER TWO

Spies and Smugglers

LET US NOW LOOK IN ON TWO CANADIAN FARMERS, JACOB MANNING AND HIS BROTHER, DAVID, WHO HAD BEEN HELD PRISONER BY THE AMERICANS IN A LOG STABLE ON BENJAMIN ROBERTS'S FARM, NEAR CHÂTEAUGUAY FOUR CORNERS, NEW YORK STATE. THAT IS WHERE WADE HAMPTON'S ARMY WAS CAMPED. ON OCTOBER 21, 1813, THE TWO FARMERS LEARNED THAT HAMPTON WANTED TO TALK TO THEM.

The brothers were spies—part of a group recruited by the British from the settlers of the townships north of the border. This was smugglers' country, where everybody knew everybody else, and where everybody was involved in spiriting goods illegally across the border. The Americans sneaked barrels of potash into Canada for sale in Montreal. The Canadians slipped over the imaginary line pulling hand sleds loaded with ten-gallon (45-l) kegs of whisky. Everyone knew about it. How could you hide the tell-tale signs? So much beef was smuggled into Canada for the British army that herds of cattle had left tracks in the woods along the frontier.

The Mannings, who had been supplying the British army with reports of the American troop movements, had been surprised in their sleep on October 2. Since then they had been held under suspicion. Now they were brought under guard to Hampton's headquarters in a tavern.

Hampton was well known for his impatience, arrogance, and bad temper. A self-made man, with all the stubborn pride of that species, he was difficult to get along with. An uneducated farm boy, orphaned early in life by an Indian raid, he was well on his way to becoming the wealthiest planter in the United States. He had a greed for land and had made his fortune in speculation, much of it shady. He owned vast plantations in South Carolina, with thousands of slaves, some of whom he had brought along on this campaign.

He had been a good politician and a good soldier during the American Revolution, but now he was in his sixtieth year and had lost much of his drive. He was so unpopular that some officers had refused to serve under him. Some, in fact, had threatened to quit the army if Hampton was placed in charge of the Niagara frontier.

His task was to cross the border and march down the Châteauguay River to the point where it joined the St. Lawrence near Montreal. The Americans thought that an attack on Kingston would confuse the British. Alternatively, Hampton's army was ready to join Wilkinson on his sweep to Montreal.

Neither side knew the other's strength. Hampton had no idea how many men the British and Canadians had. The British were just as much in the dark about the American strength and strategy. That's why Hampton had called on the Mannings. He wanted David Manning to take his fastest horse, gallop to Montreal, and bring back information about the size of the British defence force stationed there.

He had been a good politician and a good soldier during the American Revolution, but now he was in his sixtieth year and had lost much of his drive. He was so unpopular that some officers had refused to serve under him.

But when he offered Manning a handsome reward, Manning turned him down.

"Are you not an American?" Hampton demanded.

"Yes," said Manning. "I was born on the American side and I have many relations, but I am true to the British flag."

He was, in fact, a United Empire Loyalist—one of the "Tories" (as they were called) who refused to fight against the British during the American Revolution and who were forced to move north of the border.

At this response, Hampton's famous temper flared up. He told the Manning brothers they were in his power. If they didn't toe the line, he would send them to the military prison.

That didn't frighten the two backwoodsmen. They replied boldly that anything would be better than being held in a filthy stable. So Hampton tried to squeeze more information from them. Was there a fort in Montreal? They told him that there wasn't, but he refused to believe it.

He took the two men to the tavern window overlooking a farm and proudly pointed out the size of his army. Spread out before them the brothers saw an imposing spectacle: thousands of men striking their tents, cavalry cantering about, the infantry drilling in platoons. It was clear that Hampton was about to move his army across the border into Canada.

The general now asked how far the Mannings thought a force of that size could go. Jacob Manning couldn't resist a cheeky answer: "If it has good luck, it may get to Halifax," he said, for Halifax was where all prisoners of war were sent.

That infuriated Hampton, who told his officer of the guard, a local militiaman named Hollenbeck, to take the brothers back to their stable prison and to keep them there for three days so that they couldn't get word of his advance to the British.

But Hollenbeck was an old friend and neighbour, and once they were out of Hampton's earshot, he asked, "Do you want anything to eat?"

"No," said Jacob.

"Well, then, put for home," said Hollenbeck, and off the Mannings went to warn the British of the American advance.

CHAPTER THREE

The "Marquis of Cannon Powder"

THE MANNINGS WEREN'T THE ONLY ONES TO WARN OF THE AMERICAN ADVANCE. HAMPTON'S TROOPS CROSSED THE BORDER AND REACHED SPEARS'S FARM AT THE JUNCTION OF THE CHÂTEAUGUAY AND OUTARDE RIVERS ON OCTOBER 21. THERE THEY ROUTED MEMBERS OF A SMALL BAND OF CANADIAN SOLDIERS WHO ESCAPED AND SOUNDED THE ALARM.

People living near the border had been in a state of tension for weeks, not knowing exactly where the Americans would attack. Now it was obvious that Hampton would advance along the cart track that bordered the Châteauguay. His object was the St. Lawrence, and surely Montreal.

In the coming battle the defence of Canada would fall almost entirely on the French Canadian militia—citizen soldiers who supported the regular forces. More than three hundred were moving up the river road to a meeting place in the hardwood forest not far from the future settlement of Allan's Corners. Few had uniforms. Many wore homespun blouses and blue toques. Two flank companies of the notorious Devil's Own battalion wore green coats with red facings. These men had been recruited from the slums of Montreal and Quebec. The battalion got its name because of its reputation for thievery and disorder.

The following morning a more reliable force arrived. These were the Canadian Fencibles and Voltigeurs. The latter unit consisted not of habitants but of voyageurs, lumbermen, and city-bred youths. They had been drilled like regulars all that winter by their leader, a thirty-five-year-old career soldier, Lieutenant-Colonel Charles-Michel d'Irumberry de Salaberry. They wore smart grey uniforms and fur hats and were so tough that they thought nothing of fighting in their bare feet.

De Salaberry would emerge from this battle as an authentic Canadian hero. He was short in stature, big-chested, and muscular. He was a strict disciplinarian—brusque, impetuous, often harsh with his men. He had been a soldier since the age of fourteen, and three younger brothers had already died in service. His father's patron and his own was the Duke of Kent, the father of Queen Victoria.

A superior called him "my dear Marquis of cannon powder," but his Voltigeurs admired him because he was fair-minded, and they sang about him:

This is our major,
The embodiment of the devil
Who gives us death.
There is no wolf or tiger
Who could be so rough;
Under the openness of the sky
There is not his equal.

His men knew the story of the scar on de Salaberry's brow. That went back to his days in the West Indies when an arrogant German killed his best friend in a duel.

"I come just now from dispatching a French Canadian into another world," the duellist boasted.

De Salaberry replied, "We are going to finish lunch and then you will have the pleasure of dispatching another."

But it was the German who was dispatched and de Salaberry merely scarred.

For weeks he had been spying on Hampton's pickets at Châteauguay Four Corners. Now he prepared to meet the full force not far from the point where the Châteauguay meets the English River.

He had chosen his position with care. Half a dozen ravines cut their way through the sandy soil at right angles to the Châteauguay River. These would be his main line of defence. The first three lines were only two hundred yards (180 m) apart, the fourth lay half a mile (800 m) to the rear. Two more lay some distance downriver near La Fourche, where the reserve army and headquarters would be stationed, six lines of fighting men.

By noon on October 22, de Salaberry and his axemen had hacked down scores of trees, whose tangled branches formed a breastwork on the forward lip of each ravine. A mile (1.6 km) in front of the forward ravine, on Robert Bryson's farm, de Salaberry found a coulee, forty feet (12 m) deep. Here his men built another obstacle, or abatis, extending in a half-circle from the deep gorge on the left to a swamp in the forest on their right. It would be hard for the Americans to get around these obstacles and attack from the flanks. To hit at the Canadians, they would have to mount a frontal attack—always a difficult and dangerous tactic against a stubborn enemy.

They were still hacking down trees and piling up slash when an unexpected reinforcement arrived. This was the battalion of the Select Embodied Militia, a mixed bag of French Canadians and Scottish farmers who had arrived at top speed. Their commander, Lieutenant-Colonel "Red George" Macdonell, was used to quick action. When he had been asked how soon he could get underway, he had responded briskly, "As soon as my men have done dinner." The battalion made the exhausting trip in just sixty hours, without a man missing.

That same day, October 24, Hampton's main body moved deeper into Canada along a road his engineers had hacked through the bush. A spy watched them go by, carefully counted the guns, the wagons, and the troops, and immediately sent a detailed report to the British.

The spy also reported cheering news: more than fourteen hundred American militiamen had bluntly refused to cross the border and invade Canada in this silly war. That was their right under the American Constitution. No citizen soldier was required to fight on foreign soil if he didn't want to. Only regular army men were required to.

As a result Hampton's army was badly depleted. In addition, his men were poorly clothed; in fact, they had so little winter gear that they had to gamble to get greatcoats. Nor were the southerners—mostly from Virginia—used to the Canadian weather. One regiment of a thousand had already lost half its force due to sickness.

Meanwhile, Hampton learned the main attack would be on Montreal. Wilkinson was bringing his army down the St. Lawrence by boat and would join Hampton for the assault on the city. The idea of attacking Kingston was abandoned.

By this time the British were aware of the full American strategy. De

Salaberry was badly outnumbered in spite of American afflictions and illness. Hampton had assembled about four thousand men at Spears's farm. All that stood between his army and the St. Lawrence River were the sixteen hundred militiamen seven miles (11 km) downriver.

The Canadian Voltigeurs and Fencibles would bear the brunt of the attack in the forward ravine. They would wait behind a tangle of roots and branches, knowing they were heavily outgunned and that the odds against them were better than two to one. The spy had counted nine cannon, plus a Howitzer and a mortar. And he believed that more were moving down toward the Canadian lines by another route.

Who was the spy who seemed to know everything that was going on? He was, of course, David Manning, the Loyalist farmer whom Hampton believed to be safely behind bars. But Hampton hadn't reckoned with the uncertain loyalties of the border people. He didn't know and would never know that Hollenbeck, his sergeant of the guard, was not only David Manning's friend and neighbour but also an informant himself. Hollenbeck was perfectly prepared to salute the American flag in public, while secretly supplying the British with all the information and gossip they would need.

CHAPTER FOUR

The Battle of Châteauguay

MAJOR-GENERAL WADE HAMPTON REALIZED THAT HE COULD NOT STORM AROUND THE FLANK OF THE FRENCH CANADIANS AND TRY TO TAKE THEM IN THE REAR. THEIR POSITION WAS ANCHORED BETWEEN GORGE AND SWAMP. HE ORDERED ROBERT PURDY, COLONEL OF THE VETERAN U.S. 4TH INFANTRY, TO TAKE FIFTEEN HUNDRED CRACK TROOPS AND FORD THE CHÂTEAUGUAY RIVER AT ITS LOWEST POINT AND PROCEED ALONG THE OPPOSITE BANK UNDER COVER OF DARKNESS.

Hampton hoped that, in this roundabout way, they would get around de Salaberry's defences on the opposite shore. At dawn they would recross the river by way of a second ford and attack the enemy from behind their lines. As soon as Hampton heard gunfire from Purdy, he would launch a frontal attack on the barrier of trunks and branches. In this way, he thought, de Salaberry would be caught between the claws of a pincer.

It looked good on paper, but it was impossible to carry out in reality. Here was Hampton proposing that Purdy and his men plunge through sixteen miles (26 km) of a thick wood and hemlock swamp in the pitch dark. That would be difficult for anybody who knew his way around. For strangers it would be a nightmare.

The guides they took with them were worthless. In fact, they told Hampton that they didn't know the country. But Hampton was so stubbornly sure of his plan that he paid no attention. Nothing could change his mind.

The result was disaster. Hampton went along with the expedition to the first ford of the river, then returned to camp. It was a cold night. Rain began to fall. There was no moon. On the far side of the river, Purdy's men floundered in a creek, stumbled into a swamp, tripped over fallen trees, and staggered through thick piles of underbrush. All order vanished.

After two miles (3 km) the guides, too, were lost. Purdy realized he couldn't go on in the dark. And so his men spent the night in the rain, shivering in their summer clothing, not even able to light a fire for fear of being discovered.

Back at camp, Hampton received a rude shock. A letter from Washington instructed him to build huts for winter quarters right there at Four Corners, south of the border. Hampton was flabbergasted. Winter quarters at Four Corners? He had expected to spend the winter at Montreal! The high command apparently doubted the expedition would ever reach its objective, and so the fight went out of him. He tried to recall Purdy's force but realized that in that black night it could not be found.

Dawn arrived, wan and damp, the dead leaves of autumn drooping from the trees. Purdy shook his men awake in the tangle of brush and swamp where he had camped. Across the river the Americans were already setting out to move along the wagon road that led to the French Canadian position.

De Salaberry was not expecting an attack that morning. A party of his axemen, guarded by forty soldiers, was strengthening the bulwark in front of the forward ravine. Suddenly, at ten o'clock—surprise!—the first Americans came bounding across the clearing firing their muskets.

De Salaberry was well to the rear when he heard the staccato sound of gunfire. He moved up quickly with reinforcements. The workmen had already scattered, and the Americans, cheering wildly, were pushing forward, only to be halted by Canadian musket fire.

De Salaberry, a commanding figure in his grey fur-trimmed coat, moved to the top of the abatis. He climbed up on a large hemlock that had been uprooted by the wind. There, hidden from the enemy by two large trees, he watched the blue line of Americans move down the river toward him.

But the firing had sputtered out, and the expected attack did not come because Hampton was waiting to hear from Purdy across the river. His men settled down to cook lunch. On the Canadian side of the bulwark a company of French Canadian militiamen knelt in prayer and were told by their captain that, having done their duty to their God, he now expected they would do their duty to their king.

Meanwhile, de Salaberry's scouts had found a few stragglers emerging from the dense woods along the far bank of the river, revealing Purdy's pres-

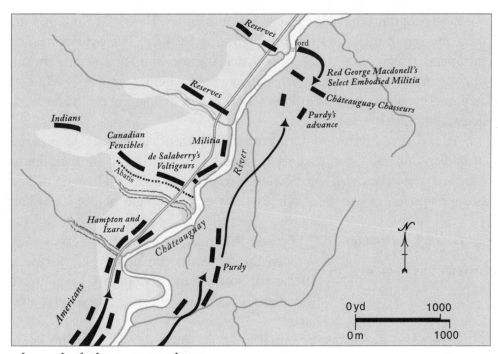

The Battle of Châteauguay, phase I

ence. Purdy was badly behind schedule. His force of fifteen hundred men had not gone far enough. In fact, at this point they were directly across from de Salaberry's forward position.

On the Canadian side, word got back to Red George Macdonell, who had been given the task of guarding the ford in the rear. Macdonell sent two of his companies across the river to reinforce a small band of Châteauguay Chasseurs—untrained local farmers conscripted into the militia for Canada.

Macdonell's men moved through the dense pine forest, peering through the tangle of naked trunks, looking for the advancing Americans. Purdy's advance guard—about a hundred men—were splashing through a cedar swamp when the two forces met. Both sides opened fire.

A scene of confusion followed. Macdonell's men stood fast, but the untrained Chasseurs turned and fled. The American advance party also turned tail and plunged back through the woods. There, Purdy's main body, thinking they were Canadians, opened fire and killed some of their own men.

Purdy thought the woods were full of enemies. He tried to regroup his men and sent a message to Hampton asking for help. The courier headed for Spears's farm, only to discover that Hampton had left and had moved upriver. At this point Hampton had no idea whether or not Purdy had achieved his objective. He couldn't tell what was happening on the far bank because the forest was so thick.

At two that afternoon Hampton finally decided to act. He ordered Brigadier-General George Izard to attack in line. Izard, another South Carolina aristocrat, was a competent professional soldier. His well-drilled brigade moved down the road toward the vast tangle of the Canadian abatis.

"Brave Canadians, surrender yourselves; we wish you no harm!"

Behind that breastwork, de Salaberry's men watched the tall American officer ride forward. Afterward, some remembered his cry: "Brave Canadians, surrender yourselves; we wish you no harm!"

In response de Salaberry himself fired. The American fell from his horse and the battle was joined.

Badly outnumbered, de Salaberry now depended on a series of deceptions to fool the Americans into believing they were facing a superior force. He called to his bugler to sound the call to open fire. The noise of exploding muskets mingled with the cries of a small body of Caughnawaga Indians hidden in the woods to the right of the Canadian line. The Americans, firing by platoons, as if on a parade ground, poured volley after volley into the woods, believing the main Canadian force was hidden there. But the lead balls whistled harmlessly through the treetops.

Now Red George Macdonell sounded his own bugles as a signal that he was advancing. Other bugles took up the refrain. De Salaberry sent buglers into the woods to trumpet in every direction. As a result the Americans thought they were heavily outnumbered.

Izard hesitated. Finally some of Macdonell's men appeared at the edge of the woods wearing red coats. They popped back into the woods, turned their jackets inside out (because they were lined with white flannel), and popped out again. The Americans thought they were a different corps.

Twenty Indians were sent to dash through the woods to the right of the

Canadian line, appearing from time to time, brandishing tomahawks. The Americans, unable to tell one Indian from another, and seeing them popping in and out, thought there were hundreds of them working in the depths.

"Defy, my damned ones!" cried de Salaberry. "Defy! If you do not dare, you are not men!"

The battle continued for an hour. The Americans fired rolling volleys, platoon by platoon. The Canadians returned the fire raggedly. There were few casualties on either side. The Americans didn't attempt to storm the barrier.

Now de Salaberry focused his attention on the far side of the river. The two Canadian companies that had driven off Purdy's forward troops were moving cautiously toward the colonel's position and tangling with his main force.

De Salaberry hurried to the bank of the river, clambered up a tree, and began to shout orders in French so the Americans couldn't understand him. He lined up his forces along with the Indians and militia to fire on Purdy's men if they emerged from the woods.

The two forces faced each other in the swampy forest. Captain Charles Daly of the Embodied Militia ordered his men to kneel before they fired. That manoeuvre saved their lives. Purdy's overwhelming body of crack troops responded with a shattering volley, but most of it passed harmlessly over the Canadians' heads.

Now Purdy's men swept forward on the river flank of the Canadians, determined to take them from the rear. The situation was critical. But as the Americans burst out of the woods and onto the riverbank, de Salaberry, watching through his glass, gave the order to fire. The bushes on the far side erupted into a sheet of flame. The Americans, badly mangled, fled into the forest. Exhausted by fourteen hours of struggle, they could fight no longer.

A lull followed. Hampton, astride his horse on the right of his troops, wasn't sure what to do. A courier had just swum the river to tell him about Purdy's predicament. That rattled the major-general.

He considered his next move. Izard hadn't tried to storm the barrier; that would cause heavy casualties. De Salaberry's ruses had fooled Hampton. The American general thought there were at least five or six

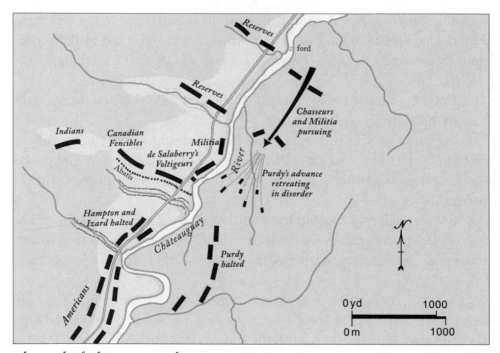

The Battle of Châteauguay, phase II

thousand men opposing him, although there were only a few hundred. De Salaberry had at most three hundred men in his advance position. Macdonell had about two hundred in reserve. The remainder were several miles to the rear at La Fourche, where the English River joined the Châteauguay. There were only six hundred of these and none were in the fight.

De Salaberry's boldness and Hampton's failure of nerve decided the outcome of the Battle of Châteauguay. Compared to other battles in this foolish war, it was really no more than a skirmish, with men on both sides peppering away at each other at long range with little effect. In fact, de Salaberry, on the other side of the river, lost only three men killed and eight wounded.

The fight had gone out of Hampton. Purdy was bogged down. The afternoon was dragging on and there was rain in the offing. Twilight was only a few hours away.

Hampton was dogged by indecision. He was jealous of Wilkinson, who he knew would gain all the glory if Hampton won the battle. He was furious at Armstrong, the U.S. secretary of war, who was resigned to defeat. Above all he lacked confidence in himself. He did not have the will to win.

Most of his force hadn't even got into the battle. He hadn't used his big guns. Izard's brigade had stopped fighting. And so Major-General Wade Hampton sent an order to Purdy to break off the engagement of the right bank and told his bugler to sound the withdrawal.

The Canadians watched in astonishment as Hampton's brigade retreated in perfect order. They made no attempt to harass it, waiting instead for the rally that never came. De Salaberry expected a renewed attack at any moment. He sent back word to all the houses along the river to prepare for a retreat and to burn all the buildings. It wasn't necessary.

Colonel Purdy, hidden in the forest, knew nothing of this. As the sun set, he started to move his wounded across the river on rafts. He sent a message to Hampton asking that a regiment be detached to cover his landing. He was shocked and angered to learn that Hampton had already retreated three miles (5 km), deserting him without support.

The next morning the once elite detachment struggled into Hampton's camp. Many had no hats, knapsacks, or weapons. Their clothing was torn, they were half-starved and sick with fatigue. Their morale was shattered.

Purdy was thoroughly disgusted. Several of his officers had behaved badly in the skirmish. But when Purdy tried to arrest them for desertion or cowardice, Hampton countermanded the orders.

Purdy reported that somebody in the commissary was selling the troops' rations, but Hampton brushed that away. In Purdy's view the sick were so badly neglected that many had died from lack of medical care. He was convinced that Hampton was drinking so heavily that he was no longer able to command.

Meanwhile, de Salaberry felt that he was being snubbed by the British high command. The French-Canadian militia had borne the brunt of the battle. One thousand fresh troops were available to harass the enemy and de Salaberry wanted to commit them, but his senior commanders wouldn't allow it. De Salaberry was embittered because he believed he had not been given the sole credit for repulsing the American invasion. Sir George Prevost, the Governor General of Canada, wanted his share of glory.

Hampton, meanwhile, ordered his entire force back across the border to

Four Corners "for the preservation of the army," a statement that would astonish the British, who were convinced that the Americans were planning a second attack. On October 28, Indian scouts confirmed that Hampton was retiring.

De Salaberry called the battle "a most extraordinary affair," and so it was: 460 troops had forced the retreat of 4,000. The victors had lost only five killed and sixteen wounded, with four men missing. The Americans lost fifty.

It was a small battle, but for Canada it was profoundly significant. A handful of civilian soldiers, almost all French Canadians, with scarcely any help had managed to turn back the gravest invasion threat of the war. If Hampton had reached the St. Lawrence to join with Wilkinson's advancing army, Montreal would likely have fallen. With Montreal gone and Upper Canada cut off, the British presence in North America would be reduced to a narrow strip in Quebec. Although the Battle of Châteauguay looks like no more than a silly skirmish, without that victory Canada could not have stretched from sea to sea.

CHAPTER FIVE

"Damn Such an Army!"

ON GRENADIER ISLAND IN THE ST. LAWRENCE, JAMES WILKINSON REALIZED, AS HE WROTE THE SECRETARY OF WAR, "ALL OUR HOPES HAVE BEEN VERY NEARLY BLASTED." HERE, ON THE FIRST OF NOVEMBER, THE GREAT FLOTILLA DESIGNED TO CONQUER MONTREAL WAS STUCK. THE TROOPS WERE DRENCHED FROM THE INCESSANT RAIN. BOATS WERE SMASHED, STORES SCATTERED, HUNDREDS SICK, SCORES DRUNK.

Wilkinson, of course, had to put the best face on these disasters. He relied on God to solve his problems: "Thanks to the same Providence which placed us in jeopardy, we are surmounting our difficulties and, God willing, I shall pass Prescott on the night of the 1st or 2nd proximo, if some unforeseen obstacle does not present to forbid me."

But there were plenty of unforeseen obstacles. On the journey from Sackets Harbor to Grenadier Island—a mere eighteen miles (29 km)—the American flotilla had been scattered by gales so furious that great trees were uprooted on the shores. Some boats hadn't even arrived.

A third of all the rations had been lost. It was impossible to disentangle the rest from the other equipment. Shivering in the driving rain, some of the men had torn oilcloths off the ration boxes for protection, so the bread became soggy and inedible. Hospital stores were pilfered; hogsheads of brandy and port wine, which the doctors believed essential for good health, were tapped and consumed. The guard was drunk, and the officer in charge found he couldn't keep his men sober.

The boats were badly overloaded. They became difficult to row or steer. Sickness increased daily. One hundred and ninety-six men were so ill that they had to be sent back to Sackets Harbor. Wilkinson himself was flat on his back with dysentery.

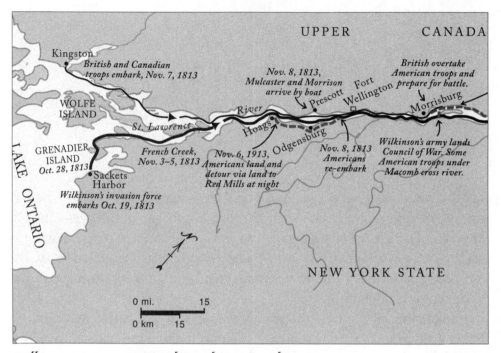

Wilkinson moves on Montreal, October–November 1813

In spite of the meagre food, the American islanders preferred to sell their produce to the British on the north shore. One fourteen-year-old drummer boy, Jarvis Hanks, tried to buy some potatoes from a local farmer for fifty cents a bushel. The man refused. He said he could get a dollar a bushel in Kingston. So that night Hanks and his friends stole the entire crop.

Some of the officers still half-believed that Wilkinson intended to attack at Kingston and not Montreal at all. It wasn't until October 30 that Wilkinson made up his mind to join with Hampton and head for the French Canadian capital.

The head of the American fleet, Commodore Isaac Chauncey, was "disappointed and mortified" when he heard that. He didn't believe the plan had much chance of success with the winter coming on.

Finally the troops set out down the St. Lawrence. Three brigades headed for the next rendezvous point at French Creek on the American side of the river directly opposite Gananoque. One made it; the weather forced the other two back.

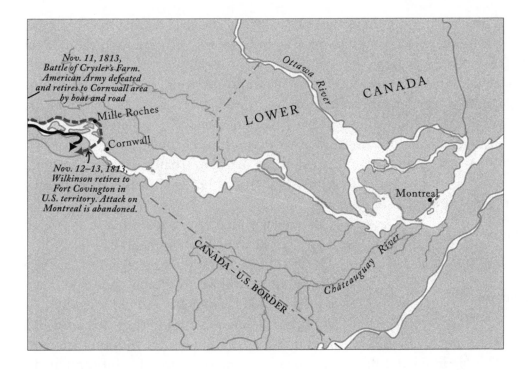

Nov. 11, 1813,
Battle of Crysler's Farm.
American Army defeated
and retires to Cornwall area
by boat and road

Mille Roches

Cornwall

Nov. 12–13, 1813,
Wilkinson retires to
Fort Covington in
U.S. territory. Attack on
Montreal is abandoned.

Ottawa River

LOWER CANADA

Montreal

CANADA - U.S. BORDER

Châteauguay River

The bulk of the army arrived on November 3, but Wilkinson was now so ill he had to be carried ashore. Meanwhile British gunboats skirmished with the Americans, which delayed the assault still further. The full flotilla didn't reach French Creek until November 5.

The valley of the St. Lawrence was bathed in an Indian summer glow. Six thousand men in 350 boats formed a procession five miles (8 km) long to slide down the great river with flags flying and brass buttons gleaming, fifes and drums playing, and boatmen singing. There was only one drawback: British gunboats were not far behind.

By November 6, the flotilla reached Morristown, four days late. Wilkinson had to halt now because he feared the British guns at Prescott, a dozen miles (19 km) downstream. He decided to strip his boats of all armament, march his men along the riverbank, hauling the supplies in wagons, and pass Prescott with the lightly manned boats under cover of darkness. That would delay him another day.

While the boats were being unloaded and the troops formed, he issued a proclamation to the British settlers along the river, urging the farmers to stay home, promising that persons and property of those who didn't fight would be protected.

He might as well have been talking to the wind, for this was Loyalist country. The settlers were already priming their muskets to harass the American flotilla. The river shortly became a shooting gallery, with gunfire exploding from the bushes at every twist of the channel.

At noon, Wilkinson learned of the defeat at Châteauguay. He was told that "our best troops behaved in the most rascally manner."

"Damn such an army!" Wilkinson cried. "A man might as well be in hell as command it."

"Damn such an army!" Wilkinson cried. "A man might as well be in hell as command it."

However, with Hampton's forces intact, the two armies numbered close to eleven thousand men. Surely that would be enough to seize Montreal.

At eight that night, with the river shrouded in a heavy fog, the flotilla began to move out into the water with muffled oars. The fog lifted and the leading boat was subjected to a fearful cannonade. Fifty twenty-four-pound (11-kg) balls were hurled at her from the Canadian shore but with no effect, because the guns were out of range and set too high to do any damage.

The flotilla halted and waited for the moon to set. Its pale light, gleaming on the bayonets of the troops trudging along the shore, had helped to identify the manoeuvre to the British, as had signal lights flashed in the homes of certain Ogdensburg citizens friendly to the British cause.

In the midst of this uproar, Colonel Winfield Scott arrived. Wilkinson had left him in charge of a skeleton command at Fort George on the Niagara frontier until relieved by New York State militia. Now he had ridden for thirty hours through the forests of northern New York in a sleet storm.

Taken aboard Wilkinson's passage boat, Scott felt stimulated by the bursting of shells and rockets. He found it sublime though he distrusted and despised his general, whom he called an "unprincipled imbecile." He was convinced that Wilkinson was drunk. But the fact was he was probably intoxicated with doses of opium, prescribed to ease his dysentery.

Wilkinson's condition was so serious he finally was forced to go ashore.

Benjamin Forsyth of the rifle company met him and helped him up the bank with the aid of another officer. Wilkinson was muttering to himself, hurling insults at the British, threatening to blow the enemy's garrison to dust and lay waste the entire countryside.

The two officers sat him down by the hearth, posted a guard at the door to keep the spectacle from prying eyes, and tried to decide what to do. By this time Wilkinson was singing bawdy songs and telling obscene stories, until he began to nod, and to the relief of all, allowed himself to be put to bed.

November 7 dawned bright and clear—a perfect day for sailing. But the British had reinforced every bend with cannon and sharpshooters. Wilkinson detached an elite corps of twelve hundred soldiers to clear the bank, with Forsyth's riflemen detailed as rearguard. By nightfall the flotilla had only moved eight miles (13 km).

Wilkinson was now losing his nerve as Wade Hampton had before him. In his weakened condition he believed himself to be in the grip of forces he could not control. He had little faith in his own army. He knew that he had been held up too long, giving the British a chance to catch him from the rear. Already the word was that two army schooners and seven gunboats had reached Prescott, carrying at least a thousand men.

In his fevered imagination, the general magnified the forces opposed to him. The farmers on the Canadian shore had purposely been stuffing the heads of their American interrogators with wild stories about the dangers ahead. They described terrifying rapids, batteries of guns at every narrows, savage Indians prowling the forest, and no fodder for the horses. It was said that the army would face five thousand British regulars and twenty thousand Canadian militiamen. That was a fantastic overstatement, but it fooled the doddering major-general.

On the following day, Wilkinson, who could hardly get out of his bunk, called a council of war. It was finally agreed to carry on to Montreal. He was still concerned about the forces on the Canadian side. He ordered one of his commanders, Jacob Brown, to disembark his brigade and take command of the combined forces clearing the Canadian shore.

Ahead lay the dreaded Long Sault rapids, eight miles (13 km) of white water in which no boat could manoeuvre under enemy fire. Brown's job was to clear the banks so the flotilla could make it through the rapids without fear of attack. With the British at his rear, Wilkinson couldn't get underway until Brown reached the head of the rapids. Wilkinson moved eleven miles (18 km), but with the British nipping at his heels he stopped again.

On November 10, the British gunboats moved into the attack at the same time. Brown's force on the shore ran into heavy resistance. By the time he'd cleared the bank, the pilots refused to take the boat through the white water.

The American flotilla moved two miles (3 km) past John Crysler's farm to Cook's Point, a mile or two (2 or 3 km) above the rapids. The troops built fires on the shore, tearing off the farmers' rail fences. All night they shivered in the rain and sleet. Jarvis Hanks, the drummer boy in the 11th, pulled a leather cap over his head and curled up so close to the fire that by morning both his cap and his shoes were charred.

Meanwhile, Brown had gone aboard Wilkinson's boat to find exactly who was in charge. But Wilkinson was too sick to see him. It had taken eight days for the fleet to move eighty miles (128 km). A log drifting down the river could make the same distance in two.

CHAPTER SIX

The Battle of Crysler's Farm

IT WOULD BE PLEASANT TO BE ABLE TO VISIT THE SCENE OF ONE OF THE GREAT BRITISH-CANADIAN VICTORIES ON THE SHORES OF THE ST. LAWRENCE AND FOLLOW THE TACTICS OF THE TROOPS THAT DAY. ALAS, JOHN CRYSLER'S FARM IS NO MORE. THE BROAD FIELD WHERE THE BATTLE TOOK PLACE IS UNDER WATER, PART OF THE ST. LAWRENCE SEAWAY. BEFORE THE AREA WAS FLOODED, SOIL WAS DUG FROM THE SITE AND A MOUND CONSTRUCTED NOT FAR AWAY ON WHICH A MONUMENT WAS PLACED TO RECORD THE BATTLE. ABOUT A HALF MILE (800 M) DISTANT, UPPER CANADA VILLAGE STANDS — A COLLECTION OF VENERABLE HOUSES MOVED FROM THE SEAWAY SITE TO GIVE SOME IDEA OF THE WAY PEOPLE LIVED DURING THE EARLY DAYS OF THE NINETEENTH CENTURY.

On November 11, 1813, dawn broke, bleak and soggy. John Loucks, a militiaman and one of the three troopers in the Provincial Dragoons posted with three companies of the Canadian Voltigeurs and a few Indians a mile (1.6 km) ahead of the main British force, spotted a movement through the trees ahead. A party of Americans was advancing from Cook's Point, where the American flotilla was anchored. A musket exploded in the woods on Loucks's left, where a party of Indians was stationed. The Americans replied with a volley that kicked sand in front of the troopers' horses. Young Loucks drove off at a gallop to warn the British commander, Lieutenant-Colonel Joseph Wanton Morrison.

As the troopers dashed through the ranks of the 49th Regiment, Lieutenant John Sewell was toasting a piece of breakfast pork on the point of his sword. He needed the hot nourishment because he had slept on the cold ground all night with his gun between his legs to protect it from the icy rain. Now he realized there would be no time for breakfast as his company commander shouted, "Jack, drop cooking, the enemy is advancing."

The British scrambled into position behind a stout rail fence, but the warning was far too early. All that Loucks had seen was an American scouting party.

Back at his headquarters in the Crysler farmhouse, Morrison assessed his position. He had been chasing Wilkinson and the gunboats for five days, ever since word had reached Kingston that the American attack would be on Montreal. Finally he had caught up with him. Would the Americans stand and fight? Or would the chase continue? With a force of only eight hundred men to challenge Wilkinson's seven thousand, Morrison wasn't eager for a pitched battle.

However, he realized if he did have a battle, it would be on ground of his own choosing. It would be a European-style battle on an open plain where his men could manoeuvre as on a parade ground, standing shoulder to shoulder in parallel lines, each man occupying twenty-two inches (55 cm) of space, advancing with a bayonet, wheeling easily when ordered, or into a staggered series of platoons, each one supporting its neighbour.

This was the kind of warfare for which his two regiments had been trained—the Green Tigers, known for the fierceness of their attack, and his own regiment, the 89th. Morrison was an old soldier who had learned his trade well. Like his father before him, he had served half his life in the British army, shifting from continent to continent whenever his country called him.

He understood battle tactics. He had chosen his position carefully, anchoring his thin line between the river on his right, where the gunboats would give him support, and a black ash swamp about half a mile (800 m) to his left, which nobody could penetrate. His men were protected by a heavy fence of cedar logs five feet (1.5 m) high. Ahead for half a mile (800 m) a muddy field stretched, covered with winter wheat, cut with gullies, and bisected by a stream that trickled out of the swamp to become a deep ravine running into the St. Lawrence.

Behind the fence on the right was the 49th, close to the river and to the King's Highway that ran along the bank. On the left was the 89th. Its soldiers wore the scarlet, but the battle-seasoned 49th hid its distinctive green tunics under grey overcoats.

Half a mile (800 m) forward of this were light troops, including the

Canadian Fencibles. Another half mile (800 m) farther on, the skirmishers—Indians and Voltigeurs, the latter almost invisible in their grey homespun, were concealed behind rocks, stumps, and fences.

Morrison was heavily outnumbered. But he counted on the ability of his troops to hold fast against the more individualistic Americans. It was here that the contrast between the two countries became apparent.

Wilkinson's men were experienced bush fighters. They were brought up with firearms and blooded in frontier Indian wars. They were used to taking individual action in skirmishes where each man would have to act on his own if he was to escape with a whole skin.

On the other hand, the British soldier was drilled to stand unflinchingly with his comrades in the face of exploding cannon, to hold his fire until ordered so that the maximum effect of the spraying muskets could be felt, and then to move in machinelike unison with hundreds of others, each man an automaton.

The British regulars followed orders implicitly. The Americans were less obedient, sometimes to the point of anarchy.

Morrison had one advantage, though he didn't know it. The American high command had collapsed. The chief of the invading army and his second-in-command both lay deathly ill, unable to direct any battle.

Wilkinson's deputy, Morgan Lewis, was dosing himself on blackberry jelly, but he was even less capable than his superior. Wilkinson couldn't get out of his bunk. He waited to hear from Jacob Brown on shore that the rapids ahead had been cleared of British troops.

At half past ten, a dragoon arrived to tell him the rapids were clear. But the commander-in-chief was in a quandary. The British gunboats were just behind him: What if they should just slip past?

He gave an order for the flotilla to get underway and told Brigadier-General John Boyd, on land, to begin marching his men toward Cornwall below the rapids. But even as he did that he was alerted to the presence of the British on Crysler's field. At the same time, the British gunboats began to lob shot in his direction. So Wilkinson held up and decided to try to destroy the small British force before moving on.

Boyd was not happy with that. All that morning he had been given a series of conflicting orders. At noon a violent storm had reduced the morale of his troops, who had been under arms for nearly two days. Boyd rode impatiently to the riverbank, where he finally received a pencilled order to put his men in motion in twenty minutes, as soon as the guns could be put ashore. That was the last order he got from Wilkinson.

In the battle that followed, Boyd would be in charge of the Americans. He had once been a soldier of fortune, who for twenty years had sold his services to a variety of Indian princes. He exchanged his turban and lance in 1808 for a colonel's commission in the U.S. 4th Infantry. He was a brigadier-general at the opening of the war, but he did not enjoy the trust of his leaders.

Brown couldn't stand him. Scott thought he was an imbecile. Lewis described him as "a combination of ignorance, vanity, and petulance, with nothing to recommend him but that species of bravery in the field which is vaporing, boisterous, stifling reflection, blinding observation." In short, Brigadier-General Boyd was not the best man to put up against highly trained British soldiers.

Boyd's first move was to send in Colonel Eleazar Ripley's regiment

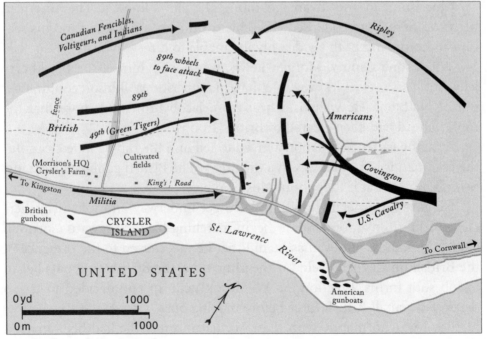

Battle of Crysler's Farm, Phase I

across the muddy fields and over a boggy creek bed to probe Morrison's forward skirmishes in the woods on the British left. Ripley advanced half a mile (800 m) when a line of Canadian Voltigeurs suddenly rose from concealment and fired two volleys at his men.

Ignoring the cries of their officers, the Americans leapt behind stumps and began to open individual fire until their ammunition was exhausted. After that they ran back out of British range. Ripley retired with them but soon returned to the attack with reinforcements and drove the Voltigeurs back.

John Sewell, the British lieutenant whose breakfast was so rudely interrupted, was standing with his fellow Green Tigers in the thin line formed by the two British regiments when he saw their grey-clad Voltigeurs burst from the woods on his left, chased by the Americans. The situation was critical. If Ripley's men could get around the 89th, which held the left flank, and attack the British from the rear, the battle was as good as lost.

Morrison now executed the first of a series of parade-ground manoeuvres. The 89th Regiment was facing east. He wheeled them about to face north. As they poured out of the woods, the Americans ran into this solid line of scarlet-coated men, all firing their muskets in unison. That volley of hot lead caused them to break and run.

The contrast between the fire of the opposing forces was so distinct that the women and children hiding in Captain John Crysler's cellar could easily tell the American guns from the British. The American guns made a steady *pop-pop-pop.* The latter, at regular intervals, resounded "like a tremendous roll of thunder."

Unable to turn the British left wing, Boyd advanced his three main brigades across the open wheat fields to try to seize the British right wing. A forty-five-year-old Marylander, Leonard Covington, who commanded the 3rd Brigade, was fooled by the grey coats of the 49th right in front of them.

"Come, lads, let me see how you will deal with these militiamen," he shouted. But the disguised Tigers were already executing another drill. They moved in a series specifically arranged to meet this kind of threat. The right wing simply wheeled *backwards* to the left until it faced the line of cavalry. Sewell noted that the entire movement, which the Americans thought was a

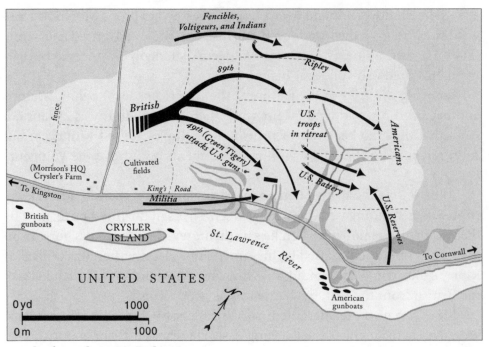

Fencibles,
Voltigeurs, and Indians

Ripley

89th

British

49th (Green Tigers)
attacks U.S. guns

U.S.
troops
in retreat

Americans

fence

(Morrison's HQ)
Crysler's Farm

Cultivated
fields

U.S. Battery

← To Kingston

King's Road
Militia

U.S. Reserves

British
gunboats

CRYSLER
ISLAND

St. Lawrence River

To Cornwall →

UNITED STATES

American
gunboats

0 yd   1000
0 m   1000

Battle of Crysler's Farm, Phase II

retreat, was carried out with all the coolness of a parade-ground review as the commands rang out over the crash of grapeshot and canister; *Halt … Front … Pivot … Cover … Left wheel into line … Fire by platoons from the centre to the flank*. The effect was shattering as the wounded American horses, snorting and neighing, floundered about with their saddles empty.

At the same time, a company of 89th, stationed well ahead of the main ravine, charged the American guns, captured a six-pounder (3-kg), and killed its crew. By now the whole American line was crumbling and the retreat was saved from becoming a rout only by the presence of the American reserves. The Battle of Crysler's Farm was over. Again, a small force of British and Canadians had beaten a superior American army.

CHAPTER SEVEN

A Bitter Ending

MAJOR-GENERAL JAMES WILKINSON HAD SPENT THE ENTIRE DAY IN HIS BUNK, LAMENTING HIS ILL FORTUNE AT NOT BEING WITH HIS MEN. HE TRIED TO PRE-VENT THE PELL-MELL RUSH TO THE BOATS, EXCLAIMING THAT THE BRITISH WOULD SAY THE AMERICANS WERE RUNNING AWAY AND CLAIM THE VICTORY. HE SENT A MESSAGE TO BRIGADIER-GENERAL BOYD ASKING HIM IF HE COULD HOLD THE BANK UNTIL THE NIGHT TO PRESERVE SOME VESTIGE OF AMERICAN HON-OUR. BOYD'S ANSWER WAS A CURT *NO*. THE MEN, HE SAID, WERE EXHAUSTED AND FAMISHED, AND THEY NEEDED A COMPLETE NIGHT OF REST.

Boyd now busied himself with the necessary report of the day's action, which, as always in defeat, was a masterpiece of doubletalk. He couldn't claim victory but he came as close to it as he could, larding his account with a series of alibis. Boyd admitted the result of the action was "not so brilliant and decisive as I could have wished." But he blamed the bad weather, the fatigue of the troops, the lack of sleep, the superiority of the enemy (which was untrue), the superior position of the British, the presence of the gun-boats, the surprise, the lack of American guns, and so on.

Wilkinson, however, didn't shilly-shally in his report to the secretary of war. He inflated the British strength from a realistic 800 to 2,170. He bumped up the British casualties from 170 to 500, and said that "although the imperious obligations of duty did not allow me sufficient time to rout the enemy, they were beaten."

But it was Wilkinson who was beaten. "Emaciated almost to a skeleton, unable to sit my horse, or to move ten paces without assistance," he was looking for an excuse to give up the grand campaign. He got it the follow-ing morning after the battle in the form of a letter from Major-General Hampton.

The two armies—Hampton's and Wilkinson's—were supposed to meet below the Long Sault, at St. Regis just opposite Cornwall. Wilkinson's flotilla made the passage but Hampton was not there, nor would he ever be.

He wrote that it was impossible to get troops to transport enough supplies to the big river to feed the army. His arrival would only weaken the existing forces, and the roads were impractical for wheeled transport. His troops were raw, sick, exhausted, dispirited.

Hampton intended—or so he reported—to go back to Plattsburgh on Lake Champlain and strain every effort to continue the invasion south of Montreal. Actually, he intended to do nothing.

That gave Wilkinson the scapegoat he needed to protect his own reputation. Montreal was just three days down the river, virtually defenceless. Hampton's sudden withdrawal at Châteauguay had convinced the British high command to withdraw the bulk of British troops to Kingston. Wilkinson still had some seven thousand soldiers. But neither he nor his generals had the will to continue. A hastily summoned council of war agreed to abandon the enterprise.

Wilkinson went to some effort to make it clear that the grand plan was entirely Hampton's fault. In his general order on November 13, he announced that he was "compelled to retire by the extraordinary unexampled, and apparently unwarrantable conduct of Major-General Hampton."

He wrote to Secretary of War John Armstrong that with Hampton's help he could have taken Montreal in eight or ten days, but now all his hopes were blasted: "I disclaim the shadow of blame because I have done my duty … To General Hampton's outrage of every principle of subordination and discipline may be ascribed the failure of the expedition … "

The American army now drifted eighteen miles (29 km) down the St. Lawrence to Salmon Creek and moved up the tributary to the American hamlet of French Mills, soon to be known as Fort Covington in honour of the dead brigadier-general. Here, in the dreary wilderness of pine and hemlock, with little shelter and hard rations, the Americans passed a dreadful winter.

Sickness, desertions, and greed did more damage than any British force. Clothing was hard to come by. Little Jarvis Hanks, the drummer boy, had no pantaloons and was forced to tailor himself a pair out of one of his two precious blankets. Driven to subsist on polluted bread, the men sickened by the hundreds and died by the score.

So many men died that funeral music was banned from the camp for reasons of morale. By the end of December, almost eighteen hundred were ill. The food was so scarce the sick had to subsist on oatmeal, which was originally ordered for poultices.

All the efficient officers had gone on furlough or were themselves ill with pneumonia, diarrhoea, dysentery, typhoid, or atrophy of the limbs, a kind of dry rot. The remainder, ex-politicians mostly, fattened their pocket-books by selling off army rations to British and Americans alike, and drawing dead men's pay.

The defeat on the St. Lawrence wrecked the careers of the men who bungled the attack. Wilkinson, convalescing in his comfortable home at Malone, New York, and bitterly blaming everybody but himself for the defeat, must have known his days were numbered. Hampton, to the relief of all, would shortly quit the army. Lewis and Boyd had each taken a leave of absence and would never be heard of again.

Along the St. Lawrence, the settlers began to rearrange the fragments of their lives. The north shore had been heavily plundered of cattle, grain, and winter forage. Fences had been ripped apart to build fires—the sky so lit up that it sometimes seemed as if the entire countryside was ablaze. Cellars, barns, and stables had been looted.

Stragglers, pretending to search for arms, rummaged through houses, broke open trunks, stole everything from ladies' petticoats to men's pantaloons. Fancy china, silver plate, jewellery, books—all these went to the plunderers in spite of Wilkinson's proclamation that private property would be respected.

The Americans left a legacy of bitterness. Dr. William "Tiger" Dunlop, an assistant surgeon with the 89th working with the wounded of both armies in the various farmhouses that did duty as makeshift hospitals, discovered he could not trust some of the Loyalist farmers near the stricken Americans. So great was their hatred of the enemy that they might have killed off the wounded.

Fortunately, this brief explosion in their midst marked the last military excursion down the great river. For John Crysler and his neighbours, the war was over. In spite of James Wilkinson's hollow boast that the attack on Montreal was merely suspended and not abandoned, the St. Lawrence Valley would never again shiver to the crash of alien musketry.

INDEX

About Fifth House

Fifth House Publishers, a Fitzhenry & Whiteside company, is a proudly western-Canadian press. Our publishing specialty is non-fiction as we believe that every community must possess a positive understanding of its worth and place if it is to remain vital and progressive. Fifth House is committed to "bringing the West to the rest" by publishing approximately twenty books a year about the land and people who make this region unique. Our books are selected for their quality and contribution to the understanding of western-Canadian (and Canadian) history, culture, and environment.

Look for the following Fifth House titles at your local bookstore:

Canada Moves West
    Pierre Berton
Exploring the Frozen North
    Pierre Berton
The Golden Trail: The Story of the Klondike Rush
    Pierre Berton
Homemade Fun: Games & Pastimes of the Early Prairies
    Faye Reineberg Holt
Monarchs of the Fields: The Story of the Combine Harvester
    Faye Reineberg Holt
The Nor'Westers: The Fight for the Fur Trade
    Marjorie Wilkins Campbell
Prairie Sentinel: The Story of the Canadian Grain Elevator
    Brock V. Silversides
The Savage River: Seventy-one Days with Simon Fraser
    Marjorie Wilkins Campbell
Settling In: First Homes on the Prairies
    Faye Reineberg Holt
Threshing: The Early Years of Harvesting
    Faye Reineberg Holt

Pierre Berton's History for Young Canadians

"*The stories are so real that it's as though Berton is leading us down the surveyor's mountain paths, helping us swing the hammer on the rails, or cut the sod along with the pioneers.*"
–from the foreword by Arthur Slade, author of *Dust* and the
     Canadian Chills series.

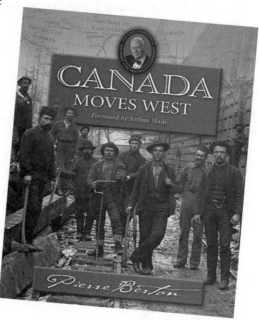

The first book in Fifth House's *Pierre Berton's History for Young Canadians* series is *Canada Moves West*, a rousing collection of five young-adult, non-fiction books by revered author Pierre Berton. These books describe how, back in the days of the pioneers, the Canadian West was won—with blood, sweat, tears, and sheer determination.

Originally printed as separate volumes in the *Adventures in Canadian History* series, the titles in *Canada Moves West* include:

> *The Railway Pathfinders*
> *The Men in Sheepskin Coats*
> *A Prairie Nightmare*
> *Steel Across the Plains*
> *Steel Across the Shield*

Riveting history abounds in the books. Find out about:
* The romantic and gritty adventures of railway pathfinders such as the indomitable Walter Moberly, and railway builders,

Joseph Whitehead and Harry Armstrong, who fought their way from the gnarled rocks of the Canadian Shield to the passes of three mountain ranges in British Columbia;

* The epic tales of the immigrants in sheepskin coats from eastern Europe, who braved hardship and discrimination to create new lives in a new land, successfully settling the wide open spaces of the Canadian prairies;

* The story of those whose lives were forever changed by the coming of the railway: the Cree and Blackfoot peoples, led by Chiefs Piapot, Big Bear, and Crowfoot.

ALSO AVAILABLE—*Exploring the Frozen North*

"Pierre Berton is the perfect writer to take you north. His words pull you into the experience—suddenly you are there ... don't miss the northern adventures recounted in Exploring the Frozen North. *Pierre Berton makes them come alive."*—from the foreword by Eric Wilson, author of the Tom and Liz Austen Mysteries

Exploring the Frozen North is the second omnibus in the *Pierre Berton's History for Young Canadians* series. It documents the amazing lives of the men and women who mapped the Arctic at great personal cost. Berton tells the stories of the explorers, but he does not ignore those people living in the Arctic—the Inuit. The titles in this omnibus include:

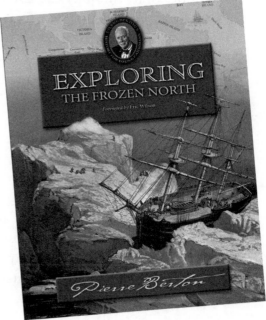

Parry of the Arctic
Jane Franklin's Obsession
Dr. Kane of the Arctic Seas
Trapped in the Arctic

In *Exploring the Frozen North* incredible Arctic adventures come alive. Join Berton as he writes about:

* William Edward Parry, the first white man to attempt exploration of the Arctic islands;
* Jane Franklin and her relentless search for her lost explorer husband, John Franklin;
* Elisha Kent Kane, the sickly American doctor, who sought the legendary ice-free passage to the North Pole; and
* Robert John McClure, whose ambitious and aggressive race for the North West Passage almost ended when he and his crew were trapped in the ice for two long years.

COMING SOON—*The Great Klondike Gold Rush*

Telling the stories of the prospectors, the gold seekers, and the gold that drove them mad, *The Great Klondike Gold Rush* is the acclaimed six-book history of North America's last great gold rush.
Included in the fourth and final omnibus
in this exciting series are:

> *Bonanza Gold*
> *The Klondike Stampede*
> *Trails of '98*
> *City of Gold*
> *Before the Gold Rush*
> *Kings of the Klondike*

Join Pierre Berton as he writes about the:
* discovery of gold on an obscure northern creek
  by Robert Henderson, the professional prospector, and
  George Carmack, the amateur gold-seeker and salmon fisherman;

* thousands of men and women who clawed their way to Canada's "golden" north in the summer of 1897, when the story of Yukon's gold drove the world mad;
* hardship and folly, courage and despair of the would-be prospectors, who braved the terrible White and Chilkoot Passes, determined to get rich on gold;
* glory of the boomtown Dawson City, a mud-spattered collection of shacks full to brimming with the craziest characters on the Yukon River;
* lives of the prospectors, who "craved the widest possible freedom of action," characters such as Salt Water Jack, Jimmy the Pirate, Pete the Pig, and Cutthroat Johnson; and
* kings of the Klondike, those larger-than-life gold-rush characters (whose millions were spent as quickly as they were won), such as Big Alex McDonald, who gave away gold nuggets from a bowl, and Curly Munro, who fed his husky puppies thousands of kilograms of bacon, fish, and flour.

More Inspiring Canadian Nonfiction from Fifth House Publishers ...

The Golden Trail: The Story of the Klondike Rush
Pierre Berton

"Canadian history is alive and well, thanks in a large part to Pierre Berton."–Arthur Slade

The Golden Trail is the exciting story of the Klondike gold rush of 1896, written by legendary Canadian historian Pierre Berton. Within these pages is a gripping tale of unbelievable hardship and super-human effort. Through story and anecdote, Berton passionately describes the fever that overcame usually sane men as word spread about the discovery of gold in Yukon Territory. Once gold was discovered along the Klondike River, the mad rush began. Men left their jobs and loved ones in the quest for Yukon gold, only to meet with misery as they struggled up the brutal White and Chilkoot Passes. When—and if—they arrived at a claim, it was incredibly hard work to find gold. Berton's story of the men who gambled it all for a taste of gold is truly a story of rags to riches to rags again.

The Savage River: Seventy-one Days with Simon Fraser

Marjorie Wilkins Campbell

On 28 May 1808, Simon Fraser's company of adventurers left Fort George on an unfamiliar river in the heart of British Columbia, headed—they hoped—for the Pacific. The young fur trader's mission was to find the quickest route west for the North West Company's valuable goods, giving them an advantage over their rivals, the Hudson's Bay Company. Seventy-one days later, Fraser brought his exhausted men back to the fort. They had achieved their goal and reached the ocean, but they also brought back the bad news that the river was too wild to be of use to the North West Company.

The Savage River is Marjorie Wilkins Campbell's gripping account of one of the greatest adventures in Canadian history. First published in 1968, the book is based on Simon Fraser's journal of his remarkable journey on the river that now bears his name.

The Nor'Westers:
The Fight for the Fur Trade
Marjorie Wilkins Campbell

"Thanks to this new edition of *The Nor'Westers* one of Canada's most exciting stories will live on."—Fred Stenson, from the *Foreword*

The fur trade was a risky business. With few provisions, traders travelled by canoe and foot through the dangers of Canada's northwest to find furs for European markets. It was a hard life. While the trade made men into explorers and heroes, it also brought them and their families to the brink of starvation. Because the work was so difficult, one group of traders decided to join forces in 1779. They called themselves the North West Company and soon became known as the Nor'Westers. It was the beginning of an empire.

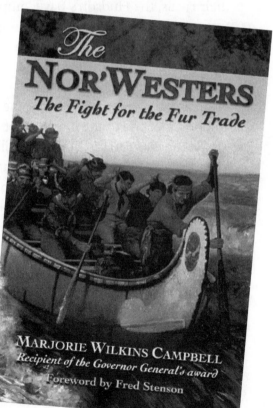

In her award-winning book, Marjorie Wilkins Campbell captures the drama of the fur trade from 1779 until the Hudson's Bay Company took over the North West Company in 1821. *The Nor'Westers* is an exciting portrayal of those who braved the Canadian wilderness.

Marjorie Wilkins Campbell was the author of eight books on the West for both adults and younger readers, including *Silent Song: A Tribute to a Reluctant Pioneer Mother* and *The Savage River: Seventy-one Days with Simon Fraser*. She received a Governor General's award for *The Nor'Westers* in 1954.